Gender and Politics

Series Editors
Johanna Kantola
University of Tampere
Tampere, Finland

Sarah Childs
Birkbeck, University of London
London, UK

The Gender and Politics series celebrated its 7th anniversary at the 5th European Conference on Politics and Gender (ECPG) in June 2017 in Lausanne, Switzerland having published more than 25 volumes to date. The original idea for the book series was envisioned by the series editors Johanna Kantola and Judith Squires at the first ECPG in Belfast in 2009, and the series was officially launched at the Conference in Budapest in 2011. In 2014, Sarah Childs became the co-editor of the series, together with Johanna Kantola. Gender and Politics showcases the very best international writing. It publishes world class monographs and edited collections from scholars—junior and well established—working in politics, international relations and public policy, with specific reference to questions of gender. The 15 titles that have come out over the past five years make key contributions to debates on intersectionality and diversity, gender equality, social movements, Europeanization and institutionalism, governance and norms, policies, and political institutions. Set in European, US and Latin American contexts, these books provide rich new empirical findings and push forward boundaries of feminist and politics conceptual and theoretical research. The editors welcome the highest quality international research on these topics and beyond, and look for proposals on feminist political theory; on recent political transformations such as the economic crisis or the rise of the populist right; as well as proposals on continuing feminist dilemmas around participation and representation, specific gendered policy fields, and policy making mechanisms. The series can also include books published as a Palgrave pivot.

More information about this series at
http://www.palgrave.com/gp/series/14998

Jennifer Thomson

Abortion Law and Political Institutions

Explaining Policy Resistance

palgrave
macmillan

Jennifer Thomson
University of Bath
Bath, UK

Gender and Politics
ISBN 978-3-319-96168-2 ISBN 978-3-319-96169-9 (eBook)
https://doi.org/10.1007/978-3-319-96169-9

Library of Congress Control Number: 2018948813

Cover credit: tenra/getty images
Cover designed by Akihiro Nakayama

This Palgrave Macmillan imprint is published by the registered company
Springer Nature Switzerland AG
The registered company address is: Gewerbestrasse 11, 6330 Cham, Switzerland

Acknowledgements

With full knowledge that it will provide little comfort, this book is dedicated to the hundreds of women who travel from Northern Ireland to England (or elsewhere) every year to terminate pregnancies. Their journeys are a simple injustice, and one that could be easily rectified—I hope that this will soon be the case.

This book began its life as a Ph.D. thesis in the School of Politics and International Relations, Queen Mary University of London, where I was supervised by Prof. Rainbow Murray and Dr. Judith Bara. Both were incredibly supportive of this project from day one, and I am so grateful to have had them guiding me through the Ph.D. process. Thanks also to Prof. James Dunkerley, Dr. Sophie Harman, Dr. Brendan O'Duffy, Dr. Madeleine Davis and Dr. Peter Allen, who all read and commented on my thesis at various points in its genesis, and whose support and kind words were greatly appreciated. I am indebted to Dr. Melanie Hoewer and the Institute of British-Irish Studies at University College Dublin for providing a welcoming intellectual home in late 2015. My thesis was examined by Profs. Fiona Mackay and Eric Kaufman, and I am very thankful for their support as I concluded my Ph.D.

I am deeply grateful to the Economic and Social Research Council for the grant (ES/J500124/1) which enabled me to undertake this doctorate, as well as their award of additional funding to undertake an Overseas Institutional Visit in Dublin. I am also thankful for the over fifty individuals and representatives of various organisations who took time out of busy schedules to talk with me for this research. I could offer little to recompense them for their time or help, but this work would not exist without their generosity.

After Queen Mary, this project then moved with me to De Montfort University's Department of Politics and Public Policy. Thanks to Prof. Alasdair Blair and the department for my short stay there. This book is completed as I begin life in the Department of Politics, Language and International Studies at the University of Bath. I am deeply grateful for the supportive and friendly scholarly environment that I have found there.

Several components of this book have been published elsewhere—Chapter 4 is an expanded version of Jennifer Thomson, 2016, "Explaining Gender Equality Difference in a Devolved System: The Case of Abortion Law in Northern Ireland," *British Politics*, Volume 11, Issue 3, pp. 371–388. It also expands upon Jennifer Thomson, 2018, "A 'United Kingdom?': The 1967 Abortion Act and Northern Ireland" in Colleen MacQuarrie, Claire Pierson, Shannon Stettner and Fiona Bloomer (eds.) *Troubled Waters: Abortion in Ireland, Northern Ireland and Prince Edward Island*, Island Studies Press: UPEI, Charlottetown. Chapter 6 draws in part on Claire Pierson, Ronan Kennedy and Jennifer Thomson, 2016, "Challenging Identity Hierarchies: Consociational Power-Sharing and Gendered Political Representation," *British Journal of Politics and International Relations*, Volume 18, Issue 3, pp. 618–633. Chapter 7 expands upon Jennifer Thomson, 2018, "Resisting Gendered Change: Feminist Institutionalism and Critical Actors," *International Political Science Review*, Volume 39, Issue 2, pp. 178–191.

Heartfelt thanks to friends and family who have supported me in so many spoken and unspoken ways during the writing of this book. Most especially I thank my parents, who have been unfailingly supportive in every way, but most especially with regard to my education—my Dad, Jim, who is always willing to argue with me, and my Mum, Jane, who has always gone above and beyond to support me, and who is the centre around which our extended family revolve. Thanks also to Ruth, for being irrepressibly herself—but mostly because I know she will be angry if she doesn't see her name here.

Special thanks to Bryan Marshall who, in the course of a month during which he and Carol were evacuated from a hurricane, and in which he also underwent emergency surgery to fit a pacemaker, still found time to read this book and deliver some wonderfully supportive comments.

Thanks finally to Brad. He has lived with this project over three continents and too many years and remains my favo(u)rite. 사랑해.

Praise for *Abortion Law and Political Institutions: Explaining Policy Resistance*

"In this fascinating book, Jennifer Thomson examines abortion policy in Northern Ireland through the prism of feminist institutionalism for the first time. She shows us how and why the 1967 Abortion Act has not been extended to Northern Ireland, and highlights the wider implications for our understanding of why gendered institutional change does or does not occur."

—Georgina Waylen, *Professor, Politics, University of Manchester, UK*

"The critical puzzles at the heart of this compelling book are those why and how progressive change does not happen. Why, in contrast to the rest of the United Kingdom and more recently the Republic of Ireland, does Northern Ireland retain its highly restrictive abortion laws? And why has no-one been talking about it? Jennifer Thomson's new book illuminates the political, multi-level institutional, and legal dynamics—and the critical actors and veto players—that have maintained the gendered status quo on abortion in Northern Ireland for more than fifty years. Taking a Feminist Institutionalist approach, she argues that non-decision making and silencing around abortion in Northern Ireland are distinctly gendered, and are important mechanisms of gendered power.

Abortion Law and Political Institutions: Explaining Policy Resistance is comprehensive, rigorous, and passionate. It represents a significant original empirical contribution to the literature on politics in Northern Ireland, and well as the international gender and politics literature. In applying an institutionalist gender lens, Thomson also contributes an important new case study to the Feminist Institutionalist field."

—Fiona Mackay, *Professor of Politics, University of Edinburgh, UK*

Contents

Acronyms

ALRA	Abortion League Reform Association
BMA	British Medical Association
BPAS	British Pregnancy Advisory Service
CEDAW	Convention on the Elimination of All Forms of Discrimination Against Women
DFID	Department for International Development, UK
DHSSPS	Department of Health, Social Services and Public Safety, Northern Ireland
DUP	Democratic Unionist Party
FPA	Family Planning Association, Northern Ireland
GFA	Good Friday (Belfast) Agreement
MLA	Member of the Legislative Assembly, Stormont, Northern Ireland
MP	Member of Parliament, Westminster
NIALRA	Northern Ireland Abortion League Reform Association
NILT	Northern Ireland Life and Times Survey
NIWEP	Northern Ireland Women's European Platform
OFMDFM	Office of the First Minister and the Deputy First Minister, Northern Ireland
PIRA	Provisional Irish Republican Army
PSNI	Police Service of Northern Ireland
PUP	Progressive Unionist Party
RCM	Royal College of Midwives
RCN	Royal College of Nurses
SDLP	Social Democratic and Labour Party
SPUC	Society for the Protection of the Unborn Child
UUP	Ulster Unionist Party
WRDA	Women's Resource and Development Agency, Northern Ireland

List of Tables

CHAPTER 1

Introduction

In Belfast in 1984, Catherine[1] is 27 years old, and married to a man in jail for membership of the Provisional Irish Republican Army. Still active in republicanism, albeit within the remit of her role as prisoner's wife and mother to three young children, she has a brief affair with a man she is helping to hide from British authorities. She falls pregnant but manages to get money to travel to England to an abortion clinic. She worries about being arrested en route as a result of the Prevention of Terrorism Act. She isn't stopped and makes it to England to have the termination. On her return, she is questioned when re-entering Northern Ireland. Interrogated by police, she admits that she travelled for an abortion. "'You're a murderer, a Fenian whore and a murderer!'", they tell her, "'you're all the same – you IRA bitches'". A 'good cop/bad cop' routine ensues, in which attempts are made to encourage her to turn informant, further insults are thrown, and threats made that her children will be removed from her. She is terrified at the thought of this.

In Belfast in late 2013, Sarah Ewart, a recently married woman from East Belfast, pregnant but carrying a foetus suffering from anencephaly,[2] is denied an abortion. Having been told that she is ineligible under the strict legal framework provided for by Northern Irish law, she contacts a major BBC radio and television presenter in the region and is filmed as she travels to England for a termination. Her case receives much media attention in the province, reigniting debate around abortion, with public attitudes generally sympathetic to her situation and, indeed, incredulous that it could occur in contemporary Northern Ireland.

J. Thomson, *Abortion Law and Political Institutions*, Gender and Politics, https://doi.org/10.1007/978-3-319-96169-9_1

These are two very different stories, from very different periods within Northern Ireland's contemporary history—one taking place when violence within the province was still prevalent and a peace settlement, with or without a political institutional element, appeared impossible; one taking place over a decade after the Good Friday Agreement,[3] during a period of minimal violence and in the second full term of the Northern Irish Assembly. Yet both have the same ending—the impossibility of a termination within Northern Irish territory or law. Northern Ireland is a near anomaly in Western Europe in terms of its abortion laws. Until the referendum to repeal the 8th amendment to the Irish constitution passed overwhelmingly in May 2018, this conservative position extended across the border between the Republic and Northern Ireland. Yet Northern Ireland remains part of the UK, the rest of which has had liberal abortion laws since 1967. This book asks why this is the case. Why does Northern Ireland remain distinct from the rest of the UK as far as the termination of pregnancy is concerned? Why has the 1967 Abortion Act, which allows for terminations in England, Scotland and Wales, never been extended to Northern Ireland? Why, despite Northern Ireland now being a fundamental part of the multi-level governance structures of the UK, does it remain distinctly different on this issue?

Northern Irish society has changed dramatically from the early 1980s, the period in which this book begins. The region has moved from one of the bloodiest conflicts seen in post-World War Europe, to twenty years of post-peace agreement stability. Although still markedly poorer than the rest of the UK (as might be expected given the decades long conflict), Northern Ireland boasts major international tourist attractions (Giant's Causeway, the Belfast Titanic centre), world-class universities and, in 2013, played host to the meeting of G8 countries in Lough Erne. All of the above are often cited by those who praise Northern Ireland's transition to "peace" as providing a global benchmark for other countries emerging from conflict (Wilson 2010). As a society, its proponents argue, Northern Ireland's post-conflict stability and achievements are unsurpassed: so why, of all issues, does abortion remain so contentious and laws regarding it so strict?

Going hand in hand with this developing peace, Northern Ireland's politics and governance have changed dramatically in the period which this book considers. The devolution of political powers to Northern Ireland following the peace agreement in 1998 embraced the province within a complex multi-level governance set-up in the UK. A devolved government has been enacted, at once giving Northern Ireland greater local powers but also enmeshing it further into a UK-wide system. Northern Ireland, although with key important differences,[4] now elects regional representatives on the same time frame and with many of the same powers as Welsh and Scottish residents. Similarly, it continues to be represented at the national parliament at Westminster.[5] Why, even though it is a key component of the UK both territorially and in terms of its governance structures, is Northern Ireland allowed to be different in this regard? And why has central government at Westminster, heavily involved in the peace process and post-conflict management, had markedly little interest in this issue?

Why Institutions?

This book approaches the issue of abortion and Northern Ireland from an institutional perspective. Much literature on gender and politics has focussed on women *in* politics (Kenny 2013, 34; Mackay 2004, 114). It has considered, for example whether women can be said to act for women when in office (Childs 2001; Childs and Krook 2006; Childs and Withey 2006; Celis *et al.* 2008; Dovi 2002; Mansbridge 1999; Phillips 1995), how women's movements interact with the state (Banaszak *et al.* 2003; Stetson and Mazur 1995) and how institutions can encourage greater female representation (Krook 2009; Murray 2010). Yet there has been little work on "other aspects of political architecture, such as how unitary functions are shared or divided between different levels of government, in unitary, devolving or federal systems" (Sawer and Vickers 2010, 3). There has been less interest in how complex multi-level set-ups (such as the devolved UK) affect gendered policy-making.

Contemporary governance in the UK operates along a unique system of devolved governance. This system is often taken to be gender-neutral, or to have no gender-specific outcomes. Indeed, broader considerations of federalism or multi-level governance are very rarely gendered (Sawer and Vickers 2010, 3), making gendered thinking around devolved or multi-level institutions "a new and under-researched field" (Mackay 2010, 155). The nature of formal political structures in Northern Ireland—a regional Assembly and a national government, set within the framework of European institutions and international treaty obligations—creates a complex multi-level governance set-up as seen in Cardiff and Edinburgh. Furthermore, the specific nature of governance in Northern

Ireland—the power-sharing consociational arrangements—are a very different type of government than that seen elsewhere in the UK. Northern Ireland thus presents a clear example of multi-level governance through which its gendered implications can be considered.

Studying the issue of abortion through the lens of multi-level governance is particularly key given that institutional accounts of abortion rarely form part of academic work on the subject. Because of the broader concerns which are often drawn into the debate on abortion (as outlined below—largely opinions on female sexuality, the family and motherhood), the majority of work on abortion in the social sciences tends to address it as a social or legal, rather than a political, issue. Abortion has been considered from an understanding of new technologies and the way in which they have changed the social construction of termination of pregnancy (Roberts 2012), or via the role of international organisations and globalised human rights discourse (Bloomer and Fegan 2014; Cook and Dickens 2003). Work on abortion tends to address it from the ground up, looking at citizen activism and discourse (Bloomer 2013; Smyth 2005), not from the top down, looking at the way political institutions create discourse and legislation.

Indeed, cultural factors (especially religiosity and the social status of women) are important when considering a policy such as abortion. Regarding the social status of women, Northern Ireland would not appear to be so different from much of the rest of the Western world, with women enjoying equal citizenship and employment rights protected in law. Moreover, women occupy key public positions, most notably DUP leader Arlene Foster, and the leader of Sinn Féin in Northern Ireland, Michelle O'Neill. There have now been five female Lord Mayors of Belfast, and in 2017 the largest number of female MLAs ever was elected.[6]

Religion is perhaps a more important factor in the province, given the relatively high levels of religiosity reported. According to data from 2016, only 19% of Northern Irish residents do not consider themselves to belong to a religion, and 51% attend a church service at least once a month.[7] Christianity, of various denominations, continues to dominate the province, not only in the make-up of its citizenry,[8] but in the role that it plays structurally. Schools run by the Catholic Church serve the vast majority of the province's Catholic residents, with state schools tending to cater to the Protestant community.[9] As a result, education remains largely segregated by religious community. The Christian religion, in various denominations, continues to exert huge personal and structural force in the province.

This book does not deny that such factors are important when considering abortion, in this particular case study, or more generally. Nor does it deny that, as the above statistics suggest, Northern Ireland is, in general, more socially conservative than the rest of the UK. It has, however, consciously chosen to adopt an institutionalist lens to address this topic. Not only is the institutional aspect of abortion policy rarely considered in academic studies, but it is institutions which ultimately maintain the final say on this issue. They alone have the capacity to change the legal situation. An institutional lens is thus appropriate, because it helps to address the central concern of this book—why fundamental legislative change has not occurred.

Furthermore, the academic frameworks in which abortion tends to be analysed "seldom highlight political institutions; instead they take them for granted and treat them as natural occurrences" (Halfmann 2011, 5). This book takes political institutions seriously and offers, akin to Halfmann, "a rereading of conventional accounts of abortion policy and politics" (ibid.). As such, it acknowledges not only that institutions matter, but that the make-up of these institutions is fundamental to understanding how the issue is addressed: as Htun writes, "The configuration of democratic institutions - 'authoritarian enclaves', coalitional dynamics, political-party systems, executive legislative relations, and electoral systems – shape patterns of policy on gender issues" (Htun 2003, 174; see also Halfmann 2011, 5). This is especially important given that feminist institutionalism, whilst used to consider other aspects of gender and devolution in the UK (Kenny 2011, 2013; Mackay 2010; Mackay and Charles 2013), has rarely been used to analyse Northern Ireland. Most importantly, an institutional approach allows for the question of not only *why* the 1967 Act has never been extended to Northern Ireland, but *how* political structures and institutions have hindered the Act's extension. How have institutions, inter-institutional relationships and the particular multi-level governance set-up acted to inhibit change in the Northern Irish context?

Why Abortion?

Abortion is a specifically gendered topic, in that "so long as pregnancies occur in women's bodies" (Petchesky 1990, x), it is an issue that will affect women most centrally. As a result, many women will understand abortion "as a necessity, if not a 'right'" (ibid.), intrinsic to their ability to live their lives independently. Abortion policy draws attention to the blurring of lines between women's public lives as citizens and private lives as individuals. Aspects of human existence which have been hitherto defined as private (the body, sexuality, family) are "in fact preconditions of women's full and free access to the public sphere" (Lister 1997, 126). Abortion highlights the inherently patriarchal nature of most legal systems, in that women need to be treated "differently" (i.e. given specific rights) in order to be able to interact in the public realm. Whilst still often framed in public and political discourse as a private issue, the right to abortion is thus understood within feminist and liberal political theory as an exercise in bodily autonomy, and intrinsic to women's ability to exist equally alongside men in the public sphere (Held 1989, 201–202; Lister 1997, 126).

Access to safe and legal abortion has also long been understood as fundamentally important to women's health within national and international health policy. The World Health Organisation (WHO) declares that:

> Whether abortion is legally restricted or not, the likelihood that a woman will have an abortion for an unintended pregnancy is about the same. Legal restrictions on abortion do not result in fewer abortions, nor do they result in significant increases in birth rates. However, a lack of legal access to abortion services is likely to increase the number of women seeking illegal and unsafe abortions, leading to increased morbidity and mortality. (WHO 2015, 2)

Similarly, the Department of International Development of the United Kingdom (DFID) is distinctly liberal in its policy regarding reproductive rights and its work in the developing world. It argues that "Women and adolescent girls must have the right to make their own decisions about their sexual and reproductive health and well-being, and be able to choose whether, when and how many children to have" (DFID 2014, 3). Even in countries where abortion is not legal, DFID will "help make the consequences of unsafe abortion more widely understood, and can consider supporting processes of legal and policy reform" (ibid.).

Within international health policy and British development policy, abortion is thus understood as a fundamental component of women's health services.

Regardless of these arguments, abortion is rarely a non-controversial topic for political conversation. Abortion is discussed in Presidential debates in the USA; it is subject to extensive transnational campaigning, both for and against it; it struggles to be recognised in international law or human rights treaties (Htun and Weldon 2018, Chapter 6). It has come to symbolise, in many Western societies, "a much broader ideological struggle" (Petchesky 1990, xi) around which ideas such as population control, the family, motherhood, women's sexuality and indeed "the value of life" (Halfmann 2011, 7) are debated and defined. Debate around abortion has often become polarised between conservative and liberal thinking, in which a "clash of absolutes" (Tribe 1992) occurs, most especially in North America. As a result of all these additional issues, the central concern in abortion—women's lives, health and rights—is often obscured in broader political debate.

To date, the vast majority of work on institutions and gender has focussed on political recruitment and the descriptive representation of women (Kenny 2013; Mackay and Krook 2011). There has been less consideration of how different political institutional make-ups influence gendered policy issues, such as abortion, and women's substantive representation. Simultaneously, much literature on abortion and reproductive rights tends to work from the perspective of legal discourse or social movement activism, largely overlooking political institutions (Halfmann 2011). This book thus provides a key new direction for both literature on feminist institutionalism, providing a case study of how a substantive policy issue can be addressed using this framework, and the broader academic consideration of abortion rights.

Why Northern Ireland?

Northern Ireland's politics and society, especially in the years during the Troubles, have been much studied. However, as Eilish Rooney writes, "the preoccupation of most writers on the Northern Irish conflict has been in the more marketable arena of 'power politics', with the personalities, political parties and armed groups" (2006, 358) receiving most of the attention. Women and gender have played little role in this narrative. As such, the specific insights that can be gained from thinking about Northern Irish politics from a gendered perspective are largely under-considered.

Although there has been a substantial amount of work looking at women in Northern Irish politics, this largely focuses on the level of descriptive representation (Braniff and Whiting 2015; Galligan 2006, 2013). There has been some consideration of individual political parties, and women within them (Braniff and Whiting 2015; Tonge *et al.* 2014). There has been much less analysis of women's substantive representation, and of gendered policy issues more broadly. Work which specifically references "gender" (as a structural force) as opposed to "women" in Northern Irish politics has been especially marginalised. Ashe (2007, 2008, 2009a, b, 2012, 2014) and Racioppi and See (2000, 2001, 2006) have been most prolific in developing the idea of gender as a structural influence on Northern Irish society, looking at the role of gender in recent events such as the Holy Cross dispute[10] (Ashe 2006), or Iris Robinson's[11] public comments on homosexuality (Ashe 2007), although this has produced few book-length studies. In terms of structural explanations for Northern Irish society and conflict, gender is a late addition to the field and has had little influence on more orthodox explanations of the conflict and Northern Irish politics (McGarry and O'Leary 1995; Tonge 2005, 2014).[12]

With substantive gender issues given less consideration, abortion has been especially overlooked. Reproductive rights are occasionally mentioned in the literature on gender and Northern Ireland (O'Rourke 2013, 205), but only with a peripheral focus. Academic work on abortion in Northern Ireland is so far limited and has largely only been written within the last few years. It has tended to emerge from activist-academics, looking at the ways in which lack of abortion impacts citizenship rights in Northern Ireland (Horgan and O'Connor 2014), or the injustices of travelling for terminations (sometimes referred to as "abortion tourism": Bloomer and O'Dowd 2014). Whilst there has been some interest in activism around abortion (Bloomer 2013), there has been far less consideration of it as a political issue. It is given some consideration in Tonge *et al.*'s analysis of the DUP (2014): with this exception, political attitudes, formal political debates and changing policy on abortion have been given no sustained attention in scholarship on Northern Ireland. Yet abortion has been debated multiple times in the devolved Northern Irish Assembly (as Chapter 7 shows) and has received considerable attention in the legal system. Abortion debates have seen unusual meetings of politicians across the ethno-national divide (particularly around the issue of the Marie Stopes clinic), been subject to discussion on the part of international human rights mechanisms and have seen a huge amount of grass-roots political activism, both for and against liberalisation, including an annual March for Life which attracts thousands from across the island of Ireland. Abortion is a pressing political issue with much to tell us about contemporary Northern Irish politics. This book sets out to do so.

Within the feminist literature on post-conflict societies and governance, reproductive rights have been afforded less attention. Yet in their consideration of post-conflict law reform, Ní Aoláin *et al.* argue that reproductive rights are a "crude but effective measure" (2011, 220) for explaining how gender-friendly a post-conflict society has become: "reproductive rights capacity and access is one of the core benchmarks that … requires consistent inclusion to measure the full and transformative effect of transition from conflict to peace for women" (ibid., 222). Although a niche policy area, as they rightly point out a consideration of reproductive rights is a key indicator into the status of women and their rights within the peace and post-conflict process.

Aside from abortion, there are several other gendered policy issues on which Northern Ireland differs from the rest of the UK. Domestic violence and childcare legislation lag behind England, Scotland and Wales. Whilst same-sex marriage has been legal in the rest of the UK since 2013,[13] these laws have not been replicated in Northern Ireland. Equally, whilst legislation around sexually active gay men donating blood has been relaxed in the rest of the UK, until 2016 gay men were forbidden from donating blood in Northern Ireland. In 2014, attempts were made to enact a "Conscience Clause" in Northern Irish legislation, allowing for differential treatment on the basis of strongly held religious beliefs. A ban on same-sex couples adopting children was only struck down in 2013, and after an attempt by then Health Minister Edwin Poots to have the decision overturned.

Yet none of these policy areas have as precise an impact on women alone as abortion does. Furthermore, the policies referenced above are all relatively new. Abortion has been legal under the 1967 Act in England, Scotland and Wales for almost 50 years, yet Northern Ireland has remained rigid in its lack of liberalisation. The region has changed dramatically in both its society and politics in this period, and whilst, as this research explores, the discourse around abortion has also changed, the practical effects of abortion laws and their impact on women have not.

Although abortion has historically faced similar restrictions on both parts of the island of Ireland, this book does not consider the Republic. This is due to the very different legal, political and historical framework which exists there—the referendum of 2018; the prior reference to the "right to life of the unborn" in the Irish Constitution; the ramifications of the "X" case.[14] As a result of these significant differences, and the now divergent policy position across the two parts of Ireland, the Republic is not addressed in this book.

Book Overview

Moving on from this introduction, Chapters 2 and 3 provide a consideration of the conceptual and methodological framework used in the text. Chapter 2 explains the book's feminist institutionalist framework, drawing predominantly from literature which considers the gendered implications of multi-level governance structures, and contemporary devolution in the UK. Chapter 2 also details the methods and fieldwork employed in this research, explaining the ways in which both textual analysis of political debates and interviews with key stakeholders provide the evidence base for this book. Chapter 3 provides an outline of contemporary Northern Irish history, and the role of women and gender within that history. It also details abortion law in the UK, and Northern Ireland's unique place within this legal set-up.

The empirical chapters open by considering what role Westminster has played in this issue. Chapter 4 looks at national institutional factors, by analysing how central government has addressed (or failed to address) the issue of abortion and Northern Ireland since the 1967 Abortion Act. It draws from formal political debates at Westminster and interviews with Northern Irish Members of Parliament (MPs).

The book then moves to consider regional political institutions, most especially the devolved Northern Irish Assembly in Belfast. Chapter 5 looks at the movement towards peace from the 1980s onwards and explores why women's rights, and abortion rights more specifically, were not given greater consideration in the peace process. Chapter 6 considers the devolved Northern Irish Assembly created following the Good Friday Agreement. It looks at the conceptual basis of the Assembly, the gendered nature of consociational power-sharing (which provides the structure for the new political institutions in Northern Ireland) and the impact that this has on political space for issues such as abortion.

Chapter 7 then turns to consider how abortion has been treated as an issue in political debate in the Assembly, and the actions that have been taken to address it within formal politics, from 1998 to 2016. It looks at the micro-level of debates within the Assembly to ask how the issue of abortion has been addressed in the institution, and what role key individual politicians have had.

The book concludes by arguing that the complex multi-level governance make-up in the UK provides a means by which central government can avoid controversial issues such as abortion. It elucidates the gendered nature of post-conflict power-sharing at work in Northern Ireland, and how this impedes feminist activism and movement around women's issues. It argues further that feminist institutional theory can be merged with a consideration of "critical actors" to provide key insights into the gendered nature of power-sharing in post-conflict polities such as Northern Ireland. In doing so, the book illustrates how feminist institutional theory can be expanded beyond women's descriptive representation, to explore the gendered nature of substantive representation and gendered policy-making.

Notes

1. This is a pseudonym used by the authors of *Only the Rivers Run Free* (Fairweather *et al.* 1984), in which Catherine's story features. The quotes used here are from the same source, pp. 47–48.
2. Anencephaly is a condition where the foetus' brain and skull do not fully develop; babies with this condition rarely survive birth, and if they do, live for only very short periods of time. It can only be detected later in pregnancy, from around 20 weeks onwards.
3. The peace agreement of 1998 which reinstated devolved governance in the province. It is sometimes referred to as the Belfast Agreement, particularly within the Unionist/Loyalist community, but, for ease of understanding, is referred to as the Good Friday Agreement here throughout.
4. Largely the consociational power-sharing arrangements, not present in either Cardiff or Edinburgh. This is discussed in greater detail in Chapter 6.
5. Although Sinn Féin do not take their seats at Westminster.
6. Although, due to the suspension of the Assembly, have yet to take their seats.
7. Northern Ireland Life and Times Survey (NILT), 2016. http://www.ark.ac.uk/nilt/2016/Background/RELIGION.html, http://www.ark.ac.uk/nilt/2016/Background/CHATTND2.html. Accessed 2 February 2018.

8. The NILT of 2016 records only 2% of Northern Irish citizens belonging to a religion other than a Christian denomination. http://www.ark.ac.uk/nilt/2016/Background/RELIGION.html. Accessed 2 February 2018.
9. 2015 NILT data show that only 16% of respondents attended an "integrated" school. http://www.ark.ac.uk/nilt/2016/Background/SLFMXSCH.html. Accessed 2 February 2018.
10. Holy Cross is a Catholic primary school for girls in a prominently Protestant area in north Belfast. In 2001 and 2002, girls walking to school were regularly picketed by Loyalist protestors, eventually leading to pupils being escorted to school by riot police and soldiers.
11. Iris Robinson is a former DUP MLA. She is married to the former First Minister, Peter Robinson. Speaking from a deeply conservative perspective, she was strongly outspoken on issues regarding sexuality and abortion until her retirement from formal politics in 2009.
12. Class as a structural explanation for the conflict has a much longer academic history—see Whyte (1990)—yet race is equally neglected.
13. Same-sex marriage was legalised in England and Wales in July 2013 via the Marriage (same-sex couples) Act, and in Scotland in March 2014 via the Marriage and Civil Partnership (Scotland) Act. Civil partnerships are legal in Northern Ireland and have been since 2004, the same time at which legislation was brought in covering the rest of the UK. This similarity with the UK is largely due to the fact that Northern Ireland was then under Direct Rule from Westminster. Both main unionist parties (the DUP and the UUP) objected to civil partnership legislation being extended to Northern Ireland.
14. Like Northern Ireland, abortion in the Republic was, until further restrictions in the last thirty years, regulated primarily by the 1861 Offences Against the Person Act which originated from the era of British colonialism. A referendum held in 1983 added the Eighth Amendment to the Irish Constitution, which declared that "The State acknowledges the right to life of the unborn and, with due regard to the equal right to life of the mother, guarantees in its laws to respect, and, as far as practicable, by its laws to defend and vindicate that right." Implicit in this amendment was a tension between the right to life of the mother and the foetus—in cases where both cannot be saved, no guidelines for appropriate practice were present.

    This highly restrictive state of affairs in Irish abortion legislation, and the emphasis on foetal rights as opposed to women's rights, remained until the X case of 1992. X was a fourteen-year-old pregnant rape victim who was initially denied the right to travel for an abortion by the Irish Supreme Court (Smyth 2005). Subsequent referendums enshrined the right to travel for a termination, and for Irish-based organisations to provide information on abortion available outside of Ireland. The national soul-searching which ensued after the X case was mirrored in the wake of the tragic death of Savita Halappanavar in 2012. Denied a termination in a Galway hospital even though she was miscarrying, Ms. Halappanavar's death from septicemia acted to highlight the impracticality of the legal situation. As a result of Ms. Halappanavar's death, the Protection of Life During Pregnancy Act was instated, clarifying when abortion is legally permitted in Ireland for the first time since the 1983 amendment.

However, the procedure remained highly restricted. "Miss Y," an anonymous woman seeking asylum in Ireland in spring 2014, became pregnant as a result of rape in her home country. Due to her immigration status, limited English and lack of financial resources, she had difficulty arranging travel for a termination abroad. She eventually travelled to Liverpool by ferry but was arrested for illegally entering the UK. Hospitalised back in Dublin in her second trimester of pregnancy with severe mental health problems, including the threat of suicide, she refused food and water. She underwent a caesarean section in a Dublin hospital in her third trimester. The full facts around her case remain unclear, but illustrate that, even with the Protection of Life During Pregnancy Act, access to abortion in even the most extreme cases remained incredibly restricted in the Republic of Ireland.

The impact that the X case has had on public discourse also means that the issue of suicide in pregnancy has become central to the debate in Ireland, in a way that has not been replicated in Northern Ireland. Ireland's constitutional legal structure meant that any change would be subject to extensive campaigning and a public referendum; change in Northern Ireland could transpire via political or legal action with little public involvement, creating a very different set of circumstances. The Republic also has a different political framework in terms of the structure of both institutions and parties. Ireland has an elected head of state and a bicameral system, both of which are very different from the situation in Northern Ireland. Of all the political parties on the island of Ireland, only Sinn Féin field candidates on both sides of the border. The ethno-national division in Northern Ireland is not replicated in the Republic where the legacy of the Irish Civil War has a far greater impact on the formal party structure. Politically, the two parts of the island are very different.

A public referendum on abortion in the Republic of Ireland took place on the 25 May 2018. Ireland voted to repeal the 8th amendment to the constitution, by 66.4 to 33.6%, with a turnout of 64.13%. Legislation to allow abortion on request up to 12 weeks, and in limited circumstances after this point, is expected to be introduced.

Bibliography

Ashe, F. 2006. The McCartney Sisters' Search for Justice: Gender and Political Protest in Northern Ireland. *Politics* 26 (3): 161–170.

———. 2007. Gendering Ethno-Nationalist Politics in Northern Ireland. *Ethnic and Racial Studies* 30 (5): 766–786.

———. 2008. Gender and Ethno-Nationalist Politics in Northern Ireland. In *Northern Ireland After the Troubles*, ed. Colin Coulter and Michael Murray, 45–60. Manchester: Manchester University Press.

———. 2009a. Iris Robinson's Excitable Speech: Sexuality and Conflict Transformation in Northern Ireland. *Journal of Politics* 29 (1): 20–27.

———. 2009b. From Paramilitaries to Peacemakers: The Gender Dynamics of Community-Based Restorative Justice in Northern Ireland. *British Journal of Politics and International Relations* 11 (2): 298–314.

———. 2012. Gendering War and Peace: Militarized Masculinities in Northern Ireland. *Men and Masculinities* 15 (3): 230–248.

———. 2014. Gendering Demilitarisation and Justice in Northern Ireland. *British Journal of Politics and International Relations* 17 (4) (November): 665–680.

Banaszak, Lee Ann, Karen Beckwith, and Dieter Rucht (eds.). 2003. *Women's Movements Facing the Reconfigured State*. Cambridge: Cambridge University Press.

Bloomer, Fiona. 2013. Protests, Parades and Marches: Activism and Extending Abortion Legislation to Northern Ireland. In *Performing Feminisms in Contemporary Ireland*, ed. Lisa Fitzpatrick. Dublin, Ireland: Carysfort Press.

Bloomer, Fiona, and Eileen Fegan. 2014. Critiquing Recent Abortion Law and Policy in Northern Ireland. *Critical Social Policy* 34 (1): 109–120.

Bloomer, Fiona, and Kellie O'Dowd. 2014. Restricted Access to Abortion in the Republic of Ireland and Northern Ireland: Exploring Abortion Tourism and Barriers to Legal Reform. *Culture, Health & Sexuality* 16 (4): 366–380.

Braniff, Maire, and Sophie Whiting. 2015. 'There's Just No Point Having a Token Woman': Gender and Representation in the Democratic Unionist Party in Post-agreement Northern Ireland. *Parliamentary Affairs* 69 (1): 93–114.

Celis, K., Johanna Kantola, and Mona Lena Krook. 2008. Rethinking Women's Substantive Representation. *Representation: Journal of Representative Democracy* 44 (2): 99–110.

Childs, Sarah. 2001. In Their Own Words: New Labour Women MPS and the Substantive Representation of Women. *British Journal of Politics and International Relations* 3: 173–190.

Childs, Sarah, and J. Withey. 2006. The Substantive Representation of Women: Reducing the VAT on Sanitary Products in the UK. *Parliamentary Affairs* 59: 10–23.

Childs, Sarah, and Mona Lena Krook. 2006. Should Feminists Give up on Critical Mass? A Contingent Yes. *Politics and Gender* 2 (4): 522–530.

Cook, R.J., and B.M. Dickens. 2003. Human Rights Dynamics of Abortion Law Reform. *Human Rights Quarterly* 25 (1): 1–59.

DFID. 2014. United Kingdom Department for International Development. *Safe and Unsafe Abortion: The UK's Policy Position on Safe and Unsafe Abortion in Developing Countries.* London: DFID. https://assets.publishing.service.gov.uk/government/uploads/system/uploads/attachment_data/file/324590/safe-unsafe-abortion2.pdf. Accessed 29 May 2018.

Dovi, S. 2002. Preferable Descriptive Representatives: WILL Just Any Woman, Black or Latino Do? *American Political Science Review* 96 (4): 729–743.

Fairweather, Eileen, Roisin McDonagh, and Melanie McFadyean. 1984. *Only the Rivers Run Free: Northern Ireland: The Women's War.* London: Pluto.

Galligan, Yvonne. 2006. Women in Northern Ireland's Politics: Feminizing an 'Armed Patriarchy'. In *Representing Women in Parliament: A Comparative Study*, ed. Marian Sawer, Manon Tremblay, and Linda Trimble. Abingdon: Routledge.

———. 2013. Gender and Politics in Northern Ireland: The Representation Gap Revisited. *Irish Political Studies* 28 (3): 413–433.

Halfmann, Drew. 2011. *Doctors and Demonstrators: How Political Institutions Shape Abortion Law in the United States.* Chicago: University of Chicago Press.

Held, David. 1989. *Political Theory and the Modern State.* Cambridge: Polity.

Horgan, Goretti, and Jennifer O'Connor. 2014. Abortion and Citizenship Rights in a Devolved Region of the UK. *Social Policy and Society* 13 (1): 29–49.

Htun, Mala. 2003. *Sex and the State: Abortion Divorce and the Family Under Latin American Dictatorships and Democracies.* Cambridge: Cambridge University Press.

Htun, Mala, and S. Laurel Weldon. 2018. *The Logics of Gender Justice: State Action on Women's Rights Around the World.* Cambridge: Cambridge University Press.

Kenny, Meryl. 2011. Gender and Institutions of Political Recruitment: Candidate Selection in Post-devolution Scotland. In *Gender, Politics and Institutions: Towards a Feminist Institutionalism*, ed. Mona Lena Krook and Fiona Mackay. London: Palgrave Macmillan.

———. 2013. *Gender and Political Recruitment: Theorizing Institutional Change.* London: Palgrave Macmillan.

Krook, Mona Leda. 2009. *Quotas for Women in Politics: Gender and Candidate Selection Reform Worldwide.* Oxford: Oxford University Press.

Lister, Ruth. 1997. *Citizenship: Feminist Perspectives.* Basingstoke: Palgrave Macmillan.

Mackay, Fiona. 2004. Gender and Political Representation in the UK: The State of the 'Discipline'. *British Journal of Politics and International Relations* 6: 99–120.

———. 2010. Devolution and the Multilevel Politics of Gender in the UK: The Case of Scotland. In *Federalism, Feminism and Multilevel Governance*, ed. Melissa Haussman, Marian Sawer and Jill Vickers, 155–170. London: Ashgate.

Mackay, Fiona, and Mona Lena Krook (ed.). 2011. *Gender, Politics and Insitutions: Towards a Feminist Institutionalism*. Basingstoke: Palgrave Macmillan.

Mackay, Fiona, and Nickie Charles. 2013. Feminist Politics and Framing Contests: Domestic Violence Policy in Scotland and Wales. *Critical Social Policy* 33 (4): 593–615.

Mansbridge, Jane. 1999. Should Blacks Represent Blacks and Women Represent Women? A Contigent 'Yes'. *Journal of Politics* 61 (3): 628–657.

McGarry, John, and Brendan O'Leary. 1995. *Explaining Northern Ireland*. Edinburgh: Blackwell.

Murray, Rainbow. 2010. *Parties Gender Quotas and Candidate Selection in France*. Basingstoke: Palgrave Macmillan.

Ní Aoláin, Fionnuala, Dina Francesca Haynes, and Naomi Cahn. 2011. *On the Frontlines: Gender, War and the Post-conflict Process*. Oxford: Oxford University Press.

O'Rourke, Catherine. 2013. *Gender Politics in Transitional Justice*. Abingdon: Routledge.

Petchesky, Rosalind. 1990. *Abortion and Women's Choice: The State, Sexuality, and Reproductive Freedom*. Lebanon, NH: Northeastern University Press.

Phillips, Anne. 1995. *The Politics of Presence: The Political Representation of Gender, Ethnicity and Race*. Oxford: Oxford University Press.

Racioppi, L., and K.O. See. 2000. Ulstermen and Loyalist Ladies on Parade: Gendering Unionism in Northern Ireland. *International Feminist Journal of Politics* 2 (1): 1–29.

———. 2001. "This We Will Maintain": Gender, Ethno-Nationalism and the Politics of Unionism in Northern Ireland. *Nations and Nationalism* 7 (1): 93–112.

———. 2006. Engendering Democratic Transition from Conflict: Women's Inclusion in Northern Ireland's Peace Process. *Comparative Politics* 38 (2): 189–208.

Roberts, Julie. 2012. *The Visualised Foetus: A Cultural and Political Analysis of Ultrasound Imagery*. London: Ashgate.

Rooney, E. 2006. Women's Equality in Northern Ireland's Transition: Intersectionality in Theory and Place. *Feminist Legal Studies* 14: 353–375.

Sawer, Marian, and Jill Vickers. 2010. Introduction: Political Architecture and Its Gender Impact. In *Federalism, Feminism and Multilevel Governance*, ed. Melissa Haussman, Marian Sawer, and Jill Vickers. London: Ashgate.

Smyth, Lynda. 2005. *Abortion and Nation: The Politics of Reproduction in Contemporary Ireland*. Ashgate: Aldershot.

Stetson, Dorothy McBride, and Amy Mazur. 1995. *Comparative State Feminism*. Thousand Oaks: Sage.

Tonge, Jonathan. 2005. *The New Northern Irish Politics?* London: Palgrave Macmillan.

———. 2014. *Comparative Peace Processes*. Cambridge: Polity Press.

Tonge, Jonathan, Maíre Braniff, Thomas Hennessey, James W. McAuley, and Sophie A. Whiting. 2014. *The Democratic Unionist Party: From Protest to Power*. Oxford: Oxford University Press.

Tribe, Laurence. 1992. *Abortion: The Clash of Absolutes*. London: Norton.

WHO. 2015. World Health Organisation. *Safe Abortion: Technical and Policy Guidance for Health Systems—Legal and Policy Considerations*. Geneva, Switzerland: WHO. http://apps.who.int/iris/bitstream/10665/173586/1/WHO_RHR_15.04_eng.pdf.

Whyte, John. 1990. *Interpreting Northern Ireland*. Oxford: Oxford University Press.

Wilson, Robin. 2010. *The Northern Ireland Experience of Conflict and Agreement: A Model for Export?* Manchester: Manchester University Press.

CHAPTER 2

Gendering Institutions and Devolution

This book considers abortion in contemporary Northern Ireland, asking specifically why the 1967 Abortion Act has never been extended to the region. It does so from within a feminist institutionalist framework to address how political institutions have framed and constrained potential for change. This research situates itself within literature which considers the gendered implications of multi-level governance, most especially devolution as it has unfolded in the modern-day UK.

In order to do so, this chapter gives a brief summary of the conceptual literature on multi-level governance, followed by a consideration of its gendered effects. A discussion of the gendered nature of devolution in the UK then follows. Feminist institutionalism is then introduced as the overarching conceptual framework to this book, followed by a discussion of its application here.

Multi-level Governance

Whilst federal systems and theory have been in existence for centuries, an understanding of multi-level governance has emerged in a far more contemporary setting, largely to explain the developing role of the European Union and UK-wide devolution. In response to the major structural reforms of the EU in 1988, Gary Marks first used the term in 1992. Bache and Flinders (2004) argue that multi-level governance must be understood as a component of its parts: "multi-level" refers to the growth and influence of supranational and extra-state bodies (such as

J. Thomson, *Abortion Law and Political Institutions*, Gender and Politics, https://doi.org/10.1007/978-3-319-96169-9_2

the European Union) but also global bodies (such as the World Bank). "Governance" refers to the "hollowing out" (Rhodes 1997) of the state, and the greater role that non-governmental bodies have had in both moulding public policy and delivering it (Bache and Flinders 2004, 97). The state no longer carries complete supremacy, concerned instead with coordinating as opposed to directly administering and controlling policy (ibid.). Multi-level governance thus has both "vertical and horizontal dimensions" (ibid., 96). The vertical level sees action at sub-, supra- and national bodies, whilst the horizontal level sees services and provisions more widely spread out amongst a diverse group of policy actors such as non-governmental organisations and charities. Policies can be "uploaded" to the supranational, downloaded to the subnational or laterally loaded to non-governmental groups (Banaszak *et al.* 2003, 4–5). Viewed in this way, multi-level governance provides an "organising perspective" which encourages a reconceptualisation of how we define the distinction between "'domestic' and 'international' policy" (Bache and Flinders 2004, 94).

Devolution in the British context has introduced a very specific form of multi-level governance to the UK. A quasi-federal system replaced the previously dominant Westminster model of strong centralised government. Devolution in the UK has not merely been the result of power devolved from the centre to the regions—British regions now have greater autonomy to forge links with other regions within the European Union and thus to act independently from central government. The "upwards-downwards" hierarchical language of multi-level governance (ibid., 105) obscures in British devolution "greater evidence of a bargaining executive, rather than a strong executive; of interdependence between territorially distinct state organisations, rather than hierarchy; of multiple and confused accountability, rather than clear lines of accountability; of a quasi-federal state, rather than a unitary state" (ibid.). Furthermore, devolution in the UK framework has been uneven in the powers it has distributed amongst the regions. The devolution of powers has been, and continues to be, "ad hoc and reactive to territorially distinct dynamics, and asymmetrical and disjointed in outcomes" with little consideration of how reforms in Scotland, Wales and Northern Ireland, in addition to the continuing devolution of powers to English cities and regions, affect governance from the centre (Mackay 2010, 157).

Gender and Multi-level Governance

The limited (but growing) work on gender and federalism/multi-level governance suggests that there is no "one size fits all" to understand devolved or layered political design and women's rights. Individual political cultures play a key role, so that "national particularities in state architecture" (Kenny and Mackay 2011, 285), the possible retention of a centralised political party structure (ibid.) and the potential that regional or devolved government may be weaker and less able to exact change (Sawer and Vickers 2010, 5) can limit the scope of subnational institutions for feminist change.

Equally, with the establishment of devolved or new federal bodies, institutional practices must be learned anew, with the necessary "learning costs associated with newness" (Celis *et al.* 2012, 46). This breakdown of centralised control may result in "jurisdictional overlaps and blurred boundaries" thus enabling politicians and institutions to sideline or ignore gender issues (ibid.). "Multi-level games" (ibid., 51) can be distracting and demand widespread financial and human resourcing from feminist lobbyists. "Centrifugal dynamics" (ibid., 58) have the potential to see women's movements less interested in the centre and thus setting back feminist causes across the nation state as a whole.

These critiques aside, however, scholarship has largely suggested great potential for women's rights in devolved and federal democracies. Multiple governments mean more sites for citizens to interact with decision-makers and to influence legislation. The possibility of so-called venue-shopping (Vickers *et al.* 2010, 237) means that women's activists can move between different arenas of government to aim their attempts at the Forum which they think will provide the most friendly environment for their proposed policy changes (Chappell 2002, 97, 152; Vickers *et al.* 2010, 229). In this way, feminists can take advantage of different political spheres to avoid an anti-change "blockage at one level of government" (Sawer and Vickers 2010, 11). For example, work considering the unitary British state prior to devolution found that the centralised structure hindered attempts to further women's rights by providing no alternative sphere for lobbying. Bashevkin (1998, 10) found that the long period of Conservative rule from 1979 to 1997 made feminist lobbying at Westminster difficult and that successes were largely only possible due to the ability to lobby and involve certain aspects of the European structure. In general, therefore, the literature on gender and multi-level governance is positive about the potential inherent in different avenues for political action and lobbying presented by non-centralised political structures. Following these findings, the make-up of the devolved UK might be expected to be of great help to feminist campaigning and lobbying.

Gender and Devolution in the United Kingdom

Yet devolution in the UK, in the limited work which considers its gendered effects, has been shown to have varied outcomes for women-friendly policymaking.[1] Some scholarship suggests that devolution is encouraging limited, territorially specific feminist action rather than work across the UK as a whole. Celis *et al.* (2012) found that Scottish women's organisations had conducted little lobbying or action outside of Scottish political institutions, suggesting that they were abandoning national women's concerns. Furthermore, despite the key successes in women's descriptive representation in the devolved bodies (see Table 2.1), there is a sense from the literature that the urgency around gendered issues is fading. Kenny and Mackay argue that the Scottish Parliament now suffers from a "halo effect," in that the success of female politicians within all of the main parties[2] has "arguably engendered a sense of complacency among the political parties and made it increasingly difficult for feminist party activists to press the case for further reform" (2014, 880). This is set within a context in which the "new politics [is] a spent force" (ibid., 879) in Scotland and a return to an older model of "politics as usual" is gradually occurring. A version of Prime Minister's Questions was introduced into the Scottish Parliament in the form of First Minister's Questions, bringing a theatrical, combative style of debate into a chamber which had hitherto been based around principles of a more consensual politics (Mackay 2014, 562). Similarly, Kenny (2013) argues that candidate recruitment in post-devolution Scotland has been susceptible to erosion and drift, with resistance to more gender-friendly political recruitment.

Beyond these setbacks, there is a greater sense from the literature that a distinct territorial advantage to women-friendly politics and policymaking exists in the post-devolution landscape. Indeed, the level of women's descriptive representation in the new institutions alone appears indicative of more feminised bodies (see Table 2.1). Early work on the newly

Table 2.1 Women's representation in the devolved UK bodies and the Irish Daíl, 1997 to present day

Year of election	*House of commons*	*Scottish Parliament*	*National Assembly for Wales*	*Northern Ireland Legislative Assembly*	*Greater London Assembly*	*Irish Daíl*
1997	18.2	–	–	–	–	–
1998	–	–	–	17	–	–
1999	–	37.2	38.3	–	–	–
2000	–	–	–	–	40	13
2001	17.9	–	–	–	–	–
2003	–	39.5	50	19	–	–
2004	–	–	–	–	40	13
2005	19.7	–	–	–	–	–
2007	–	33.3	46.7	16.7	–	13
2008	–	–	–	–	32	–
2010	23	–	–	–	–	–
2011	–	35	40	19	–	15
2015	29	–	–	–	–	–
2016	–	35	42	28	–	22[a]
2017	32	–	–	30[b]	–	–

[a]The Republic of Ireland introduced laws requiring political parties to stand at least 30% female candidates in 2012

[b]Although the Assembly elected in 2017 has yet to sit

Adapted from Mackay (2010), Potter (2013), Russell (2000), Centre for the Advancement of Women in Politics, Queen's University Belfast, http://www.qub.ac.uk/cawp/observatory.html. Accessed 5 February 2018

devolved institutions found that not only has devolution provided different spaces for political activism, but it has done so in "new" environments which are "less likely to carry the embedded masculine institutional norms that have operated as such a barrier in Westminster and Whitehall" (Chappell 2002, 96). Writing in 2006, Mackay found that the new parliament in Edinburgh with its "apparent 'regendering' of political norms has a culture of civility and mutual respect and has largely avoided the 'yah boo' adversarial practices of Westminster" (Mackay 2006, 179; see also Malley 2012). Moreover, new politicians elected via devolution were "overtly feminist in outlook" and "actively pursued 'women friendly' policies" (Chappell 2002, 96). This positive outlook has largely continued. Writing in 2012, Mackay and McAllister found that female representatives in Edinburgh and Cardiff felt "a strong sense of entitlement and belonging; in turn, their presence is regarded as normal and unremarkable" (731). Indeed, devolved politics appears remarkably feminised. From 2016, both Scotland and Northern Ireland boasted female First Ministers. In the televised debates prior to the General Election of 2015, Nicola Sturgeon of the SNP and Leanne Wood of Plaid Cymru acted as the voices of their respective nations. Sturgeon has become especially associated with a gender equality stance, attending the first ever same-sex marriage conducted in Scotland, and adopting gender-equal representation in her first Cabinet appointments. Devolved politics, and especially their leadership, are significantly feminised, especially when compared to the slower growth in women's representation seen at Westminster.

There has been less academic work considering the substantive representation of women in the new institutions. Mackay (2006, 181) argues that the greater presence of women MSPs (Members of the Scottish Parliament) has helped to reframe childcare and domestic violence as mainstream issues. Similarly, Chaney found that female Welsh Assembly Members repeatedly ensured that new policies and legislation were considering gender (2006, 199). The devolved UK bodies also have vastly different powers, and thus different abilities to enact policy. Gendered policy achievements have therefore been uneven across the three devolved regions. In Wales, for example, domestic violence has become understood in a gender-neutral way, whilst in Scotland it has been interpreted in "a more radical feminist framing" (Mackay and Charles 2013, 603) as an issue of men's violence against women. This has been largely due to the fact that, as criminal justice policy is devolved to Scotland but not to Wales, Scotland has greater scope over how it can frame the issue (ibid. 2013, 611).

Northern Ireland, Devolution and Gender

In this picture of devolution in the UK and gender, Northern Ireland is both largely absent and an aberration. As Birrell notes, "'intergovernmental relations' has a popular connotation of referring mainly to relations with the Irish government" (2012, 271) and the relationships between Westminster, Stormont and the Irish Daíl have dominated multi-level governance understandings of Northern Ireland.

Northern Ireland, as the only part of the UK that had prior devolution, did not see completely new political institutions created, but rather an (albeit radically) rebooted version of the old parliament at Stormont.

The lack of common political parties between Northern Ireland and the rest of the UK means that the relationship between Stormont and Westminster can be categorised in some ways as one of competition rather than cooperation (Vickers *et al.* 2010, 237). The support afforded to the Conservative government by the DUP in the wake of the 2017 General Election, uncertainty over the Irish border following the EU membership referendum and the ensuing difficulties that have occurred in attempts to restart power-sharing governance in Northern Ireland illustrate the tensions between the national and devolved legislatures.

From a gendered perspective, none of the positive aspects found in the other devolved institutions appear to have helped in Northern Ireland. Already carrying a 50-year history of prior devolved governance in the province, the absence of a fully "new" institution has not resulted in a more woman-friendly approach to political representation as seen in Scotland and Wales. Women's descriptive representation in Northern Ireland has always been poor (Brown *et al.* 2002, 76). In the historic election of 1997, the region returned not a single female MP (ibid.). Women's representation in the new iteration of Stormont remains the worst of all devolved institutions in the UK and performs only slightly better than the Irish Daíl (see Table 2.1). Despite a clear commitment to women's representation in the Good Friday Agreement, "the promise of women's full and equal political participation is largely unfulfilled" (Galligan 2013, 415). The particular nature of politics in Northern Ireland, both its "robust and often sectarian style" (Galligan 2013, 430), and the fact that the legacy of divided politics has left less space for "other" types of politics, such as feminism (Brown *et al.* 2002, 80), have been blamed for this (this is discussed further in Chapters 5 and 6).

The Northern Irish Assembly can thus be understood as an example of "nested newness" (Mackay 2014; see also Chappell 2014a). This concept signifies that no institution, no matter how radically new, can avoid its immediate historical legacy and context. As Mackay describes it, institutions are:

> … the carriers of multiple – sometimes contradictory – interests and ideas; they are marked by past institutional legacies and are shaped by initial and ongoing interactions with already existing institutions … within which they are "nested" and interconnected. (2014, 567)

Mackay argues that, as they evolve, institutions have the capacity to remember the "old" and forget the "new." In this way, former practices can be remembered (or adapted, such as the introduction of a replica of Prime Minister's Questions into the new Scottish Parliament [Mackay 2014, 562–563]), whilst positive gendered change can be forgotten (equal opportunities were one of the key principles around which the new Scottish institution was founded, but has gradually been forgotten; equally, the crèche in the parliament building, heavily symbolic of a positive gendered outlook, has been continually put forward for closure in order to save money [Mackay 2014, 564–565]). In the continued absence of the Bill of Rights, and the lack of attention paid to women's right to political participation, both of which are enshrined in the Good Friday Agreement, the Northern Irish Assembly has also been good at forgetting the new. Similarly, in the dominance of ethno-national politics, the complete lack of any collective social or political understanding of the past in the province, and the continued relative absence of women from positions of power, remembering the old is a daily occurrence in the province's political institutions. "Old" and "new" exist uncomfortably and "stickily" alongside each other in the new bodies in Northern Ireland (Chappell 2014a; Kenny 2013; Mackay 2014).

Greater regional powers for Northern Ireland have thus, unsurprisingly, not provided venues for women's rights or LGBT activism, such that abortion and same-sex marriage legislation still lag far behind the rest of the country.[3] The absence of the dominant British parties has also made it difficult for feminists to "venue-shop" (Vickers *et al.* 2010, 237), with failures at Stormont not resulting in an easy movement to lobbying at Westminster, due to the very different political party make-up of the institutions. Rather than doubling the number of political institutions for women's rights activism and action, Northern Ireland has instead been the victim of a back and forth effect, with politicians and policymakers shifting the responsibility for abortion between institutions (Celis *et al.* 2012, 45; Vickers *et al.* 2010, 232).

Institutional Theory

In the light of this empirical literature considering gender, multi-level governance and devolution, institutional theory provides, particularly in its feminist guise, the key framework for this book.

As Steinmo writes, "institutional theory is as old as the study of politics" (2008, 118). "New institutionalism," in its various forms, is established as a key methodological framework within the social sciences, working from the basic understanding that "the organisation of political life makes a difference" (March and Olsen 1984, 747). "New" institutionalism distinguishes itself from "old" institutionalism in its greater critical stance and methodological nuance. In response to "an overemphasis on agency without structure … or, worse, on agency without sentient agents or structures" (Schmidt 2008, 313), new institutionalism aimed to bring the state "back in" (Skocpol *et al.* 1985) to an understanding of politics. Whilst previously "the focus on institutions was a matter of common sense, an obvious starting point for studying a country and, therefore, there was no need to justify it" (Rhodes 1997, 63), "new" institutionalism tries to problematise this taken-for-granted basis for research. Prior institutional work tended to have a static understanding of what political institutions were, with a "focus upon formal rules and organisations rather than informal conventions; and upon official structures of government rather than broader institutional constraints on governance" (Lowndes 2002, 92). Political institutions and their study were unquestioned, and often normatively driven within British political science as part of an acceptance of the superiority of the Westminster model. Such work was categorised by its "over emphasis on the political elite, its narrow conception of politics, its simplistic assumptions about the location and focus of power … and its essentially insular (domestic) focus" (Bache and Flinders 2004, 95).

From the 1980s onwards, political science moved towards a "new" understanding of the institutionalist methodology. Lowndes outlines six key changes that have occurred in the movement from "old" to "new" institutionalism:

(i) From a focus on organisations to a focus on rules
(ii) From a formal to an informal conception of institutions
(iii) From a static to a dynamic conception of institutions
(iv) From submerged values to a value critical stance
(v) From a holistic to a disaggregated conception of institutions
(vi) From independence to embeddedness (Lowndes 2002, 97).

"New" institutionalism is concerned with an understanding of institutions as fluid entities, based on the formal and informal rules which sustain them. It is less concerned with institutions as having "concrete" as opposed to "living" existences. Yet it is far from a single coherent framework and, as such, "does not constitute a unified body of thought" (Hall and Taylor 1996, 936). There are broadly four approaches to new institutionalism: rational choice, sociological or organisational, discursive or constructionist and historical (Mackay *et al.* 2010, 574–575; see also Hall and Taylor 1996).

Rational choice institutionalism does not see institutions as shaping behaviours, but rather that behaviour is endogenously determined (Lowndes 2002, 95). It posits that individuals within the institution act "to maximize the attainment of a set of goals given by a specific preference function and, in doing so, behave strategically" (Hall and Taylor 1996, 939). Rational choice institutionalism thus focusses on the micro-level of individual action, emphasising the "coordinating functions of institutions" (Thelen 1999, 371) and arguing that institutions provide incentives for collective action by offering ways to maximise results for those involved. Sociological institutionalism has a broader conception of what an institution can be. In distinction to rational choice institutionalists, sociological institutionalists ask not "'what do I get out of X?', people first ask themselves 'What should I do? What is appropriate?'" (Steinmo 2008, 163). Sociological institutionalism also further distinguishes itself from either rational choice or historical institutionalism by stressing the interrelationship between the institution and the individual. Institutions are seen as creative of individual behaviour, action and taste (Hall and Taylor 1996, 948).

Discursive or constructionist institutionalism is the most recent iteration of new institutionalism. Discursive institutionalism works from the premise that "ideas and discourse matter" (Schmidt 2008, 305) to the actions of political institutions. It argues that there must be "greater emphasis on the role of ideas and discourse in influencing actor interests, preferences and behaviour" (Mackay *et al.* 2010, 575). It positions itself as better placed than the other iterations of institutionalism (particularly historical institutionalists' reliance on the notion of path-dependency) in its ability to understand how and why institutions change or develop (Schmidt 2008, 314, 322; 2010, 2).

Finally, historical institutionalism works from an understanding of context specificity and the historical embeddedness of institutions. It "emphasises the extent to which individuals turn to established routines or familiar patterns of behaviour to attain their purposes" (Hall and Taylor 1996, 939), stressing the "path-dependency" of institutions. Historical institutionalism has a "problem-driven approach" (Waylen 2011, 148) and is interested primarily in "real world outcomes" (Steinmo 2008, 157). As outlined below, of the four varieties of new institutional theory, historical institutionalism has had the clearest influence on work which considers gender and institutions.

Feminist Institutionalism

As Kenny notes, new institutionalist approaches have often "underplayed ... insights into gender relations" (2007, 91; see also Kenny and Mackay 2009). The majority of the work falling into the above four categories has largely been gender-blind. This has meant that major changes to how political institutions function in recent years—such as gender quotas, gender mainstreaming with regard to policy, state feminist initiatives, the inauguration of ministerial (or the equivalent) positions focussing on women or equality—have largely been overlooked by new institutionalism. The development of a feminist institutionalism is an attempt to address this oversight, but also to think more fundamentally about the role of gender in political institutions.

A clear definition of gender is required here. As Chappell writes, "the challenge for each of us attempting to develop this field is to ensure that we avoid eliding the terms 'gender' and 'women' (which can so easily occur)" (2010, 184). In this research, an understanding of gender is adopted which is interested not in biological difference (e.g. only concerned with the presence or absence of men and women in political institutions) but in gender as a *structural* force within society and politics. This echoes the understanding of gender as it has been employed in much contemporary social science literature, which has "moved from 'measuring' gender as a discrete and dichotomous variable to understanding gender as a complex frame of reference" (Kenny 2007, 93). A similar understanding of gender to that expressed by many other feminist institutionalist scholars is followed here (Kenny 2007; Mackay *et al.* 2010), by adopting the definition of R. W. Connell. Connell builds on the work of other key thinkers to define gender as a "linking concept" (1987, 140) which acts to join together the social world and the private practices of childbirth, parenting, etc. In this definition, gender is a "process rather than a thing" (Connell 1987, 140; see also Beckwith 2005), with particular institutions (such as the state or the family) having their own gendered "regime." Such an understanding links closely to Chappell's argument that institutions often carry a "gendered logic of appropriateness" (2006): the particular code of conduct both for individual behaviour and for what is acceptable for broader discussion within an institution is gendered. Gender acts as a "process" or a "logic of appropriateness" through which certain issues (such as abortion) come to be endowed, or not, with importance in political discussion. Why did Westminster not intervene on abortion in Northern Ireland for so long? Why do blurred boundaries of responsibility for this issue exist? In general, abortion has not been considered an "appropriate" or key issue for action.

Following the brief outlines provided in the previous section, feminist institutionalism draws heavily from discursive and sociological institutionalism, but most especially from historical institutionalism, which is also reflected in this book's contribution.[4] The focus that sociological and discursive institutionalism have on meaning, values and norms complements the structural understanding of gender that feminist institutionalism carries (Kulawik 2009; Mackay *et al.* 2009). Historical institutionalism, like much feminist political science, seeks out "real world puzzles" (Waylen 2009, 246) and is often concerned with institutional development. Much feminist institutionalist work explicitly draws on historical institutionalist frameworks and concepts (Kenny 2013; Waylen 2007, 2011). This is not to suggest that feminist institutionalism merely borrows from conceptual frameworks that precede it. As outlined below, feminist institutionalism, developing from the rich tradition of feminist social science, brings its own specific considerations to bear and "may have more to offer the new institutionalism that the other way around" (Kenny and Mackay 2009, 278).

Feminist institutionalism makes four specific contributions to institutional theory, which this book adds to in the following ways.

An Understanding of Gender

Like "new" institutionalism more broadly, feminist institutionalism is concerned with how "formal structures and informal 'rules of the game' [are] structured" (Mackay and Krook 2011, 1). Further to this, and working from an understanding of gender as outlined above, feminist institutionalism works from the basis that all institutions are gendered and that this "means that constructions of masculinity and femininity are intertwined in the daily culture or 'logic' of political institutions" (Mackay and Krook 2011, 6; see also Acker 1992). As such, feminist institutionalism can help to understand how the outputs of institutions, the relationships between institutions and actors and the experiences of men and women within these institutions are gendered (Chappell 2010, 183). Feminist institutionalism does not therefore merely "add" gender to an understanding of new institutionalism but acts to question the very foundations of both new institutional theory (Kenny 2007, 97) and of institutions themselves.

This book thus explores how the institutions of Northern Irish politics are gendered. It moves beyond an understanding of sexed bodies within the Assembly to a consideration of the ways in which the gendered political structure influences decision-making and action (see Chapter 6). Akin to the understanding of gender described above, it perceives gender as a "process" (Connell 1987, 140) or "logic of appropriateness" (Chappell 2006) which encourages certain issues (such as abortion) to be invested with less attention in political bodies and decision-making.

A Greater Understanding of Informal Institutions, Rules and Norms

Feminist institutionalism also allows for a gendered understanding of the ways in which formal and informal politics interact. Whilst new institutionalism also considers this interaction, this is again rarely done with an appreciation of gender. Following the understanding of a gender "regime," feminist institutionalists argue that a "gendered logic of appropriateness" (Chappell 2006) acts to prescribe (and proscribe) acceptable modes of behaviour such that "the masculine ideal usually dominates political and legal settings" (Chappell 2010, 184). The debating style in the British Houses of Parliament is one such example of a very traditional masculine style of rhetoric forming what is implicitly understood as the norm for national politics.

As Kenny writes, this interest in informal politics is important because "gender is not always easy to 'see' in institutions" (2014, 679). Equally, these "barely visible" (Mackay *et al.* 2010, 583) gender dynamics of political institutions have largely gone unacknowledged and unconsidered by the mainstream literature (ibid., 579; Chappell 2006, 223). As Waylen notes, there is a "hidden life of institutions" which is "not always perceived" (2014a, 213, 216). A gendered appreciation can help to understand the subtle relationships which create the more opaque rules of institutions (ibid.). Similarly, as Chappell notes in her consideration of the International Criminal Court, it is "as important to account for *actions not undertaken* as it is to analyse those that have" (Chappell 2014b, 193, emphasis in the original), an observation which is especially important in research such as this which analyses why change has *not* occurred. The "importance of monitoring *inaction*, *silences*, and *lacunae*" (ibid.) is also vital to understanding how unspoken, informal gender norms may be at work.

This understanding is especially important for this research given the absence of movement around abortion law in Northern Ireland. As discussed above, the distinction between what is and is not acted on in political discussion has gendered implications. As such, the importance of considering "inaction" and "silences" (ibid.) is highly important for this book, which focusses centrally on an issue on which there has been very little legal change. Much like informal mechanisms, to study a lack of action requires more than observation of the outcomes decided upon by the institution (as such, in-depth interviews were the key research method applied—this is discussed in greater depth below). Like new institutional theory more broadly, a consideration of inaction and the informal mechanisms which exist in institutions requires a more dynamic understanding of how institutions function.

A Greater Understanding of Change/"Newness"

As the outline provided above of work on gender and devolution in the UK suggests, and in line with the transformative aims of most feminist political science (Waylen 2014a), feminist institutionalism is also concerned with innovation and how change can be enacted within new institutions (Kenny and Mackay 2009). Institutional theory has been slow to provide frameworks or explanations for why institutional change occurs, and often creates a "static" picture, "concerned more with institutional continuity than with institutional change" (Kenny 2007, 92). A growing body of work is interested to gender this theorising of institutional change (Waylen 2014b). As Waylen notes, new political institutions create potentials to adopt more equitable gender "regimes": "the creation of new institutions can offer opportunities for gender concerns to be incorporated more easily and fundamentally at the outset of an institution's life than it is to 'add them in' at a later stage" (Waylen qtd. in Chappell 2010, 187). As a result of this, much feminist institutionalist work has been interested in new bodies, including the devolved British institutions (Kenny 2013; Mackay 2014; Mackay and Waylen 2014; Malley 2012).

An understanding of novelty is central to this book in that it is largely concerned with a new body, the devolved Assembly of Northern Ireland. The Assembly was part of a broad new understanding of governance in the contemporary UK—new institutions were developed in Belfast, Edinburgh and Cardiff and the constitutional face of the country was profoundly changed. Yet, as feminist institutionalist theorists have argued, new institutions can still be "nested" in older understandings of politics. The Assembly is a clear example of "nested newness" (Mackay 2014) in that, whilst being a new set of structures, it is still very constrained by past understandings of politics in the province—most notably the continued presence of key individuals and the dominance of ethno-national voting patterns. This "nested" element to devolved Northern Irish politics has meant that different issues (especially gender issues, such as same-sex marriage and abortion) struggle for serious inclusion in the political sphere, as old concerns maintain their dominance.

A Greater Understanding of Power

Furthermore, feminist institutionalism has a keener understanding of power than is present in the various guises of new institutionalism. New institutionalism more broadly does not place overt emphasis on the role of power (Kenny 2007). An appreciation of gender as described above, however, puts an understanding of power at its centre. Given the gendered premise from which it begins, feminist institutionalism also "foregrounds power" (Kenny and Mackay 2009, 275; Mackay *et al.* 2010, 573). Gendered power dynamics frame decision-making and access to hierarchies within institutions: "the power relations that sustain political processes are produced and reproduced through gender" (Mackay *et al.* 2010, 583).

In this research, power is closely related to decision-making. Power in this case study is linked to the issue of informality and "silences" outlined above. The various "silences" and lack of attention to the issue of abortion, notably from national government, highlight this as a topic on which there has largely been a absence of decision-making, and a lack of a clear policy direction. The deferrals, obstructions and foot-dragging which have been seen at the devolved level (see Chapters 6 and 7) have also been a site of power through the exercise of non-decision-making.

Feminist Institutionalism, Northern Ireland and Abortion: Why Hasn't Change Happened?

As already discussed, the central aim of this book is to understand why the 1967 Abortion Act has not been extended to Northern Ireland. Following the description of feminist institutional theory above, Northern Ireland presents an appropriate case study by which to employ (and question) feminist institutionalist concepts for several reasons.

Firstly, feminist institutionalism has rarely been employed in a Northern Irish context. Whilst there has been much work on women's descriptive representation in the region (Braniff and Whiting 2015; Cowell-Meyers 2003, 2011; Galligan 2006, 2013; Matthews 2014), there has been less consideration of substantive representation, and little by way of addressing the manner in which the unique institutional make-up impacts women and gendered representation. Northern Ireland thus provides a fruitful new direction for feminist institutionalism, given that not only is it the final piece of the puzzle of devolution in the UK to consider, but it also includes many factors which feminist institutionalism has not addressed to date (its situation as a post-conflict polity; the unique power-sharing institutional arrangements). Using a feminist institutionalist analysis provides exciting new directions for this literature to consider, as well as completing the picture described above of other accounts of devolution in the UK.

Secondly, feminist institutionalist work to date has largely only looked at one institution (Kenny 2013), one level of multi-level governance (Mackay 2010), or a comparative study of different institutions (such as the Scottish Parliament and the Welsh Assembly; Mackay and McAllister 2012). This study explores the links between the various levels of multi-level governance at work in the UK, a factor which has often been overlooked in work on gender and devolution. The inter-institutional relationships within the complex multi-level structures here are important, especially given how fitful governance in Northern Ireland has been (and continues to be) since devolution.

Thirdly, the Northern Irish Assembly provides another example of a "new" institution. As discussed above, new institutions and institutional design have been a key consideration for feminist institutionalism (Chappell 2015; Kenny 2013; Mackay 2014). Having been suspended for the majority of the 2000s, the Northern Irish Assembly is still a relatively new body, continuing to evolve and develop in its working practices. A consideration of how it was designed, and how it functions at this point, can help to understand how gendered regimes are being adopted or challenged within its institutional workings. At the same time, however, the "new" Northern Irish Assembly is essentially a (dramatically) revamped version of the Stormont Parliament of 1920 to 1974. Hence, it provides a means by which the concept of "nested newness" (Mackay 2014) can be further examined—how are old practices and concepts enmeshed in the new institution?

Finally, this case study allows further consideration of the role of power and the structure/agency debate within institutions. Feminist institutionalism has, in general, been interested more in structures and institutional processes, than the broader sweep of feminist political science which has been interested in agency (e.g. the extensive literature on the women's movement—Banaszak *et al.* 2003—or the literature considering "critical mass" and "critical actors" within political institutions—Childs and Krook 2006; Dahlerup 1989, 2006). Historical institutionalism more generally has given extensive consideration to the structure/agency debate—Thelen and Mahoney (2010) in particular are interested in how agents work within institutions to create gradual change. Although less of an immediate concern, feminist institutionalism has addressed the notion of agency and has made clear contributions to the gendered implications of the structure/agency debate within institutional theory. In Chappell's consideration of the influence of feminist activism on the federal structure in Australia and Canada, she argues that "the relationship between feminists and political institutions is co-constitutive, with agency and structures continuously informing each other" (2002, 4). In later work (2015, Chapter 5), she has considered the importance of individual feminists within the International Criminal Court. Elsewhere, feminist institutionalism has considered how "key women, particularly feminists, are often central" (Waylen 2009, 251) to policy change—Waylen (2011) cites the Health Minister in the first post-apartheid South African government, a well-placed feminist who helped ensure that liberal abortion laws were passed.

These examples reflect broader research interests in feminist institutionalist thinking: it remains centrally focussed on how things change, and how new institutions develop. As a result of the transformative potential inherent in this work, and the normative concerns of feminists working in this field, it has largely focussed on "positive change" (Waylen 2011, 149): changes that illustrate how oppressive structures, norms or policies can be challenged and adapted. Yet the focus of this research is largely not an example of "positive change." This book considers, not progressive change or key movements towards gender equality, but rather stasis and obstruction. This concern is echoed in contemporary trends in feminist institutionalist thinking which address the ways institutions can be sites of resistance to positive gendered change (Kenny's consideration of the struggle against women's political recruitment in post-devolution Scotland [2013]; Mackay's conceptual framework of "nested newness" as a means to understand why institutions revert to older practices or ignore gendered considerations [2014]; Waylen on the way in which informal institutions can "subvert gender equitable change" [2014a, 213]; Chappell's consideration of gendered "silences" and "inactions" in the International Criminal Court [2014a, b, 2015]). This book thus expands feminist institutionalism's understanding of structure/agency, by considering how resistance to change on abortion in Northern Ireland has happened within political institutions. It asks why the 1967 Abortion Act has *not* been extended to Northern Ireland—Why has change been so elusive? Why has liberalising policy been resisted? What has encouraged stasis and the absence of any coherent movement in this area? As such, this book provides a key case study for this developing feminist institutionalist interest in what we can gain from looking at actions *not* undertaken (Chappell 2014b), as much as those that have been.

A Framework for Feminist Institutionalist Research

This section considers how to turn the theoretical and empirical concerns of feminist institutionalism as described above, into the methodological base for an empirical research project.

Feminist research and methodology have long been fuelled by an interest in real-world problems (Ackerly and True 2010; Goertz and Mazur 2008; Hesse-Biber *et al.* 1999; Ramazanoglu 2002). "A commitment to problem-driven, real world research" (Mackay *et al.* 2010, 584) likewise also extends to feminist institutionalist literature. This in turn reflects the strong methodological links that feminist institutionalism has to historical institutionalism (Pierson and Skocpol 2002, 697). Much feminist institutionalist work has worked from a historical institutionalist perspective, in the sense that it places great importance on "the overarching context" (Waylen 2011, 151) of an institution. Feminist institutionalism also takes history seriously, placing "politics in time" (Pierson 2004; Pierson and Skocpol 2002, 695) and taking care to "look at forests as well as trees" (Pierson and Skocpol 2002, 711). Reflecting this, and as reiterated in the historical background provided in the following chapter, a longitudinal historical lens is also applied in this research.

The historical bent of historical and feminist institutionalism is not without critique. The in-depth approach that such work takes often means that they rely on small *n* sample sizes (Waylen 2007), or, as is the case with this research, often even a single case study (Kenny 2013). A predominant critique of this type of research is that case studies cannot avoid selection bias; that they allow the researcher to confirm already strongly held beliefs or opinions, and that, as a result, they lack scientific merit (Flyvbjerg 2006, 234). Yet qualitative researchers often argue that these fears of selection bias are "overstated" (Bennett and Elman 2006, 462), and, indeed, choosing cases based on the outcome or the particular features is intrinsic to the type of feminist research described above. Research which employs single case studies often has different motivations, which are not acknowledged in these critiques. Such research largely does not work from a positivist framework. It is interested in theory building, not theory testing (Kenny 2013; Smyth 2005; Waylen 2007). Furthermore, such critiques ignore the many benefits of case study research within the social sciences. As Bent Flyvbjerg writes, "the advantage of large samples is breadth, whereas their problem is one of depth" (2006, 241). Flyvbjerg also stresses the importance of "context-dependent knowledge" (ibid., 222) emerging from case study work which, he argues, is the best type of knowledge that social science has shown itself able to produce: "social science has not succeeded in producing general, context-independent theory and, thus, has in the final instance nothing else to offer than concrete context-dependent knowledge" (ibid., 223). Case study research thus provides a key method for producing valuable, context-based knowledge.

Feminist institutionalist work, and much feminist social science more generally, is context-driven. It works from a strong appreciation of historical background and frequently conducts small *n* research, interested in a process of theory building rather than testing existing ideas or concepts. As a result of these concerns, it frequently employs a mixed-methods approach that relies heavily on qualitative data, reflecting the "theoretical eclecticism, multiple analytic techniques, and a broad comparative and historical purview" (Pierson and Skocpol 2002, 698) of historical institutionalism. A consideration of the specific methods employed in this research continues below.

Language and Feminist Institutionalist Research

Although, as outlined in the following sections, this work employs several methods, it emerges largely from an analysis of discourse and language. Much feminist social science research works from a poststructural understanding of language which argues that it is not reflective, but rather *constructive* of reality (Hansen 2010; Kenny 2013). Language is not, in this view, the "private property of the individual but … a series of collective codes and conventions that one needs to employ to make oneself comprehensible" (Hansen 2006, 18). In other words, it is only through language that things (objects, emotions, places) have meaning. As such, Hansen continues, language has clear political functions, as it is the site where ideas and identities are simultaneously excluded and reproduced (ibid., 19). Acknowledging language in this way helps to move from a realm of unconsciously accepted truth (e.g. the idea that women are inherently weaker, or innately more peaceful) to a space where ideas can be understood as constructed, and thus contested. In this sense, an employment of discourse analysis through a feminist lens is implicitly critical, in "that it aims to reveal the role of discursive practice in the maintenance of the social world, including those social relations that involve unequal relations of power" (Jorgensen and Phillips 2002, 63).

As outlined above, discursive (or constructionist) institutionalism is the newest iteration of new institutionalism and has had, to date, less influence on feminist institutionalist work, particularly that which has considered the devolved UK. Discourse, its proponents argue, is "constitutive" (Kulawik 2009, 269) of political ideas and relationships.[5] A central argument of discursive institutionalism is that it can better help to explain institutional change. As Schmidt argues,

> … if everyone follows rules, once established, how do we explain institutional change? And how do we explain agency? Rational institutionalism, historical institutionalism and sociological institutionalism effectively leave us with "unthinking" actors who are in an important sense not agents at all. This subordination of agency (action) to structure (rules) is the key problem. (Schmidt 2008, 314).

Discursive institutionalism helps to incorporate an understanding of individual action which other forms of institutionalism are often critiqued as glossing over, rendering "a discursive account … helpful in reformulating the relation between agency and institutions in a nondeterministic manner" (Kulawik 2009, 268). Discursive institutionalism further argues that it can more effectively explain change due to its focus on ideas and norms (ibid., 322), and the implicit focus that this places on agency and action rather than rules and "path-dependent structures and unexplainable critical moments" (ibid.).

Despite the lack of an explicit institutional focus, discourse analysis has played a key role in feminist methodologies more generally, particularly through the work of Carol Lee Bacchi. Bacchi works from a similar poststructural feminist discourse analysis as outlined above, most notably in her "What's the problem?" approach (1999). Although Bacchi does not explicitly employ institutionalist language, her technique can be usefully incorporated into a feminist institutionalist framework. Bacchi proposes a deconstructionist framework which questions the ways in which policy is portrayed through language. We should not ask, she argues, how do we fix this problem, but rather how has the problem been constructed in political discourse: "what's the problem represented to be?" (ibid., 1). According to Bacchi, "we need to shift our analysis from policies as attempted 'solutions' to 'problems', to policies as constituting competing interpretations or representations of political issues" (ibid., 2). Debate around abortion here is considered in this light: how is abortion understood to be a "problem"? What contributes to this diagnosis, and what is left out? What are the effects of this representation of abortion? (ibid., 12–13).

A critical discourse analysis as outlined above is thus important as it allows us to get beyond the surface level of the debates on abortion to what is implicitly being discussed. It helps us to understand the issue of abortion in Northern Irish politics not as a neutral topic, but something which is being continually constructed in both the language of the interviewees that were spoken to in this project, and the discourse used to debate the issue in public forums, including the House of Commons and the Northern Irish Assembly. Through an appreciation of the institutional structure in which this discourse is deployed, as outlined in the discursive institutionalist work above, it also aids an understanding of how institutions encourage or impede certain types of discourse, and how language can help us to greater appreciate the interplay between structure and agency (Schmidt 2008, 2010).

Process Tracing

As reflected in the historical and contextual anchoring of much feminist institutionalist research outlined in the previous chapter, this book works primarily from process tracing. This method has often been co-opted by feminist institutionalist scholars (Kenny 2013; Waylen 2014b). George and Bennett define process tracing as the "method [that] attempts to identify the intervening causal process – the causal chain and causal mechanism – between an independent variable (or variables) and the outcome of the dependent variable" (2005, 206). In other words, it allows for long-scale historical analysis that looks at the mechanisms which cause change (or impede it in this case study). The long-lens analysis encouraged by process tracing helped to create an in-depth, historical perspective when considering the ways in which abortion has been discussed.

Yet George and Bennett's depiction of process tracing here still relies on a type of language and certain concepts (notably their reliance on the idea of variables) which are redolent of research conducted more in the vein of positivism or theory testing. Similarly, Büthe's (2002) argument for process tracing hinges on very positivist understandings of the primacy of "modelling" to political science. This is reflected in a variety of positivist work which employs process tracing as a means to test hypotheses (e.g. Bush 2011). Yet, as Levy argues, much process tracing works along a "different logic of inference" (2008, 14), with case studies chosen via a "well-developed theoretical framework" (ibid.). This reflects broader understandings of process tracing which understands it as working from an interpretive perspective, in which topics for analysis are guided and informed by theory, and thus help to expand upon existing ideas. Falleti argues that process tracing needs to be guided by theory: "the function of the method is to illustrate how the theory or formal model works in the real world rather than to generate theories" (2006, 4). Such is the manner in which the method is adopted here.

Furthermore, George and Bennett define causal mechanisms as "ultimately unobservable physical, social or psychological processes through which agents with causal capacities operate, but only in specific contexts or conditions, to transfer energy, information, or matter to other entities" (2005, 137). The emphasis on "unobservable" phenomena allows for consideration of gender as a factor, in the understanding of gender as a social structure/process outlined above as opposed to an observable male/female dichotomy (Lovenduski 1998). This also emphasises that change does not have to be initiated at the individual level as previous descriptions had done (George and McKeown 1985) but can be rooted at the institutional or social level (Falleti 2006, 2).

Process tracing does not necessarily only work from qualitative data, nor is it incompatible with quantitative findings (Collier 2011, 825), including that which considers gender and women (Bush 2011). However, the vast majority of process-tracing work relies on qualitative methods and data. Given the importance that a feminist institutionalist framework places on informal dimensions, methods employed often stress the need for in-depth, time-intensive involvement with the institutions being researched (Kenny 2013). Furthermore, as the above description of the depth of research required for process-tracing research suggests, process tracing requires large amounts of data, and intensive, in-depth research with a long-term historical focus, creating a "thick" description (Geertz 1973) of events. This was provided in this research through a range of methods which brought depth of study to the project: in-depth interviews across the political spectrum in both Northern Ireland and London, archival research, and analysis of government debates and documents produced by key stakeholders (including NGOs and service providers). These are considered in greater depth below.

Methods for Data Collection

Having considered the methodological framework, this section turns to the specific methods used in this research.

Interviews

George and Bennett suggest that "in process-tracing, the researcher examines histories, archival documents, interview transcripts" (2005, 6). Similarly, Tansey argues that, for process tracing, "the most appropriate sampling procedures are thus those that identify the key political actors that have had most involvement with the processes of interest" (2007, 2). Elite interviews are therefore one of the most appropriate research techniques because "the goal with process tracing is to reduce randomness as much as possible, and work to ensure that the identities of the most important actors are established, and that they are approached directly for interview" (ibid., 15). Tansey argues that a "snowballing" technique for identifying interviewees is the most appropriate for the purposes of process tracing, because it helps to establish those individuals who are central to the topic at hand, and that "chain-referral" references from elites can help to identify "influential players who researchers may not initially have presumed relevant to the study" (ibid., 20). In accordance with this logic, in-depth interviews were conducted with key figures in the organisations, activists and politicians surrounding this issue. Following Tansey (2007), key figures were identified prior to fieldwork but a "snowballing" technique was adopted to gain access to as wide an interview base as possible. Interviews were semi-structured in that they often began with "grand-tour" questions (Spradley 1979) and from there would move to "example" questions and "prompts" (Leech 2002). This also helped to facilitate a broad discussion about the ways in which formal, visible practices interacted with more informal norms and rules (Kenny 2014).

In this sense, this study explores the "beliefs, ideas and discourses" (Bevir and Rhodes 2002, 131) of the individuals and the institutions that are most central to this issue. Reflecting the section discussing language and discourse above, the interviews were employed with an aim to understand why the discussion around abortion in Northern Ireland has been constructed in the various ways it has, and how these constructions work to constrain or encourage action within politics in the region. In contrast to work which employs process tracing and which tends to work from positivist frameworks, this research is thus strongly interpretive, particularly with regard to interview data. Although interviews were conducted in order to "obtain information about well-defined and specific events and processes" (Tansey 2007, 2), this was not their sole purpose. Interviews were also conducted to gain a broader appreciation of how the actors involved defined and framed the issue in their own language. For example, even though party policy on abortion could often be gleaned from websites or party literature, all interviews with politicians began by asking them to outline their party's stance on the issue. This helped gain a better sense of how the party had come to this position, the ways in which it may have been contested or debated within the party, and the individual's particular opinion regarding his/her party's policy. In other words, and following Bacchi's (1999) framework as outlined above, rather than taking the parties' positions for granted, this question provided a sense of how the policy and its particular wording had been constructed.

Over fifty interviews were conducted with key stakeholders: MLAs, MPs, feminist activists, representatives of women's organisations and the women's sector, medical professionals and representatives from medical

Unions. The focus that this research has on the gendered nature of institutions, as outlined above, meant that women and men were consciously approached for interview.

Debate/Archival Research

With regard to formal political debates, extensive searches were conducted using the online Hansard search facilities for both the House of Commons[6] and the Northern Irish Assembly at Stormont.[7] Key debates and questions asked within parliament to be analysed were thus identified.

Additionally, archival research was conducted at the Linen Hall Political Collection at the Linen Hall Library in Belfast. Documents obtained there (mostly political party literature and NGO pamphlets and booklets) helped to gain a picture of, and to prioritise in terms of interviewees approached, the "specific events and processes" (Tansey 2007, 2) that were the most important to be considered.

Conclusion

This chapter has provided an overview of the literature on multi-level governance and devolution, with particular attention paid to work which considers the gendered aspects of these institutional make-ups. Although there is a developing body of literature on gender and multi-level governance, and devolution in the UK in particular, there has been little consideration of Northern Ireland. This chapter has explored why the region, with its unique power-sharing make-up and new institutions, is an important, yet underexplored, case study.

It then turned to institutional theory, and to feminist institutionalism in particular, which underpins a large amount of work to date which addresses gender and devolution in the UK. Feminist institutional theory also forms the framework for this book. The chapter explained why a feminist institutional framework is especially pertinent for this research, and the ways in which this case study can broaden the scope and evidence base of feminist institutionalist theory to date. It explored the key contributions to feminist institutionalism that this book makes—primarily an expansion of the understanding of nested newness, and a greater appreciation of the structure/agency debate within the feminist institutionalist literature. Furthermore, this book adds to the developing feminist institutionalist literature which explores obstruction and foot-dragging around gendered political issues. In this sense, the book approaches the central research problem from a novel angle in that it asks—why *hasn't* change occurred?

Notes

1. The literature on Scotland is substantially more developed and this section draws mostly from Scottish examples.
2. Indeed, from the run-up to the Holyrood elections of 2016 until late 2017, all of the main three parties in Scotland (the Scottish Nationalist Party, Labour and the Conservatives) were led by women.
3. An interview with an LGBT advocacy organisation based in Belfast also stressed the other, multiple arenas in which the Assembly has failed to deliver on LGBT rights: "… the invisibility of LGBT people themselves, the invisibility within healthcare, the invisibility within accessing services, invisibility when it comes to politics and pretty much everything we can think of is something that we very much seek to address in our lobbying work and in our representative work." Private interview with the author, Belfast, June 2014.
4. Rational choice institutionalism has had far less of an impact on the development of feminist institutionalism, largely due to the "epistemological incompatibilities" between the understanding of individual agency in rational choice theory and the gendered, socially embedded agent in feminist political science (Kenny and Mackay 2009, 273).
5. This book does not go as far as some discursive institutionalists do, to argue that discourse is itself constitutive of institutions.
6. http://www.parliament.uk/business/publications/hansard/. Accessed 5 February 2018.
7. http://aims.niassembly.gov.uk/officialreport/officialreport.aspx. Accessed 5 February 2018.

Bibliography

Acker, J. 1992. From Sex Roles to Gendered Institutions. *Contemporary Sociology* 21 (5): 565–569.

Ackerly, Brooke, and Jackie True. 2010. *Doing Feminist Research in Political and Social Science*. New York: Palgrave Macmillan.

Bacchi, Carol Lee. 1999. *Women, Policy, and Politics: The Construction of Policy Problems*. New York: Sage.

Bache, Ian, and Matthew Flinders. 2004. Multi-level Governance and British Politics. In *Multi-level Governance*, ed. Ian Bache and Matthew Flinders. Oxford: Oxford University Press.

Banaszak, Lee Ann, Karen Beckwith, and Dieter Rucht (eds.). 2003. *Women's Movements Facing the Reconfigured State*. Cambridge: Cambridge University Press.

Bashevkin, Sylvia. 1998. *Women on the Defensive: Living Through Conservative Times*. Chicago: University of Chicago Press.

Beckwith, Karen. 2005. A Common Language of Gender? *Politics & Gender* I (1): 128–137.

Bennett, Andrew, and Colin Elman. 2006. Qualitative Research: Recent Developments in Case Study Methods. *Annual Review of Political Science* 9: 455–476.

Bevir, Mark, and R.A.W. Rhodes. 2002. Interpretive Theory. In *Theory and Methods in Political Science*, 2nd ed., ed. David Marsh and Gerry Stoker. Basingstoke: Palgrave Macmillan.

Birrell, Derek. 2012. Intergovernmental Relations and Political Parties in Northern Ireland. *British Journal of Politics and International Relations* 14: 270–284.

Braniff, Maire, and Sophie Whiting. 2015. 'There's Just No Point Having a Token Woman': Gender and Representation in the Democratic Unionist Party in Post-agreement Northern Ireland. *Parliamentary Affairs* 69 (1): 93–114.

Brown, Alice, Tahnya Barnett Donaghy, Fiona Mackay, and Elizabeth Meehan. 2002. Women and Constitutional Change in Scotland and Northern Ireland. *Parliamentary Affairs* 55: 71–84.

Bush, Sarah Sunn. 2011. International Politics and the Spread of Quotas for Women in Legislatures. *International Organisation* 65 (1): 103–137.

Büthe, Tim. 2002. Taking Temporality Seriously: Modeling History and the Use of Narratives as Evidence. *The American Political Science Review* 96 (3): 481–493.

Celis, K., Fiona Mackay, and Petra Meier. 2012. Social Movement Organizations and Changing State Architectures: Comparing Women's Movement Organizing in Flanders and Scotland. *Publius: The Journal of Federalism* 43 (1): 44–67.

Chaney, Paul. 2006. Women and Constitutional Reform: Gender Parity in the National Assembly for Wales. In *Representing Women in Parliament: A Comparative Study*, ed. Marian Sawer, Manon Tremblay, and Linda Trimble. Abingdom: Routledge.

Chappell, Louise. 2002. *Gendering Government: Feminist Engagement with the State in Australia and Canada*. Vancouver: University of British Columbia Press.

———. 2006. Comparing Political Institutions: Revealing the Gendered 'Logic of Appropriateness'. *Politics and Gender* 2 (2): 232–235.

———. 2010. Comparative Gender and Institutions: Directions for Research. *Perspectives on Politics* 8 (1): 183–189.

———. 2014a. 'New', 'Old', and 'Nested' Institutions and Gender Justice Outcomes: A View from the International Criminal Court. *Politics and Gender* 10(4): 572–594.

———. 2014b. Conflicting Institutions and the Search for Gender Justice at the International Criminal Court. *Political Research Quarterly* 67 (1): 183–196.

———. 2015. *The Politics of Gender Justice at the International Criminal Court: Legacies and Legitimacy*. Oxford: Oxford University Press.

Childs, Sarah, and Mona Lena Krook. 2006. Should Feminists Give Up on Critical Mass? A Contingent Yes. *Politics and Gender* 2 (4): 522–530.

Collier, David. 2011. Understanding Process Tracing. *PS: Political Science and Politics* 44 (4): 823–830.

Connell, R.W. 1987. *Gender and Power*. Cambridge: Polity.

———. 2002. *Gender*. Cambridge: Polity.

Cowell-Meyers, Kimberley. 2003. Women Legislators in Northern Ireland: Gender and Politics in the New Legislative Assembly. http://www.qub.ac.uk/cawp/research/assembly.PDF. Accessed 21 April 2015.

———. 2011. A Collarette on a Donkey: The Northern Ireland Women's Coalition and the Limitations of Contagion Theory. *Political Studies* 59 (2): 411–431.

Dahlerup, Drude. 1989. From a Small to a Large Minority: Women in Scandinavian Politics. *Scandinavian Political Studies* 11 (2): 275–298.

———. 2006. The Story of the Theory of Critical Mass. *Politics and Gender* 2 (4): 511–522.

Falleti, Tulia G. 2006. Theory-Guided Process-Tracing in Comparative Politics: Something Old, Something New. *APSA Newsletter*. http://www.polisci.upenn.edu/~falleti/Falleti-CP-APSANewsletter06-TGPT.pdf. Accessed 5 February 2018.

Flyvbjerg, Bent. 2006. Five Misunderstandings About Case Study Research. *Qualitative Inquiry* 12 (2): 219–245.

Galligan, Yvonne. 2006. Women in Northern Ireland's Politics: Feminizing an 'Armed Patriarchy'. In *Representing Women in Parliament: A Comparative Study*, ed. Marian Sawer, Manon Tremblay, and Linda Trimble. Abingdon: Routledge.

———. 2013. Gender and Politics in Northern Ireland: The Representation Gap Revisited. *Irish Political Studies* 28 (3): 413–433.

Geertz, Clifford. 1973. Thick Description: Towards an Interpretive Theory of Culture. In *The Interpretation of Cultures: Selected Essays*, 3–30. New York: Basic Books.

George, Alexander, and Timoth McKeown. 1985. Case Studies and Theories of Organisational Decision Making. In *Advances in Information Processing in Organizations*, ed. Robert Coulam and Richard Smith. Greenwich, CT: JAI Press.

George, Alexander, and Andrew Bennett. 2005. *Case Studies and Theory Development in the Social Sciences*. Cambridge, MA: MIT Press.

Goertz, Gary, and Amy G. Mazur. 2008. *Politics, Gender and Concepts: Theory and Methodology*. Cambridge: Cambridge University Press.

Hall, Peter, and Rosemary Taylor. 1996. Political Science and the Three New Institutionalisms. *Political Studies* XLIV: 936–957.

Hansen, Lene. 2006. *Security as Practice: Discourse Analysis and the Bosnia War*. Oxford: Routledge.

———. 2010. Ontologies, Epistemologies, Methodologies. In *Gender Matters in Global Politics: A Feminist Introduction to International Relations*. Oxford: Routledge.

Hesse-Biber, Sharlene, Christina Gilmartin, and Robin Lyndenberg. 1999. *Feminist Approaches to Theory and Methodology: An Interdisciplinary Reader*. Oxford: Oxford University Press.

Jorgensen, Marianne, and Louise Phillips. 2002. *Discourse Analysis as Theory and Method*. London: Sage.

Kenny, Meryl. 2007. Gender, Institutions and Power: A Critical Review. *Politics* 27 (2): 91–100.

———. 2013. *Gender and Political Recruitment: Theorizing Institutional Change*. London: Palgrave Macmillan.

———. 2014. A Feminist Institutionalist Approach. *Politics and Gender* 10 (4): 679–684.

Kenny, Meryl, and Fiona Mackay. 2009. Already Doin' It for Ourselves: Skeptical Notes on Feminism and Institutionalism. *Politics & Gender* 5 (2): 271–280.

———. 2011. Gender and Devolution in Spain and the United Kingdom. *Politics & Gender* 7 (2): 280–286.

———. 2014. When Is Contagion Not Very Contagious? Dynamics of Women's Political Representation in Scotland. *Parliamentary Affairs* 67 (4): 866–886.

Kulawik, Teresa. 2009. Staking the Frame of a Feminist Discursive Institutionalism. *Politics and Gender* 5 (2): 262–271.

Leech, B.L. 2002. Interview Methods in Political Science. *PS: Political Science and Politics* 35 (4): 663–664.

Levy, Jack S. 2008. Case Studies: Types, Designs, and Logics of Inference. *Conflict Management and Peace Science* 25: 1–18.

Lovenduski, Joni. 1998. Gendering Research in Political Science. *Annual Review of Political Science* 1: 333–356.

Lowndes, Vivien. 2002. Institutionalism. In *Theories and Methods in Political Science*, ed. David Marsh and Gerry Stoker. Basingstoke: Palgrave.

Mackay, Fiona. 2006. Descriptive and Substantive Representation in New Parliamentary Space: The Case of Scotland. In *Representing Women in Parliament: A Comparative Study*, ed. Marian Sawer, Manon Tremblay, and Linda Trimble. Abingdon: Routledge.

———. 2010. Devolution and the Multilevel Politics of Gender in the UK: The Case of Scotland. In *Federalism, Feminism and Multilevel Governance*, ed. Melissa Haussman, Marian Sawer, and Jill Vickers. London: Ashgate.

———. 2014. Nested Newness, Institutional Innovation, and the Gendered Limits of Change. *Politics and Gender* 10: 549–571.

Mackay, Fiona, and Mona Lena Krook. 2011. Introduction: Gender, Politics and Institutions. In *Gender, Politics and Institutions: Towards a Feminist Institutionalism*. Basingstoke: Palgrave Macmillan.

Mackay, Fiona, and L. McAllister. 2012. Feminising British Politics: Six Lessons from Devolution in Scotland and Wales. *Political Quarterly* 83 (3): 730–734.

Mackay, Fiona, and Nickie Charles. 2013. Feminist Politics and Framing Contests: Domestic Violence Policy in Scotland and Wales. *Critical Social Policy* 33 (4): 593–615.

Mackay, Fiona, and Georgina Waylen. 2014. Introduction: Gendering 'New' Institutions. *Politics and Gender* 10: 489–494.

Mackay, Fiona, Surya Monro, and Georgina Waylen. 2009. The Feminist Potential of Sociological Institutionalism. *Politics and Gender* 5 (2): 253–262.

Mackay, Fiona, Meryl Kenny, and Louise Chappell. 2010. New Institutionalism Through a Gender Lens: Towards a Feminist Institutionalism? *International Political Science Review* 31 (5): 573–588.

Malley, Rosa. 2012. Feeling at Home: Inclusion at Westminster and the Scottish Parliament. *The Political Quarterly* 83 (4): 714–717.

March, James, and Johan Olsen. 1984. The New Institutionalism: Organizational Factors in Political Life. *The American Political Science Review* 78 (3): 734–749.

Matthews, Neil. 2014. Gendered Candidate Selection and the Representation of Women in Northern Ireland. *Parliamentary Affairs* 67 (3): 617–646.

Pierson, Paul. 2004. *Politics in Time: History, Institutions and Social Analysis*. New Haven: Yale University Press.

Pierson, Paul, and Theda Skocpol. 2002. Historical Institutionalism in Contemporary Political Science. In *Political Science: The State of the Discipline*, ed. Ira Katznelson and Helen V. Milner. London: W. W. Norton.

Potter, Michael. 2013. Women in the Northern Ireland Assembly. *Northern Ireland Assembly: Research and Information Service Research Paper*. http://www.niassembly.gov.uk/assembly-business/committees/archive/office-of-the-first-minister-and-deputy-first-minister/archive/research-papers/research-papers-2013/women-in-the-northern-ireland-assembly/. Accessed 26 May 2016.

Ramazanoglu, Caroline, with Janet Holland. 2002. *Feminist Methodology: Challenges and Choices*. London: Sage.

Rhodes, R.A.W. 1997. *Understanding Governance.* London: Open University Press.

Russell, Meg. 2000. Women's Representation in UK Politics? What Can Be Done Within the Law? UCL Constitution Unit Report. http://www.ucl.ac.uk/constitution-unit/publications/tabs/unit-publications/60.pdf. Accessed 5 February 2018.

Sawer, Marian, and Jill Vickers. 2010. Introduction: Political Architecture and Its Gender Impact. In *Federalism, Feminism and Multilevel Governance*, ed. Melissa Haussman, Marian Sawer, and Jill Vickers. London: Ashgate.

Schmidt, Vivien. 2008. Discursive Institutionalism: The Explanatory Power of Ideas and Discourse. *Annual Review of Political Science* 11: 303–326.

———. 2010. Taking Ideas and Discourse Seriously: Explaining Change Through Discursive Institutionalism as the Fourth New Institutionalism. *European Political Science Review* 2 (1): 1–25.

Skocpol, Theda, Dietrich Rueschemeyer, and Peter B. Evans. 1985. *Bringing the State Back In.* Cambridge: Cambridge University Press.

Smyth, Lynda. 2005. *Abortion and Nation: The Politics of Reproduction in Contemporary Ireland.* Aldershot: Ashgate.

Spradley, James P. 1979. *The Ethnographic Interview.* Long Grove: Waveland Press.

Steinmo, Sven. 2008. Historical Institutionalism. In *Approaches in the Social Sciences*, ed. Donatella Della Porta and Michael Keating. Cambridge: Cambridge University Press.

Tansey, Oisín. 2007. Process Tracing and Elite Interviewing: A Case for Non-probability Sampling. *PS: Political Science and Politics* 40 (4): 765–772.

Thelen, Kathleen. 1999. Historical Institutionalism in Comparative Politics. *Annual Review of Political Science* 2: 369–404.

Thelen, Kathleen, and Sven Steinmo. 1992. Historical Institutionalism in Comparative Politics. In *Structuring Politics: Historical Institutionalism in Comparative Perspective.* Cambridge: Cambridge University Press.

Thelen, Kathleen, and James Mahoney (eds.). 2010. *Exploring Institutional Change: Ambiguity, Agency and Power.* Cambridge: Cambridge University Press.

Vickers, Jill, Melissa Haussman, and Marian Sawer. 2010. Conclusion. In *Federalism, Feminism and Multilevel Governance*, ed. Melissa Haussman, Marian Sawer, and Jill Vickers. London: Ashgate.

Waylen, Georgina. 2007. *Engendering Transitions.* Oxford: Oxford University Press.

———. 2009. What Can Historical Institutionalism Offer Feminist Institutionalists? *Politics & Gender* 5 (2): 245–253.

———. 2011. Gendered Institutional Analysis: Understanding Democratic Transitions. In *Gender, Politics and Institutions: Towards a Feminist Institutionalism*, ed. Mona Lena Krook and Fiona Mackay, 147–162. Basingstoke: Palgrave Macmillan.

———. 2014a. Informal Institutions, Institutional Change and Gender Equality. *Political Research Quarterly* 67 (1): 212–223.

———. 2014b. A Seat at the Table—Is It Enough? Gender, Multiparty Negotiations, and Institutional Design in South African and Northern Ireland. *Politics and Gender* 10: 495–523.

CHAPTER 3

Northern Irish Politics and Abortion

Having addressed the theoretical and methodological basis of this book in the previous chapter, this chapter now turns to Northern Ireland's contemporary history. It opens with a brief historical explanation of the fault lines in the still deeply divided society. It then considers the central political parties and their electoral support in the region, before addressing the role of religion and national identity in Northern Ireland and the impact these have on sociocultural issues. Finally, it turns to the legal history of abortion in the UK and the specific circumstances in Northern Ireland, as well as attitudes to terminating pregnancy in both the region and the UK as a whole.

Contemporary Northern Ireland

Northern Ireland remains a post-conflict society. A historical perspective is necessary to understand contemporary politics in the province yet does not suggest that Northern Ireland is impossibly tied to its past.

Ireland was a British colony from the twelfth century but was only loosely managed until the sixteenth century. Beginning under King Henry VIII, the English crown began a policy of "plantation" of English and Scottish settlers to Ireland with a view to suppressing dissent amongst the local population. Following the Reformation, this settlement "took on a religious dimension" (Sales 1997, 13), with the majority of settlers being Protestant and the majority of native Irish Catholic.

J. Thomson, *Abortion Law and Political Institutions*, Gender and Politics, https://doi.org/10.1007/978-3-319-96169-9_3

Resistance to Ireland's colonisation was strongest in Ulster, one of the four original Irish counties, and this region was most aggressively settled (ibid., 14). Following the Battle of the Boyne[1] in 1690, a series of Penal laws were enacted over the next 30 years which severely restricted Catholic rights to inheritance and property. The Act of Union in 1800 cemented Ireland as part of the UK.

Economic, religious and social divisions appeared between the north-east of Ireland and the rest of the island. By 1900, Belfast was a burgeoning port city. Protestant-dominated industry looked to the Union "both through ties to British mercantile capital, and dependence on imperial trade routes" (Sales 1997, 16). Catholics, shut out of land and employment elsewhere in Ireland, moved to Belfast in large numbers, which began a still-present pattern of religious segregation within the city.

In the late 1800s, Home Rule for Ireland was attempted on several occasions via Westminster. This was strongly resisted in the north-east of Ireland where the relative prosperity relied on British trade and imperial links. During the passing of a Home Rule Bill in the Commons in 1912, the Solemn League and Covenant was signed in Ulster by 218,000 people. In 1913, an illegal army, the Ulster Volunteer Force, was formed; the following year it imported 25,000 rifles and three million rounds of ammunition. This resulted in an upswing in sectarian violence, and some 7000 Catholics and left-wing Protestants were forced out of employment in the Belfast shipyards (Hopkinson 2004, 155). The British government capitulated, and plans for Home Rule were shelved, largely due to the development of the First World War. The organised Ulster unionists succeeded in forcing the UK's hand and instigating the advent of partition.

Following the Irish declaration of independence in Dublin in 1919, the War of Independence broke out, lasting until 1921. It was then followed by the partition of Ireland into two separate entities: six counties in Ulster remained as part of the UK, whilst the remaining three Ulster counties and the rest of the island became the Irish Free State. Partition saw an outbreak of bloody violence in Northern Ireland, especially in Belfast (Mulholland 2002, 25). 11,000 were made jobless, 23,000 homeless and £3 million worth of property damage occurred in the city in the same year (ibid.). As part of the agreement around partition, a parliament at Stormont was enacted. Politics became divided along religious lines, with unionists "marginalising Catholics politically, economically and socially" (Sales 1997, 30), and gerrymandering constituencies to ensure Protestant representation.

Northern Ireland thus entered a type of rule which could be referred to as democratic at surface level only. In addition to manipulating constituency boundaries, discrimination against Catholics in employment was rife, the Catholic education system received less funding, the police service was almost entirely Protestant, and social housing provision for Catholics was difficult to obtain. This situation was largely ignored by the outside world, including the rest of the UK and Westminster, until the civil rights movement of the 1960s (spearheaded by the Northern Ireland Civil Rights Association (NICRA), formed in 1967), led by students and Catholics, forced it onto the agenda. Civil rights marches were met with violence, and the Battle of the Bogside in 1969 in Derry saw the province request that British troops be sent to aid policing. Whilst anti-discrimination measures began to be introduced, they were largely seen by the Catholic community as an attempt to safeguard the unionist position rather than truly address past wrongs and current injustices. There was an increasingly heavy-handed stance from the British state. Internment was introduced in 1971, and 2185 people were interned without trial before 1975 (Mulholland 2002, 26). This saw an initially warm welcome from the Catholic community towards British forces, who deemed them better than the local sectarian police force, rapidly fade. Following the events of Bloody Sunday in January 1972, where 14 civilians were killed by British troops during a civil rights march, Stormont was suspended and direct rule from Westminster was established.

Violence began to develop rapidly in the 1970s, with some of the highest number of deaths from the conflict in the province seen in this decade (see Table 3.1). A reinvigorated, northern version of the Irish Republican Army (the Provisional IRA) emerged. After a long, bloody decade in which the Provisional IRA did not force British troops from Northern Ireland, but saw Britain simultaneously struggle to control the republican threat, the conflict settled into the 1980s with fewer casualties but no clear end in sight. A number of high-profile attacks on British soil (the 1982 Hyde and Regents Park bombings, the 1984 bombing of the Conservative Party conference in Brighton) kept Northern Ireland on the British political and public radar, but without an answer as to how the conflict might be brought to a close (Table 3.2).

In the 1990s, movements towards peace appeared stronger. Talks emerged in the late 1980s between unionist political parties and the British government. In 1993, the Downing Street Declaration of the British and Irish governments declared that Ireland had the right to

Table 3.1 Number of deaths caused as a result of the conflict in Northern Ireland by gender, 1969–2001

Year	*Number killed*	
	Men	*Women*
1969	16	0
1970–1979	1884	212
1980–1989	797	57
1990–1999	478	53
2000–2001	35	0
Total	3210	322

Source Sutton index of deaths, CAIN web service, http://cain.ulst.ac.uk/sutton/index.html. Accessed 29 January 2018

Table 3.2 Organisations responsible for deaths in the Troubles, 1969–2001

Organisation	*No. of deaths responsible for*
British security forces	363
Irish security forces	5
Loyalist paramilitaries	1027
Republican paramilitaries	2058
Unknown	79
Total	3532

Source Sutton index of deaths, CAIN web service, http://cain.ulst.ac.uk/sutton/index.html. Accessed 29 January 2018

self-determination and that Britain had "no selfish strategic or economic interest in Northern Ireland." Following this, in August 1994 the Provisional IRA called a ceasefire, with loyalist paramilitaries following suit six weeks later. At the same time, the election of Bill Clinton to the American Presidency in 1992 saw greater support from the USA for a peace process in Northern Ireland. In 1995–1996, Senator George Mitchell, US Special Envoy for Northern Ireland, chaired a commission which led to the Mitchell Principles of non-violence from which peace talks might begin. A Forum for Peace and Reconciliation was established, and talks containing political parties from across the island of Ireland began. Peace was given a further shot in the arm via the election of New Labour in 1997, and a provisional IRA ceasefire, which had been broken in 1996 following the Docklands bombing in London, was restored.

The Northern Ireland Forum for Political Dialogue brought discussions into a more focussed Northern Irish setting and eventually led to the Good Friday Agreement of 1998. However, to what extent the "real stuff" of the peace negotiations took place behind closed doors, rather than in these elected forums, is debated (Fearon 1999; Powell, 2009; Waylen 2014). Following a public referendum in 1998, the Good Friday Agreement was enacted and a power-sharing political assembly was established at Stormont in Belfast.

The Good Friday Agreement represented a new beginning, rather than the end of the peace process in Northern Ireland. Devolution in Northern Ireland has had a far more unstable trajectory than its equivalents in Scotland and Wales. Difficulties around the decommissioning of paramilitary weapons, especially those of the provisional IRA, dogged its early years. Revelations that provisional IRA members had been training FARC rebels in Colombia, the Northern Bank robbery[2] and the murder of Robert McCartney[3] further impeded the work of political institutions. The Assembly was suspended in 2002 and was only re-established following the St. Andrew's Agreement of 2007. Further American-led talks in 2014 resulted in the Stormont House Agreement, although difficulties in its implementation in 2015 saw formal politics in the province at its lowest point for many years. A new agreement, negotiated primarily between the two main parties, was reached in November 2015.

In late 2016, allegations emerged surrounding a Renewable Heat Incentive scheme, which was initiated under First Minister Arlene Foster, then Minister for Enterprise, Trade and Investment. Despite calls for her resignation, Foster stayed but the scandal grew in magnitude. In January of 2017, Deputy First Minister Martin McGuinness resigned, thereby suspending the Assembly and triggering an election, which, for the first time, did not return a Unionist majority. Following the snap General Election of 2017, the Conservatives failed to win an outright majority and turned to the ten DUP MPs to support their government. Furthermore, there was substantial uncertainty over what shape the Irish border was going to take following the UK's exit from the European Union in 2019. These factors had the dual effect of propelling Northern Ireland and its politics back into the British public imagination in a manner that had not been seen for years, and, with allegations that this meant that the British government was no longer a neutral party with regard to Northern Ireland, undermined talks to re-establish the Assembly. As of summer 2018, the Assembly remained suspended.

Contemporary Party Politics in Northern Ireland

Party politics within contemporary Northern Ireland cannot be approached on a left to right scale as those in the rest of the UK can.[4] Northern Irish party politics might be best described instead as an "ethnic dual party system" in which it "is only a mild exaggeration to say that at each election two simultaneous but largely separate contests take place" (Mitchell 2001, 28–29). Indeed, as reflected in the consociational make-up of the Good Friday Agreement, in spite of the use of transferable votes in the current Assembly system, votes are rarely transferred between communities (Farrington 2006; Tonge 2005; Tonge and Evans 2015). Catholics overwhelmingly vote for either Sinn Féin or the Social Democratic and Labour Party (SDLP) and Protestants for the Democratic Unionist Party (DUP) or the Ulster Unionist Party (UUP).

This section briefly outlines the history of the five largest parties in contemporary Northern Irish politics.

The Ulster Unionist Party (the UUP)

The UUP (sometimes referred to as the Official Unionist Party) ruled essentially unopposed in Northern Ireland from the province's formation until the suspension of Stormont in 1972. UUP Prime Minster of Northern Ireland, Terence O'Neill, began a series of moderate reforms in the 1960s, aimed at placating Catholic dissent within the province. These frustrated the more hardline unionists and encouraged internal dissent within the party. As a result, O'Neill called a snap election in 1969 in which he almost lost his own seat. He retired from politics the following year.

Following the suspension of Stormont in 1972, the party cut its formal links with the British Conservative party.[5] Further inner party turmoil occurred over whether or not to accept the Sunningdale Agreement of 1974, as a result of which then leader Brian Faulkner (Prime Minister of Northern Ireland from 1971 until the suspension) had to resign. Following the Anglo-Irish Agreement of 1985, the UUP formed a pact with the DUP, organising a petition and a large protest in central Belfast against it. In the late 1980s, the UUP began a process of talks about the potential future of peace negotiations with the British government. From 1992 to 1997, the party held the balance of power at Westminster, helping to prop up the Major government.

Table 3.3 Northern Irish Assembly elections since the GFA (number of seats won)

	DUP	*Sinn Féin*	*UUP*	*SDLP*	*Alliance*	*Others*
1998	20	18	28	24	6	12
2003	30	24	27	18	6	3
2007	36	28	18	16	7	3
2011	38	29	16	14	8	3
2016	38	28	16	12	8	6
2017[a]	28	27	10	12	8	5

Source CAIN web service, 'results of elections held in Northern Ireland since 1968', http://cain.ulst.ac.uk/issues/politics/election/elect.htm. Accessed 29 January 2018

[a]These were the first elections to take place after the decision to change the number of MLAs from 108 to 90

Table 3.4 Northern Irish Westminster elections since the GFA (number of seats won)

	DUP	*Sinn Féin*	*UUP*	*SDLP*	*Alliance*	*Others*
2001	5	4	6	3	0	0
2005	9	5	1	3	0	0
2010	8	5	0	3	1	1
2015	8	4	2	3	0	1
2017	10	7	0	0	0	1

Source CAIN web service, 'results of elections held in Northern Ireland since 1968', http://cain.ulst.ac.uk/issues/politics/election/elect.htm. Accessed 29 January 2018

Whilst once the dominant unionist party in the province, and key to the passing of the Good Friday Agreement, the UUP has seen its post-Agreement fortunes crumble (see Tables 3.3, 3.4, 3.5, and 3.6). Differing attitudes to the Agreement within the party have caused tensions. The party's long ties to the Orange Order, a fundamental component of unionist culture in Northern Ireland, gradually broke down over the Good Friday Agreement, with member support largely shifting to the DUP (Kaufmann 2007, 228). The UUP has not held a position in the Office of the First Minister and the Deputy First Minister (OFMDFM) since the first post-Agreement Assembly and had no representation at Westminster from 2010 to 2015. On abortion, it considers it a matter of freedom of conscience and allows elected members a free vote.

Table 3.5 Northern Irish European elections since the GFA (number of seats won)

	DUP	*Sinn Féin*	*UUP*	*SDLP*	*Alliance*	*Others*
1999	1	0	1	1	0	0
2004	1	1	1	0	N/A[a]	0
2009	1	1	1[b]	0	0	0
2014	1	1	1	0	0	0

Source CAIN web service, 'results of elections held in Northern Ireland since 1968', http://cain.ulst.ac.uk/issues/politics/election/elect.htm. Accessed 29 January 2018

[a]The Alliance Party did not stand a candidate in the 2004 European elections

[b]Jim Nicholson, elected in 1989 to the European Parliament, stood in the 2009 EU election as a candidate for the Ulster Conservative and Unionists—New Force, an electoral pact between the UUP and the conservative party, largely designed to challenge seats in the 2010 Westminster election

Table 3.6 Northern Irish local Government elections since the GFA (number of seats won)

	DUP	*Sinn Féin*	*UUP*	*SDLP*	*Alliance*	*Others*
2001	131	108	154	117	28	44
2005	182	126	115	101	30	28
2011	175	138	99	87	44	39
2014[a]	130	105	88	66	32	41

Source CAIN web service, 'results of elections held in NI since 1968', http://cain.ulst.ac.uk/issues/politics/election/elect.htm. Accessed 29 January 2018

[a]Council boundaries were redrawn in 2014, changing Northern Ireland from 26 councils to 11. As a result, the total number of councillors was reduced from 582 to 462

The Social Democratic and Labour Party (the SDLP)

The SDLP was formed in 1970, emerging from the civil rights movement in Northern Ireland. Angry at the perceived failing of nationalist politics up to this point (Farren 2010, 25), the party soon eclipsed the Nationalist Party and the National Democratic Party, the two former institutions for nationalist politics (Tonge and Murray 2005, 7–10). The SDLP wanted the Assembly to be acknowledged by Westminster as unworkable and unfair and to this end withdrew as the official opposition from Stormont in 1971 (Tonge and Murray 2005, 26). In the early 1970s, they called for a Bill of Rights and anti-discrimination legislation, as well as leading campaigns of civil disobedience (non-payment of rent, etc.) to effect change in the province.

The SDLP took part in the Sunningdale negotiations of 1973 which were aimed at finding a power-sharing solution to governance in the province. Following the failure of Sunningdale, the party were committed from the late 1970s onwards to three key elements: joint Anglo-Irish action as regards the province; that the British government should drop its unconditional guarantee to the Unionist population; and that the Irish government should be more specific in the ways in which it wanted to encourage social and economic union between the two parts of the island. The greater emphasis that the party placed on Catholic integration into (albeit reformed) existing structures, and the involvement of the British state, put it at odds with Sinn Féin's position, as a result of which the parties did not enter into an electoral pact upon Sinn Féin's rise in the early 1980s.

The SDLP remained the largest nationalist party into the early years of the Assembly. John Hume, along with David Trimble, was awarded the Nobel Peace Prize for his work leading up to the Good Friday Agreement. In many ways, the Agreement is closer to SDLP ideology than to any other party; its emphasis on human rights and the production of a Northern Irish Bill of Rights were elements of the SDLP's political discourse as far back as the 1970s. Yet, as with the UUP, the party has struggled in the post-Agreement landscape (see Tables 3.3–3.6). Its electoral fortunes have fallen dramatically, now playing second fiddle to Sinn Féin's dominance of the Catholic vote. They have also been more socially conservative, particularly on abortion, although as of 2018 they allow a freedom of conscience vote on the issue by their MLAs.

Sinn Féin

Sinn Féin emerged as the political wing of the republican movement in the early 1980s, following the electoral successes of several of the provisional IRA hunger strikers.[6] Until the early 1990s, it remained a relatively small political party, with the SDLP dominating the Catholic vote. The party dropped its policy of abstention towards the Irish Daíl in 1986. From the late 1980s, there were channels of communication between John Hume and Sinn Féin leader Gerry Adams. In 1988, groups from the two parties met at the instigation of Father Alec Reid, a Redemptorist Priest, and were adopted again with renewed vigour in 1993. These talks, combined with the Brooke talks, the Downing Street declaration and the ceasefires of 1994, made the prospect of a permanent peace appear more viable.

Within the nationalist voting bloc, Sinn Féin has always been to the left of the SDLP. In the early 1980s, Sinn Féin had strong socialist leanings, and, although less avowedly so in recent years, the party still aims for the "establishment of a democratic socialist republic."[7] Gerry Adams, party leader from 1983 to 2018, declared at the 2003 Ard Fheis (AGM) that "Equality is the most important word in the Republican vocabulary" (Maillot 2005), and the party has campaigned strongly against austerity measures in the Republic in the wake of the Irish financial crisis. The party adopts a strong equal rights-based agenda, campaigning (both North and South of the border) under the slogan "An Ireland of Equals." In line with this left economic and social position, "Sinn Féin realized that it needed women" (Galligan 2006), and the party has a clearly gendered angle to its equality stance. In Stormont, the party argue that Sinn Féin has been "leading by example" with regard to women's representation (ibid., 2), largely given that it has seen some of the highest percentages of female MLAs, returning 29% female representatives in the second election to the Assembly in 2003 (Galligan 2006). The party has also been strongly supportive of LGBT rights. Yet as Frampton argues, the trajectory of Sinn Féin in the last thirty years has to be seen in the context of the "'ultra-pragmatism' of those involved" (2008, 188). Both individual political issues, and broader party ideology, are subservient to the ultimate cause of Irish reunification. An attitude of "whatever it takes" (ibid.) prevails within the party.

This is reflected in the party's somewhat ambiguous stance on abortion. Until 2017, the party's policy was "opposed to the attitudes and forces in society that compel women to have abortions and criminalise those who do make this decision."[8] The policy was changed at the 2017 Ard Fheis (party conference) to allow abortion in cases of fatal foetal abnormality, rape, incest or grave risk to the woman's physical or mental health. The party prominently campaigned for a Yes vote in the abortion referendum in the Republic of Ireland in 2018, although this vote will probably allow for abortion in larger circumstances (on request for the first 12 weeks of pregnancy) than party policy currently allows for.

Regardless of these criticisms, Sinn Féin has grown exponentially in electoral and political clout since the Good Friday Agreement. The party has made inroads into the middle class, and more conservative, Catholic voting pool, thus cementing its status as the largest nationalist party in contemporary Northern Irish politics. It is currently the only party to contest elections in Northern Ireland and the Republic of Ireland.

Following the St Andrew's Agreement of 2007, the party entered into the Executive and the OFMDFM with the DUP, an electoral grouping which, only a few years earlier, would have appeared improbable. Whilst Deputy First Minister Martin McGuinness (Sinn Féin) appeared to enjoy amicable relations with First Minister Ian Paisley (DUP) (they were in office together from 2007 to 2008),[9] the relationship between the two parties has become more strained in recent years, and their inability to agree on certain issues (particularly legislation around Irish Gaelic) means that the devolved institution remained suspended as of summer 2018.

The Democratic Unionist Party (the DUP)

The DUP was formed by the Reverend Ian Paisley in 1971, who "dominated" (Tonge *et al.* 2014, 10) the party until stepping down in 2010. Paisley's particularly firebrand variety of Protestantism and politics saw the DUP "oppose virtually every major initiative championed by the British and Irish governments to ameliorate the Northern Irish crisis" (ibid., 2014, 16), from the Sunningdale, to the Anglo-Irish, to the Good Friday Agreement. The DUP worked alongside loyalist paramilitaries and others to bring about the Ulster Workers' Council strike of 1974 which brought down the Sunningdale agreement. They were keen to work in a system of majority rule in the Assembly of the 1980s and vehemently opposed the 1985 Anglo-Irish Agreement. The party went on to oppose the Good Friday Agreement: such a position had the support of the large number (perhaps over 50%) of Protestants who voted against it in the 1998 referendum (Tonge *et al.* 2014, 23–24).

As Protestant discontent with the Good Friday Agreement grew in the early years of the newly devolved Assembly, so did the DUP's electoral fortunes, at the expense of the UUP. Several high-profile UUP members defected to the DUP (including Jonathan Bell, future First Minister Arlene Foster, Jeffrey Donaldson and future Health Minister Simon Hamilton), angry at what they perceived to be capitulation to terrorism and nationalist interests. The DUP also became more electorally efficient in the years following the Good Friday Agreement (Tonge *et al.* 2014). The 2003 Assembly Election saw the DUP pull ahead of the UUP whilst Sinn Féin made substantial gains into SDLP territory (Cox *et al.* 2006), and into new geographical areas where they had previously had little presence (Farrington 2006, 175). The DUP has also been more successful at community-based politics than the UUP. Martyn Smyth, former

UUP Director of Information, said that, "It's getting to the people … I think at times the DUP have won the battle over us" (ibid., 40). Again, like Sinn Féin, and unlike the UUP, the DUP has a more obvious leadership and a stronger party structure, such that "UUP rebels cannot expect the freedom to dissent from party policy in the DUP; the DUP is palpably leadership driven" (Tonge 2005, 81).

In contrast to Sinn Féin, the DUP adopts no clear gender equality stance. Their level of female representatives has been substantially lower than that of Sinn Féin's (Galligan, 2008), although they can, since late 2015, boast the first ever female First Minister of Northern Ireland. The DUP also draws a great deal of support from the evangelical community and retains its roots in the Free Presbyterian Church—30% of DUP members belong to it (Tonge *et al.* 2014, 138). Consequently, a strong social conservatism can be seen amongst its membership: 53.6% of members agree that "Homosexuality is wrong," and 59.3% strongly disagree that abortion should be legalised in Northern Ireland (Tonge *et al.* 2014, 155). There is little difference between male and female members on these issues, and these opinions reflect the strongly conservative stance the party take on these issues. The party also campaigned to leave the EU during the 2016 referendum, and entered into the 'confidence-and-supply' arrangement with the Conservatives at Westminster following the 2017 General Election on the basis that they would support the Government as the UK leaves the European Union.

As can be seen in Tables 3.3–3.6, both Sinn Féin and the DUP's electoral fortunes changed after the Good Friday Agreement and have achieved mainstream political legitimacy in a way that might not once have been thought possible. As Tonge outlines (2005, 129–131), there were several possibilities for the type of relationships between parties which might have formed in the new Northern Irish Assembly. One was an SDLP-Sinn Féin alliance, which might have concretised sectarian tensions in the new assembly and made for an antagonistic nationalist-unionist institution. The second option was a centrist Coalition between the SDLP and the UUP, which would have seen the two parties occupying the middle ground formerly the reserve of the Alliance Party. The third was an alliance formed on more radical understandings of identity, such as the socialist concerns of the Progressive Unionist Party and Sinn Féin. The most common belief was that, given the long-term dominance of the SDLP and the UUP, this would continue in the new institution (Evans and Tonge 2005, 1014). Instead, the years following the Good Friday Agreement (see Table 3.3) saw rapid growth in representation of the DUP and Sinn Féin in the Assembly, such that contemporary Northern Ireland can now be characterised as a "dominant two party system" (Wilson 2010, 135).

The rise of Sinn Féin and the DUP can be explained as a result of many different factors. The years following the Good Friday Agreement saw the Provisional IRA slow to decommission weapons, a fact that the anti-Agreement DUP could exploit electorally. The DUP enjoys much greater elite control in terms of party structure and organisation and has a "strongly stated message of resistance to betrayal" (McGlynn *et al.* 2014, 280), whilst the UUP was run more as a "broad coalition of groups" (ibid., 277). Having gained, through the Good Friday Agreement and the subsequent devolved institutions that were established, much of its original raison d'être as a political party, the SDLP also struggled to present itself as a party which still had relevance and new ideas. Voters turned instead to Sinn Féin.

Demographically, support for Sinn Féin and the DUP has grown in similar areas of the Northern Irish population. Indeed, "it has become respectable—indeed, the norm, to vote for the DUP or Sinn Féin within the respective blocs in a way unthinkable prior to the peace process" (Evans and Tonge 2005). Importantly, this shift to the more "extreme" parties has happened in similar age ranges for both communities. In 2009, 73% of Catholic voters under 24 voted for Sinn Fein, whilst 75% of Protestant voters under 24 voted for the DUP (Tilley and Evans 2011). This results in a situation where a large percentage of emerging support for these parties comes from those who do not remember the Troubles and who have largely been politicised in a post-Agreement landscape.

The Alliance Party

Alliance makes up the fifth party in the Northern Irish Executive. The party was formed in 1970, founded in the belief that there was another, post-nationalist/unionist way in which politics might be conducted in Northern Ireland. In Tonge's words, it promotes a "liberal, pluralist, non-ethnic form of politics" (2005, 87) rather than the traditional nationalist-unionist divisions. In spite of its cross-community approach to Northern Irish politics, Alliance was forced to redesignate[10] in the early years of the Assembly in order to save David Trimble's position as First Minister, although this was unpopular with members (Tonge 2005, 100; Evans and Tonge 2003).

The party has struggled to make clear inroads in terms of formal political representation, however, as Table 3.3 above illustrates. They have had difficulties in gaining support outside of the Protestant middle-class community. Indeed, a party which worked along bi-confessional lines faced difficulties following the Good Friday Agreement, which, by its nature, promoted a "two communities" understanding of Northern Ireland. Party members report being labelled as secretly unionist or nationalist by opposing political parties, in order to discredit their centrist position and "unite the community *against* Alliance and for their parties" (Murtagh 2015, 558). In a divided political system such as Northern Ireland, the very notion of centrism falls under attack, as parties clearly from one side or the other see bi-confessional parties as "a threat to the dominance of their form of politics, and hence power" (ibid., 561). Yet, in recent years, Alliance has had more visibility, partly through Naomi Long dramatically winning the East Belfast Westminster seat from First Minister Peter Robinson in 2010,[11] and also via David Ford's very visible position within the Executive as Justice Minister from 2010 to 2015. Anna Lo has also maintained a clear media presence and is the only ethnic minority member ever to have served in the Assembly.

For a party which evolved from the "distinctive radical tradition" (Tonge 2005, 100) of non-ethno-national alignment, it might be expected that they would adopt strongly liberal policies on social issues. A policy on same-sex marriage was only adopted in 2012 and on abortion the party allow a free vote.

Other Political Parties in Northern Ireland

As Table 3.3 shows, parties beyond these five outlined above have had little representation at Stormont, and this has decreased markedly since 1998. In the 2010–2015 legislature, there were four additional parties represented—the Greens, Traditional Unionist Voice (the TUV), NI21 and UKIP. The TUV is led by Jim Allister MLA, who left the DUP to start his own party following the St. Andrew's Agreement of 2007 which saw the DUP and Sinn Féin enter into government together. The party is strongly conservative on its position regarding the Union, fiscal matters and social issues. The Northern Irish Greens are part of the broader political Green movement, with links to both the Irish and British Green parties. The party support liberalising abortion reform and Stephen Agnew, the party's sole MLA from 2011 to 2016, has been outspoken on the issue. NI21 emerged as an offshoot of the UUP in 2013. Liberal on social issues and aiming to promote a bi-confessional political face, the party suffered several public embarrassing events almost immediately following its establishment, and have no representation following the 2016 election.[12] UKIP also had one MLA from 2012 to 2015 after a UUP MLA defected. In 2016, two representatives of the new People Before Profit Party were elected. In addition, the Progressive Unionist Party (the PUP) have had no Assembly representation since 2010,[13] but have some local government representation.

Contemporary Northern Irish Society

As Table 3.7 illustrates, a large majority of Northern Ireland's population still identify as either Catholic or part of a Protestant denomination. This places the region in contrast to the rest of the UK, where, according to the 2011 census, over 26% of the population do not regard themselves as having a religion.[14] As might be expected, religion plays a much greater role in political discourse in Northern Ireland. The largest party, the DUP, was founded by the Free Presbyterian Minister Ian Paisley. Although the party now enjoys broad membership from outside this particular church, a Christian ethos to party policy and discussion is clear (Tonge *et al.* 2014). Several prominent Christian civil society organisations exist in Northern Ireland, largely from a Protestant standpoint, and lobby politicians on social issues such as abortion—including the Christian Medical Fellowship, the Evangelical Alliance, and the Caleb Foundation.[15]

Catholic lobbying organisations are less immediately apparent, although key figures within the Catholic Church will speak publicly on issues they feel are important and wish to influence. Archbishop Eamon Martin has made several public statements regarding the incompatibility of a Catholic representative voting for abortion laws and met with Justice Minister David Ford when he was preparing his case for legal change in 2015.[16]

Table 3.7 Self-identification by religion, Northern Irish Life and Times Survey, 2016

Religion	%
No religion	19
Catholic	41
Protestant (any denomination)	34
Other christian	2
Other	2

Source NILT 2016

Table 3.8 Self-identification by nationality, Northern Ireland Life and Times Survey, 2016

Identity	%
Irish not British	24
More Irish than British	11
Equally Irish and British	17
More British than Irish	18
British not Irish	21
Other	9
Don't know	0

Source NILT 2016

Religion is further enmeshed in Northern Ireland with national and social identities. As Table 3.8 shows, almost 50% of the Northern Irish population continue to refer exclusively to Irish or British identities. Northern Irish Catholics, with their links to the Republic, have a clear culture, nation and Gaelic language to adhere to. Irish identity has globalised, fuelled by the strong political and cultural links with the USA, and the broader Irish diaspora. In the face of this Irish Catholic cultural coherence, "only a minority of Protestants are confident that their cultural tradition is protected, whereas a majority of Catholics believe their cultural tradition has been adequately protected by the Good Friday Agreement" (Mcauley and Tonge 2007, 280). Indeed, the Good Friday Agreement, and its recognition of two distinct political identities "left unionists in a quandary" (Nic Craith 2002, 57), as there is "little common agreement as to what it means to be a unionist (or British) in Ireland" (Mcauley and Tonge 2007, 4). Until the dramatic General Election result of 2017, unionism had seen a growing distance in mainstream British politicians' attitude to the province. This has been reflected politically in support for the Good Friday Agreement: in 1998, the Agreement saw around 55% Protestant support, but by 2002 this had fallen to around 35% (Kaufman 2007, 205).

As a result of this fusion of religion, identity and culture, Northern Irish politics have, in the post-Good Friday Agreement era, been fought more "with history instead of guns" (Gallaher 2007, 87). The Good Friday Agreement has not resulted in the creation of a "third way" of Northern Irish identity (Mcauley and Tonge 2007), as Table 3.8 shows (although a substantial minority do now identify as equally British and Irish).

Within this continuing bi-cultural landscape, "the question of parity of esteem for both cultures" (Nic Craith 2002, 48) has been central. Yet the role of what have been termed the developing "culture wars" (Hunter 1992; Wuthnow 1990) in Northern Irish politics and society has had little academic consideration. Mycock and McDaid argue (2014) that the "culture wars" in the province have two distinct strands. The first is related to the public display of national beliefs and identity: the flying of flags in public space, the Irish language act and parades.[17] This strand has distinct green-orange tendencies, redolent of traditional sectarian leanings, and largely follows nationalist-unionist lines. The second strand of the "culture wars" is concerned with social and moral issues (abortion, same-sex marriage, blood donation by gay men, accommodation of ethnic/racial minorities, etc.[18]) and is less aligned to green or orange leanings or political parties. Whilst issues around clear-cut topics of nationality, such as flags and language, are clearly divided along nationalist-unionist lines, sociocultural issues such as those described here are not so easily categorised.

Abortion in the UK

Abortion was first addressed in legislation in Great Britain in the 1861 Offences Against the Person Act. This made any attempt to procure a miscarriage, or supply of drugs or other material aid to procure a miscarriage, punishable by life imprisonment. This legislation was largely untouched until 1929, when the Infant Life (Preservation) Act closed "a legal loophole" (Sheldon 1997, 15) to prohibit the killing of a child in the process of being born. The Act made illegal the destruction of a child "capable of being born alive." Read into this was a 28-week gestation limit at which point it was believed the foetus was viable outside the womb. The Act was extended to Northern Ireland in 1945 as part of the Criminal Justice (Northern Ireland) Bill.

In 1937 a prominent London surgeon, Alec Bourne, openly performed an abortion on a 14-year-old girl who was pregnant as the result of rape by a group of soldiers. Until the 1967 Abortion Act, *R vs. Bourne* was the only addition to abortion legislation, and still largely forms the basis of what constitutes a legal abortion in Northern Ireland today.[19] It states that:

> If the doctor is of the opinion, on reasonable grounds and with adequate knowledge, that the probable consequences of the continuance of the pregnancy will be to make the woman *a physical or mental wreck*, the jury are quite entitled to take the view that the doctor who, in these circumstances, and in that *honest belief*, operates, is operating for the purpose of preserving the life of the woman. (quoted in Sheldon 1997, 79, emphasis added)

The vague nature of this judgement however—the belief that a pregnancy, if continued, will result in the woman becoming "a physical or mental wreck"—resulted in a wide variation in implementation. The verdict is also framed in such a way that the issue remains medicalised, with the decision ultimately resting with the doctor, rather than the woman. This is a continued critique of present British abortion legislation, which still enshrines the right to abort as a medical one, lying with the required permission of not one, but two doctors.

It was in light of this vague verdict that there was growing pressure for more transparent legislation. At the behest of both the medical profession, frustrated with the uncertainty surrounding the procedure,[20] and a media and political discourse which painted women as the poor, helpless victims of money-grabbing backstreet abortionists, public and political opinion was behind liberalisation (Sheldon 1997). The 1967 Abortion Act allowed for abortion at up to 28 weeks with the permission of two doctors, but in a manner which continues the medicalisation of the Bourne judgement. The procedure is only legal if there is the risk of "injury to the physical or mental health of the pregnant woman." In practice, this law has been implemented quite liberally, with a broad interpretation as to what injury to physical or mental health might mean. The only addition to this legislation has been the Human Fertilisation and Embryology Act 1990, which was used to lower the time limit for abortions to 24 weeks. In May 2008, MPs voted to retain this limit. As such, the 1967 Act continues to form the legal basis upon which women access terminations today in Scotland, England and Wales.

The 1967 Abortion Act was never extended to Northern Ireland, largely because the province was at that point still governed by the Northern Irish parliament at Stormont.[21] As a result, termination in the province is still legislated by the 1861 Offences Against the Person Act, with the addition of the *R vs. Bourne* judgement of 1937 and the 1945 amendment to the Northern Irish Criminal Justice Act. The vague legal situation in the province has meant that doctors are often unsure how to act or afraid of potential legal repercussions. For example, even though a court in Belfast deemed an abortion on a teenage rape victim legal in 1993, no doctor could be found willing to perform it and the girl had to be taken to England (Side 2006). Furthermore, no legal changes have been made to the situation either before or after devolution in 1998, with the exception of the 2015 Belfast High Court ruling,[22] the enforceability of which remains to be seen. As a result, women seeking terminations will most often have to travel to England and pay for them privately (see below). In the words of Goretti Horgan, a veteran pro-choice campaigner based in Derry, "the law in the North is … a mess, and it's vulnerable women who are made to pay the price" (Rossiter 2009, 18).

Since the 1967 Abortion Act, women from Northern Ireland and the Republic of Ireland have continuously travelled to England seeking abortions. In the days before cheap air travel, women, especially from the Republic, would often travel to Liverpool due to the Dublin ferry link and the strong Irish cultural links.

Although terminations are carried out every year in Northern Ireland, interview data suggests that this is becoming more difficult as political discourse around the issue has become more prominent and conservative (see Chapter 7). Women continue to travel to England for terminations as Table 3.9 shows. Travelling for abortions has often been (and still is) a clandestine affair for the women involved, lying to family, colleagues or friends about their real reason for travelling. As a result, it is thought that official statistics collected at clinics in England may not be accurate, as women may give false addresses. In addition to transport, accommodation, and any additional costs a period away from home may entail (missed work hours, childcare, etc.), Northern Irish women had to pay for private terminations until 2017. This could cost over £1000, dependent on gestation period.[23] As Table 3.9 shows, the number of Northern Irish women seeking terminations in England fell substantially in the period 2000–2016. Interview data accredited this to the availability of the abortion pill online, rather than a fall in unwanted pregnancies.[24]

Since the 1967 Act, there has been a network of Irish (and other) women in England helping women to travel for terminations. The Irish Women's Abortion Support Group emerged out of the "alternative" Irish community in London in the 1970s and 1980s, affiliated to LGBT and left-wing Irish groups (Rossiter 2009). IWASG provided women with information about how to access abortions, and accommodation, if necessary. In the days before the Internet or mobile phones, the telephone number to access the group was publicised through the "feminist grapevine, in magazines, newsletters, on stickers surreptitiously pasted on

Table 3.9 Abortions performed in England to Northern Ireland residents 2000–2013

Year	*No. of women*
2000	1528
2001	1577
2002	1391
2003	1318
2004	1280
2005	1164
2006	1295
2007	1343
2008	1173
2009	1123
2010	1191
2011	1007
2012	905
2013	802
2014	837
2015	833
2016	724

Adapted from the FPA http://www.fpa.org.uk/sites/default/files/northern-ireland-abortion.pdf, Abortion Statistics, England and Wales 2015, https://www.gov.uk/government/uploads/system/uploads/attachment_data/file/570040/Updated_Abortion_Statistics_2015.pdf, Abortion Statistics England and Wales 2016, https://www.gov.uk/government/uploads/system/uploads/attachment_data/file/652083/Abortion_stats_England_Wales_2016.pdf. Accessed 29 January 2018

the walls of public toilets, train stations and the London underground" (ibid., 96). By the early 2000s, with the advent of the Internet, cheap air travel and the fact that in 2001, British law was changed so that non-resident women no longer had to stay overnight for the procedure, the need for their services was deemed less acute and IWASG was wound down. In the mid-2000s, a new group emerged, the Abortion Support Network. Like IWASG, ASN help women from both Northern Ireland and the Republic. In their first year, they helped 60 women, and by 2013, somewhere around 400. In their monthly supporter email from July 2015, the following anonymous examples of women the organisation had helped that month were given, showing the difficult circumstances in which (Northern) Irish women travel for terminations:

> I need some advice for a friend. She is 15 weeks pregnant, and tried a medical abortion & it was unsuccessful. She is in an abusive relationship & needs to terminate this pregnancy. She is on a low income & does not receive benefits. I am scared for her well-being.
>
> I'm going to kill myself if I don't get help. I can't have this baby. I have no money. I'm a widow with young kids and have been diagnosed with [a degenerative disease]. I was on birth control but got pregnant. I'm desperate.

It is thus apparent that the strict legal situation in Northern Ireland does not stop women having terminations, but does place substantial difficulties in their way. The only real political effort made to address this issue came in the wake of the unexpected General Election result of June 2017. The DUP decision to enter into a confidence-and-supply arrangement with the Conservative government excited great media attention in Northern Ireland and its politics, most especially the DUP's social conservatism. In response to this,[25] Labour MP Stella Creasy proposed an amendment to the Queen's Speech which would allow Northern Irish women to access free terminations on NHS England. Conscious of the cross-bench support that it had, and their small majority, the Conservative government declared that women from Northern Ireland who travelled to England for abortions would receive them at no cost. Shortly afterwards, the Scottish and Welsh governments followed suit. These announcements did not affect the legal situation in Northern Ireland at all, and it remains as restrictive as it has always been. Yet, in a somewhat strange set-up, women who travel for treatment (at their own expense) are now at least spared the cost of the procedure itself.

Social Attitudes to Abortion in Northern Ireland

Despite this harsh legal situation, there are consistently high levels of support for change from both the medical profession and the general public in Northern Ireland. A 1994 survey of around 40 gynaecologists in the region found that 55% disagreed with a direct extension of the 1967 Abortion Act, but that 70% deemed abortion was necessary if a woman's health was at risk or if she had been raped (Francome 1997). Repeating the study in 2011, 57% of gynaecologists surveyed supported a liberalisation of the law, especially in the cases of foetal abnormality or rape. In alignment with these findings, Black *et al.* (2001) found that 80% of gynaecologists surveyed believed that abortion should be

Table 3.10 Attitudes to abortion, medical, Northern Irish Life and Times Survey, 1998–2008

Results for people of different religions	*1998 (%)*			*2004 (%)*			*2008 (%)*		
	Catholic	*Protestant*	*No religion*	*Catholic*	*Protestant*	*No religion*	*Catholic*	*Protestant*	*No religion*
Always wrong	36	*	15	36	22	12	35	21	16
Almost always wrong	14	*	8	14	12	12	15	14	10
Wrong only sometimes	18	*	37	20	19	23	21	24	26
Not wrong at all	24	*	33	14	35	39	16	31	38
Can't choose	9	*	8	15	11	13	13	11	10
No answer	0	0	0	3	2	0	N/A	N/A	N/A

Source Northern Ireland Life and Times Survey, 1998, 2004, 2008

*indicates that the number of people in this category is too small to allow percentages to be calculated. 1998, $n=1800$; 2004, $n=1800$; 2008, $n=1215$

legalised in Northern Ireland either through an extension of the 1967 act, or through separate legislation originating from Stormont. These studies suggest that gynaecologists and medical professionals have not been a major obstacle to the provision of safe and legal abortion in Northern Ireland and have in fact encouraged moves towards liberalisation. Obstacles to change therefore lie elsewhere.

As Tables 3.10 and 3.11 show, the same questions on abortion were asked by the Northern Ireland Life and Times Survey on three occasions from the 1998 to 2008. One framed abortion as a medical issue (Table 3.10) and one as a social issue (Table 3.11).

Across the decade in which these questions were asked, more support can consistently be seen for abortion for medical, rather than social, reasons. Little change is seen within either religious group's attitude across the time period, nor within those of no religion (who are consistently more supportive of liberalisation in both questions). Although greater support for liberalisation is seen in both questions from Protestants than Catholics, Protestants are still conservative in their attitudes, with almost 40% in 2008 still of the belief that abortion for financial reasons is wrong.

More recently, a poll conducted on behalf of Amnesty International in 2014 found that 69% of those polled wanted abortion to be available when the pregnancy is the result of rape, 68% when it is the result of incest and 60% when the foetus has a fatal abnormality.[26] Other contemporary polling from late 2014, conducted by Lucid Talk for the Belfast Telegraph, saw similar results. When given four options in 2012, 25.9% of those polled chose the statement that "Abortion should be available to any woman who chooses it after being counselled on alternatives" and 18.6% that "Abortion should be available for rape or incest victims who choose it after counselling."[27] This showed that almost 50% of those surveyed supported liberalisation of the legislation as it currently stands. In 2016, the Northern Irish Life and Times Survey asked an extensive series (40) of questions about abortion which again showed strong support (almost 60%) for abortion in cases of fatal foetal abnormality and clear support (over 50%) for abortion in cases of rape or incest.[28] This data suggests strong (and growing) public support for more liberal laws.

The considerable support shown across the survey data cited above for abortion in certain circumstances suggests that cultural factors (like religious adherence, as detailed above) although clearly important, cannot explain the lack of movement around this policy issue. There has been consistent support for legal abortion in some limited circumstances

Table 3.11 Attitudes to abortion, social, Northern Irish Life and Times Survey, 1998–2008

Do you personally think it is wrong or not wrong for a woman to have an abortion if the family has a very low income and cannot afford any more children?	*1998 (%)*			*2004 (%)*			*2008 (%)*		
		Protestant	*No religion*	*Catholic*	*Protestant*	*No religion*	*Catholic*	*Protestant*	*No religion*
Always wrong	53	*	26	58	46	36	53	39	30
Almost always wrong	19	*	15	14	17	13	15	20	10
Wrong only sometimes	12	*	27	7	11	18	13	16	15
Not wrong at all	9	*	17	6	11	17	9	14	31
Can't choose	8	*	15	9	10	14	11	12	14
No answer	0	0	0	6	4	2	N/A	N/A	N/A

Source Northern Ireland Life and Times Survey, 1998, 2004, 2008

*indicates that the number of people in this category is too small to allow percentages to be calculated. 1998, $n=1800$; 2004, $n=1800$; 2008, $n=1215$

but no change has been enacted. Indeed, when compared to opinions on abortion in the rest of the UK, Northern Ireland does appear overly more conservative. A YouGov survey in 2013 found that 44% of British adults believe life starts at conception, and that 28% would like to see the time limit for abortion lowered to less than 24 weeks, where it currently stands.[29] This suggests a reasonably high percentage (over one quarter) of the British population take issue with current legislation as it stands, yet the issue of abortion receives distinctly little political attention. This relative similarity in social attitudes also suggests that cultural factors are perhaps less important than political and structural factors in explaining why abortion legislation has not been addressed in Northern Ireland.

Conclusion

The results of the conflict in Northern Ireland continue to ripple through politics and society—to the extent, indeed, that it is debatable whether the province can in fact be referred to as "post-conflict." The region still witnesses a strongly divided political system, which is reflective of broader societal divisions. Almost twenty years after the Good Friday Agreement, identity as Northern Irish has grown within the province but is still distinctly in the minority. Politically and socially, it remains a deeply divided place. In the wake of the collapse of the devolved structures in early 2017, and the uncertainty of what Brexit will mean for the region, Northern Ireland's political future looks rocky.

In the post-Good Friday Agreement landscape, these enduring political divisions often map onto social concerns. Cultural and social issues have become increasingly politicised in Northern Ireland. Within this, gendered issues have become embroiled in these divisions, most especially abortion and LGBT rights. The "culture wars" are now an increasingly important part of Northern Irish society and politics, and show that, whilst long-established political and societal divisions are not going away, they are changing, adopting new issues and moving in directions which might not have previously been anticipated.

Yet an academic understanding of gender as a structural force within Northern Irish society, conflict or politics has had less attention. Women's descriptive political representation has been given much consideration (Galligan 2006, 2013; Matthews 2014), but there has been far less interest in substantive political issues. Within this, abortion has been especially under-considered. Legislation in the rest of the UK is long established and has changed little since its original enactment in 1967. Since then, thousands of women have travelled from Northern Ireland, seeking terminations in England. Repeated opinion polls in Northern Ireland over many years suggest that the public and medical professionals are supportive of liberalisation. Yet, despite the funding decision taken at Westminster in 2017, neither public opinion nor the thousands of women who have travelled for terminations appear to have had any impact on political or legal attitudes, and abortion remains far more restricted in Northern Ireland than the rest of the UK.

Notes

1. The Battle of the Boyne was a battle between the Catholic James 2nd and William and Mary, who had overthrown James in 1688. James' defeat at the Boyne assured the continued Protestant ascendancy in Ireland. Its anniversary on the 12th of July continues to be celebrated annually in Northern Irish protestant communities.
2. £26.5 million was stolen from the Northern Bank headquarters in Belfast in December 2004. The PSNI and British and Irish governments have all intimated that they think the PIRA were responsible, although the organisation has denied this. The robbery remains unsolved.
3. Robert McCartney was killed in a bar in Belfast in 2005, allegedly by PIRA members. His sisters and fiancée led a high-profile campaign to find his killers. They met then US President George W. Bush on a trip to America; the same year, Sinn Féin President Gerry Adams was not invited to the White House during his St. Patrick's Day visit. See also Ashe (2006, 2007).
4. Although comparisons can be made to mainland British political parties, and indeed, some parties—such as the Alliance Party with its links to the Liberal Democrats, and the Ulster Unionist Party with its alliance with the Conservatives during the 2010 elections—have concrete links to parties in Westminster. The ways in which the parties choose to designate themselves in the EU parliament are also instructional—the SDLP as centre-left, the UUP as centre-right, the DUP as independent and Sinn Féin in the "same group as the former eastern bloc Stalinist parties" (Wilford and Wilson 2006, 10).
5. Indeed, the Conservative party's full title remains to this day the Conservative and Unionist Party. The UUP and the Conservatives once again enjoyed an (albeit brief) electoral alliance in the 2010 Westminster elections.
6. Most famous of whom was the first to be elected, Bobby Sands. Sands died in 1981 whilst on hunger strike in prison in Belfast.

7. “What Sinn Féin stands for,” http://www.sinnfein.ie/what-sinn-fein-stands-for. Accessed 30 January 2018.
8. “Defend a woman’s right to travel, to know, to live”, Sinn Féin, Linen Hall Library Political Collection, Linen Hall Library, Belfast. Sinn Féin’s position on abortion is discussed in greater detail in Chapter 5.
9. The pair were nicknamed the “Chuckle Brothers” by the press, given their apparently friendly relationship.
10. The party designate as “Other.” As per the procedural rules in the Assembly, this means that they cannot file a petition of concern on their own but can support one brought by Unionists or Nationalists.
11. She very narrowly lost her Westminster seat to Gavin Robinson of the DUP in 2015.
12. Basil McCrea, the party’s leader and sole MLA following Deputy Leader John McAllister’s departure in July 2014, was accused of sexual misconduct by a former party worker. The party’s candidate for the European elections, and daughter of a former provisional IRA prisoner, Tina McKenzie, left the party’s executive as a result on the day of the EU elections. Furthermore, two days before the 2014 EU and local elections, the party changed its designation from Unionist to Other in the Assembly, which led to a very public falling out between the party Leader and Deputy Leader. McAllister left the party shortly afterwards.
13. Then leader, and future Director of the Marie Stopes clinic in Belfast, Dawn Purvis, resigned from the party in 2010 following a murder attributed to the Ulster Volunteer forces, a loyalist paramilitary grouping, which had links to the party. She remained in the Assembly as an Independent MLA.
14. A further 7.18% did not state a religion. https://humanism.org.uk/campaigns/religion-and-belief-some-surveys-and-statistics/. Accessed 29 January 2018.
15. The Caleb Foundation was credited with lobbying the National Trust during the building of the Giant’s Causeway visitor’s centre to include information on a Creationist interpretation of the geological formation. http://www.newstatesman.com/blogs/politics/2012/07/creationism-and-political-power-northern-ireland. Accessed 29 January 2018.
16. “Archbishop Eamon Martin Meets David Ford over Abortion Laws,” BBC, http://www.bbc.co.uk/news/uk-northern-ireland-30831196. Accessed 29 January 2018. David Ford’s actions are discussed in greater detail in Chapter 7.
17. The flying of flags (especially Union Jacks/Irish Tricolours, or the flags of various paramilitary groupings) has been a continually contentious issue in Northern Ireland. It has been brought into the spotlight especially since late 2012, when the Belfast city council decided to limit the

flying of the Union Jack above Belfast City Hall to certain days, rather than all year round. A period of rioting and sustained civil disobedience followed, late into 2013, largely instigated by sections of the Protestant/Unionist/Loyalist community. The Irish Language Act, for which proposed legislation emerged in early 2015, and appeared as a strong sticking point in the negotiations to restart the Assembly in 2017–2018, has been strongly promoted by Sinn Féin and equally strongly attacked by unionist parties, most especially the Democratic Unionist Party (the DUP) and Traditional Unionist Voice (the TUV). Parading remains a contentious issue, in spite of a body specifically established to oversee parading, especially around the Orange Order celebrations on the 12th of July.

18. Five attempts have been made to extend same-sex marriage to Northern Ireland via the Assembly. All have failed, largely due to the DUP's conservative stance on the issue. Whilst blood donation by gay men is now permitted in the rest of the UK, the ban has been upheld by successive Health Ministers in Northern Ireland. The province has also struggled for years with racially motivated attacks aimed at the population's growing ethnic minority communities.
19. As recently as January 2013, during Marie Stopes International's appearance before the Committee for Justice at Stormont, this has been reiterated as the legal basis for an abortion in Northern Ireland today.
20. The medical profession has often led the charge in calls for abortion reform—"In most countries, abortion came to the public agenda, not as a women's movement demand, but as a response to demands from doctors and progressive politicians to respond to the increase in abortions outside the law" (McBride Stetson 2001, 4).
21. Direct rule from Westminster was not enacted until 1972, the British government using its powers under the *Government of Ireland Act*.
22. In late 2015 the Belfast High Court ruled that Northern Irish abortion law was incompatible with human rights legislation and instructed the Assembly to introduce legal reform to address this. This has yet to be addressed by the Assembly.
23. Although both Marie Stopes and the British Pregnancy Advisory Service provided special rates for Northern/ Irish women until the Government began funding Northern Irish women in 2017.
24. Largely accredited to the website Women on Web. Medical professional, private interview with the author. June 2014.
25. This was also a response to the Supreme Court's decision that Northern Irish women could not be allowed taxpayer funded abortions within the English NHS.
26. https://www.amnesty.org.uk/sites/default/files/milward_brown_poll_results_october_2014_final_0.pdf. Accessed 29 January 2018.

27. The other two options were "Abortion should be allowed if the mother is likely to die if the pregnancy continues" (26.5% support) and "Abortion is no better than shooting a child in the head and should be treated as murder" (2% support). http://www.belfasttelegraph.co.uk/news/northern-ireland/growing-backing-for-liberalisation-of-abortion-rules-in-northern-ireland-30634125.html. Accessed 29 January 2018.
28. The full list of questions and results can be found at http://www.ark.ac.uk/nilt/2016/Abortion/. Accessed 30 January 2018.
29. http://cdn.yougov.com/cumulus_uploads/document/a0c0uf8c2g/YouGov-Survey-University-of-Lancaster-Results-130130.pdf. Accessed 29 January 2018.

Bibliography

Ashe, F. 2006. The McCartney Sisters' Search for Justice: Gender and Political Protest in Northern Ireland. *Politics* 26 (3): 161–170.

———. 2007. Gendering Ethno-Nationalist Politics in Northern Ireland. *Ethnic and Racial Studies* 30 (5): 766–786.

Black, G., A. Hunter, and N. Heasley. 2001. A Survey of Attitudes to Abortion Law in Northern Ireland Amongst Obstetricians, Gynaecologists and Family Planning Doctors. *Journal of Family Planning and Reproductive Health Care* 27 (4): 221–222.

Cox, Michael, Adrian Guelke, and Fiona Stephen. 2006. *A Farewell to Arms? Beyond the Good Friday Agreement*. Manchester: Manchester University Press.

Evans, J.A.J., and J. Tonge. 2003. The future of the 'radical centre' in Northern Ireland after the Good Friday agreement. *Political Studies* 51 (1): 26–50.

———. 2005. Problems of Modernizing an Ethno-Religious Party: The Case of the Ulster Unionist Party in Northern Ireland. *Party Politics* 11 (3): 319–338.

Farren, Séan. 2010. *The SDLP: The Struggle for Agreement in Northern Ireland, 1970–2000*. Dublin: Four Courts Press.

Farrington, Christopher. 2006. *Ulster Unionism and the Peace Process in Northern Ireland*. London: Palgrave Macmillan.

Fearon, Kate. 1999. *Women's Work: The Story of the Northern Ireland Women's Coalition*. Belfast: Blackstaff Press.

Frampton, Martyn. 2008. *The Long March: The Political Strategy of Sinn Fein, 1981–2007*. London: Palgrave Macmillan.

Francome, Colin. 1997. Attitudes of General Practitioners in Northern Ireland Toward Abortion and Family Planning. *Family Planning Perspectives* 29 (5): 234–236.

Gallaher, Carolyn. 2007. *After the Peace: Loyalist Paramilitaries in Northern Ireland*. Ithaca: Cornell University Press.

Galligan, Yvonne. 2006. Women in Northern Ireland's Politics: Feminizing an 'Armed Patriarchy'. In *Representing Women in Parliament: A comparative study*, ed. Marian Sawer, Manon Tremblay, and Linda Trimble. Abingdon: Routledge.

———. 2013. Gender and Politics in Northern Ireland: The Representation Gap Revisited. *Irish Political Studies* 28 (3): 413–433.

Hopkinson, Michael. 2004. *The Irish War of Independence*. Dublin: Gill and Macmillan.

Hunter, James Davison. 1992. *The Culture Wars: The Struggle to Define America*. New York: Basic Books.

Kaufmann, Eric. 2007. *The Orange Order: A Contemporary Northern Irish History*. Oxford: Oxford University Press.

Maillot, Agnes. 2005. *New Sinn Fein: Irish Republicanism in the Twenty-First Century*. Abingdon: Routledge.

Matthews, Neil. 2014. Gendered Candidate Selection and the Representation of Women in Northern Ireland. *Parliamentary Affairs* 67 (3): 617–646.

McAuley, J.W., and J. Tonge. 2007. For God and for the Crown: Contemporary Political and Social Attitudes Among Orange Order Members in Northern Ireland. *Political Psychology* 28 (1): 33–52.

McBride, Dorothy Stetson (ed.). 2001. *Abortion Politics, Women's Movements, and the Democratic State: A Comparative Study of State Feminism*. Oxford: Oxford University Press.

McGlynn, C., J. Tonge, and J. Mcauley. 2014. The Party Politics of Post-devolution Identity in Northern Ireland. *British Journal of Politics and International Relations* 16 (2): 273–290.

Mitchell, P. 2001. Transcending an Ethnic Party System? The Impact of Consociational Governance on Electoral Dynamics and the Party System. In *Aspects of the Belfast Agreement*, ed. Rick Wilford. Oxford: Oxford University Press.

Mulholland, Marc. 2002. *Northern Ireland: A Very Short Introduction*. Oxford: Oxford University Press.

Murtagh, Cera. 2015. Reaching Across: Institutional Barriers to Cross-Ethnic Parties in Post-conflict Societies and the Case of Northern Ireland. *Nations and Nationalism* 2 (3): 544–565.

Mycock, and McDaid. 2014. Stem the Tide of Northern Ireland's 'Culture Wars'. https://www.opendemocracy.net/andrew-mycock-shaun-mcdaid/stem-tide-of-northern-ireland%E2%80%99s-%E2%80%98culture-wars%E2%80%99. Accessed 29 January 2018.

Nic Craith, Mairead. 2002. *Plural Identities, Singular Narrative: The Case of Northern Ireland*. Oxford: Bergahn Books.

Powell, Jonathan. 2009. *Great Hatred, Little Room: Making Peace in Northern Ireland*. London: Vintage.

Rossiter, Ann. 2009. *Ireland's Hidden Diaspora: The 'Abortion Trail' and the Making of a London-Irish Underground, 1980–2000*. London: Iasc.

Sales, Rosemary. 1997. *Women Divided: Gender, Religion and Politics in Northern Ireland*. Abingdon: Routledge.
Sheldon, Sally. 1997. *Beyond Control: Medical Power and Abortion Law*. London: Pluto Press.
Side, Katherine. 2006. Contract, Charity and Honourable Entitlement: Social Citizenship and the 1967 Abortion Act in Northern Ireland After the Good Friday Agreement. *Social Politics* 13 (1): 89–116.
Tilley, J., and G. Evans. 2011. Political Generations in Northern Ireland. *European Journal of Political Research* 50 (5): 583–608.
Tonge, Jonathon. 2005. *The New Northern Irish Politics?* London: Palgrave.
Tonge, Jonathon, and Jocelyn Evans. 2015. Another Communal Headcount; The Election in Northern Ireland. *Parliamentary Affairs* 68 (3): 117–132.
Tonge, Jonathon, and Gerrard Murray. 2005. *Sinn Féin and the SDLP: From Alienation to Participation*. London: Hurst.
Tonge, Jonathon, Maíre Braniff, Thomas Hennessey, James W. McAuley, and Sophie A. Whiting. 2014. *The Democratic Unionist Party: From Protest to Power*. Oxford: Oxford University Press.
Waylen, Georgina. 2014. A Seat at the Table—Is It Enough? Gender, Multiparty Negotiations, and Institutional Design in South African and Northern Ireland. *Politics and Gender* 10: 495–523.
Wilford, Rick, and Robin Wilson. 2006. *The Trouble with Northern Ireland: The Belfast Agreement and Democratic Governance*. Dublin: New Island.
Wilson, Robin. 2010. *The Northern Ireland Experience of Conflict and Agreement: A Model for Export?* Manchester: Manchester University Press.
Wuthnow, Robert. 1990. *The Restructuring of American Religion: Society and Faith Since World War II*. Princeton: Princeton University Press.

CHAPTER 4

The National Institution: Westminster

In June 2017, the British government announced that Northern Irish women seeking terminations in England would receive taxpayer-funded treatment. With the exception of this sudden decision, Northern Ireland has rarely figured in discussions around abortion in the national parliament at Westminster, either at the time of the historic liberalisation of the procedure in 1967 or in successive debates. This chapter asks why this is and situates Northern Ireland's limited place in the discussion since the passing of the Abortion Act. It begins by looking at the ways in which a discussion of Northern Ireland was not included in the initial 1967 legislation. It then looks at attempts made to change the Northern Irish situation at Westminster from 1967 to the present day, most especially the failed attempt to extend the Act in 2008 via the Human Fertilisation and Embryology Bill. A consideration of the discussion of Northern Ireland and abortion at the time of the debate around the shape that the devolution of powers would take in 1998 then follows.

This chapter is an expanded version of Thomson, Jennifer. 2016. Explaining Gender Equality Difference in a Devolved System: The Case of Abortion Law in Northern Ireland. *British Politics* 11 (3): 371–388. It also replicates parts of, and expands upon, Thomson, Jennifer. 2018. A 'United Kingdom?': The 1967 Abortion Act and Northern Ireland. In *Troubled Waters: Abortion in Ireland, Northern Ireland and Prince Edward Island*, ed. Colleen MacQuarrie, Claire Pierson, Shannon Stettner, and Fiona Bloomer. Charlottetown: UPEI, Island Studies Press.

J. Thomson, *Abortion Law and Political Institutions*, Gender and Politics, https://doi.org/10.1007/978-3-319-96169-9_4

This chapter argues that Northern Ireland has always been discussed with a sense of uncertainty and confusion by the majority of Westminster politicians and that this unease has, at times, and most notably in 2008, been a means to ensure that the Abortion Act is not extended. Northern Irish politics suffer from a "nested newness" (Chappell 2014a; Mackay 2014) in that, despite the advent of a peace settlement and new political institutions, an older understanding of the region's politics and society still dominates the national institution. The chapter further argues that the reticence of national government to act means that, in contemporary politics, abortion in Northern Ireland is understood first and foremost as a regional, devolved issue, rather than a women's issue, allowing Westminster to abscond responsibility and judgement around what is deemed a controversial topic. Instead of opening up new institutional avenues for action around abortion, in which activists can "venue-shop" (Vickers *et al.* 2010, 237), to find the one most appropriate, devolved Northern Ireland now instead suffers from a "ping-pong" effect whereby no action is taken on this at Stormont, but responsibility at Westminster has largely been deferred.

"Completely Passed to One Side": Northern Ireland and the 1967 Abortion Act

The Abortion Act of 1967 established termination of pregnancy as legal for the first time in the UK. Under the parameters of this legislation, terminations must be carried out with the approval of two medical professionals, who are in "good faith" that the continuance of the pregnancy would involve risk to the life or health of the woman, "greater than if the pregnancy were terminated," or that there was a risk the child would be born "seriously handicapped." A time limit was "read into" the Act via the Infant Life (Preservation) Act of 1929 which made it an offence to destroy a "child capable of being born alive" and which interpreted this with the "rebuttable assumption" that this would mean 28 weeks gestation (Sheldon 1997, 108). With minimal exceptions (the time limit was shortened to 24 weeks in 1990), this law continues to govern abortion in the contemporary UK.

In the civil society campaign for abortion liberalisation, the Abortion Law Reform Association (ALRA) was the key lobbying organisation working at Westminster. It had been campaigning for change around the legal status of abortion since the 1930s. By the 1960s, the original leadership were still in place and increasingly viewed by other ALRA members as "restrained and discrete" (Furedi and Hume 1997, 15). A new vanguard of younger social liberals ousted the ALRA leadership, and the organisation went on to conduct "a classic advocacy campaign; there was a clear focus – the reform of the abortion law; a committed group of key individuals as embodied in the executive committee and key advisers" (ibid., 20). ALRA perceived abortion law reform along permissive, rather than liberal lines:

> At that time the things they [ALRA] were really looking for were to allow abortion to protect a woman's … life and health [and] for it to be stated in law rather than implied by the rather curious wording of the 1861 Act. And they also felt it should be a right [for those] who had been sexually assaulted and become pregnant, who had been raped and they also included people who they regarded as mentally deficient because they felt that society would wish for abortion to be available for that group.[1] (see also Francome 2004, Chapter 4)

Having gained the support of David Steel of the Liberal party, who had been successful in the Private Members' Ballot and who was keen to use this to support abortion law reform, an opportunity for legislative change emerged. Steel, upon the advice of Professor Dugald Baird of the University of Aberdeen, began to drift away from the notion of a prescriptive law which specified the precise ways in which abortion was legal (rape, incest, etc.) and instead towards a more liberal piece of legislation.

Yet Steel did not advocate for a more radically liberal bill which would allow abortion at the woman's request. As he said in the parliamentary debate on the second reading of the abortion bill, his aim was "to stamp out back-street abortions, but it is not the intention of the promoters of the Bill to leave a wide-open door for abortion on request" (HC Deb 22 July 1966 vol. 732 1074). The circumstances in which a woman was allowed a termination would be broadly defined, but the ultimate decision would be made by not one, but two medical doctors. This was largely due to explicit lobbying on the part of the medical profession (Halfmann 2011, 70; Keown 1988, 166). As Professor David Paintin, advisor to Steel at the time of the 1967 Act describes it,

> …the medical people at that time saw the law as being clarified so the Doctors would now be able to make decisions that were suitable in the context of each woman, but they saw doctors very much as being in control … I think David Steel had realised very wisely that unless he had the medical establishment and the religious establishment and the political establishment on his side, the thing just wouldn't get through.[2]

The resultant Act thus enshrined abortion as first and foremost a medical issue, rather than one of female bodily autonomy. A more drastic reform which would have allowed women control over the decision appeared impossible, not only because of Steel's personal stance but also broader political opinion: in 1966 Steel "had to withdraw a clause which had provided for abortion where the woman's capacity as a mother might be overstrained" (Francome 2004, 66; see also Halfmann 2011, 70) because of objections. In this sense, as Keown argues, "the Abortion Act of 1967 not only respected medical discretion but, by rendering its exercise virtually unchallengeable … allowed its variable and extensive exercise" (Keown 1988, 163).

Where in this picture of reform was Northern Ireland? The only reference to the province in the entirety of the Abortion Act is the final sentence, which baldly declares that "This Act does not extend to Northern Ireland." Professor David Paintin recalls an earlier meeting with Lord Silkin regarding an unsuccessful attempt at abortion reform through the Lords:

> And just at the very end of the meeting he said in almost an aside, "Of course it won't apply in Northern Ireland." And none of us said anything … But nobody during any of the debates from that morning onwards mentioned Northern Ireland again. It just completely passed to one side.[3]

Similarly, Lord Steel himself recalled little mention of Northern Ireland once he took up the cause of abortion reform, believing to have simply been informed by the Home Office that it was the responsibility of Stormont and not Westminster.[4] Northern Ireland was thus not a consideration in the course of the reform. In a volume of interviews with the key reformers undertaken in the late 1990s, Northern Ireland is mentioned briefly in passing ("It was scandalous that Northern Ireland wasn't included, as long as it continued to be part of the United Kingdom, but at that time we nearly lost Scotland too. It was only because David Steel was a Scottish MP that we did not" [Madeleine

Simms in Furedi and Hume 1997, 21]), suggesting it was not really of central concern to them at the time. Whilst the central individuals all had close ties to medical and political institutions (Vera Houghton, the Chair of ALRA, was the wife of Labour MP, Douglas Houghton[5]), their ties were to London-based institutions. Furthermore, there were no similar debates in Stormont whatsoever. The Northern Irish Parliament of 1922–1974 does not record one debate at all with any substantial reference to abortion. With no pressure at Westminster or Stormont, Northern Ireland was neglected in the legislation.

Indeed, in the aftermath of the 1967 Act, British activists were too busy fighting to retain what had been gained to think about attempting to extend it to Northern Ireland. Several attempts were made in the immediate aftermath of the 1967 Act to curtail its power, including the James White Bill, the Corrie Bill and the Lane Committee Report, all in the 1970s.[6] As Professor Wendy Savage, a gynaecologist and a London-based abortion rights activist, recalls:

> I think probably whilst we were fighting off all these attacks on the 1967 Act that we were so busy defending the status quo that we didn't really take all that much notice.[7]

Northern Ireland remained at a remove from both legislative change and activism in London-based politics. With worries over protecting the Act from potential political and legal pushback in the 1970s, any consideration of extending the Abortion Act to the province was not a central concern.

Attempts at Change in Westminster: 1967–1998

The issue of abortion in Northern Ireland was only rarely discussed at Westminster following the 1967 Act. This was largely due to the very different political institutions which existed in Northern Ireland as opposed to the rest of the UK. The Northern Irish Parliament of 1921–1972 was the UK's first foray into devolution. The little literature which exists on relations between Stormont and Westminster during the first iteration of Stormont suggests that Westminster was happy to leave Stormont at arm's length from national government. Both institutions had a vested interest in avoiding discussion of the constitutional question, and there was little attempt to consider the "subordinate" (Birrell 2012, 271) position of the provincial government, or how its relations with the national government fully functioned. Britain, even once direct rule was re-established, showed little desire to align Northern Ireland with the centre (ibid., 476), and, by the early 1970s, the British Parliament had given Stormont such a loose leash for so long that reform proved difficult (ibid., 490). Instead, Westminster was left with the threat of direct rule, and given that the Northern Irish parties were minor players outside of the province, national parliament had little direct relevance to on-the-ground Northern Irish politics. Indeed, from the establishment of the Parliament at Stormont in 1921, "Westminster devoted an average of 2 hours a year to Northern Ireland" which "corresponded with ignorance in Great Britain about the province" (Bogdanor 2001, 79). Simultaneously, with the main political parties from Westminster having no public presence in Northern Ireland, the province never had a say in the make-up of the national government.[8] Furthermore, the separate Belfast-based parliament meant that the wave of liberalising legislation described above which was enacted at Westminster in the late 1960s had no impact in Northern Ireland. "On matters of mores, Northern Ireland took her own path, declining to follow the rest of the United Kingdom in modifying her divorce, abortion or homosexuality laws in the 1960s," also deciding not to abolish capital punishment when the rest of the UK did in 1965 (ibid., 89).

If Westminster had little influence on Northern Irish politics, equally Northern Ireland had little influence on Westminster. The Northern Irish presence in national government during this period appears to have achieved little. Rush's (2001) analysis of the contributions of MPs from the region at selected points from 1928 to 1962 reveals a pattern of very little activity, with Northern Irish members far less likely than other MPs to ask questions or contribute in debates. Furthermore, the Ulster Party (the only political party present in the Commons from Northern Ireland in this period) appeared to lack a coherent viewpoint on both their role in Westminster and their relationship with Stormont. Whilst they followed the Tory whip, Stormont was more likely to want to see spending on social welfare and public goods (Jackson 2011, 465). Moreover, Northern Irish MPs drew almost exclusively from one small segment of the Northern Irish Protestant population. Only 2 female MPs were elected from Northern Ireland in this period out of a total of 57. MPs tended to be upper class, well connected and frequently from professional backgrounds in the Press or Law. "Dynastic succession" (ibid., 457) was frequent, with various male relatives present in different, or the same, time periods.[9] Drawing from such a narrow pool, a diverse range of views from Northern Ireland was lacking.

Against this backdrop, it is not surprising that the situation of abortion in Northern Ireland received scant discussion. Abortion with relation to the exclusion of Northern Ireland from the 1967 Act was rarely mentioned from 1967 until devolution, even following the suspension of Stormont in 1972. The majority of references in this period come from simple written questions from backbenchers to the Secretary of State for Northern Ireland with an equally simple answer in response that there was at that given moment no policy regarding any change. A question asked in 1972 is broadly representative of these:

> Mr. Parker: asked the Secretary of State for Northern Ireland whether he will take steps to bring abortion law in Northern Ireland into line with that in other parts of the United Kingdom.
> Mr. Channon: No. (HC Deb 8 June 1972 vol. 838 c123)

Questions from various backbenchers of both main political parties came sporadically in 1974, 1980, 1982, 1984, 1986 and 1987. On equally irregular occasions, backbenchers also inquired into the statistics regarding numbers of Northern Irish women coming to Britain to seek terminations, such as the following to then Secretary of State for Social Services Kenneth Clarke:

> Mr. John David Taylor: asked the Secretary of State for Social Services what is the estimated number of women from Northern Ireland who have had to go elsewhere in the United Kingdom for abortions in each of the last 10 years. (HC Deb 5 March 1984 vol. 55 cc446–7W 446W)

Occasionally, other statistics were requested: the number of women who had died as a result of illegal abortions in Northern Ireland, 1985 (HC Deb 7 March 1985 vol. 74 c591W 591W), the Regional Health Authorities in which Northern Irish women had sought terminations, 1986 (HC Deb 26 November 1986 vol. 106 cc291–2W 291W). Questions emerged equally from members who appeared against the 1967 Act or any future liberalisation (the question from 1985 came from

Reverend Martyn Smyth UUP MP and appeared an intentional comment on the lack of "back-street" abortions in Northern Ireland) and those who wanted to prompt a discussion about Northern Ireland's unique position (Mo Mowlam MP asked several pointed questions in the early 1990s, which appear directed at the provision (or lack) of sex education, contraception and abortion for young people in the province [HC Deb 30 January 1995 vol. 253 c487W]). The majority of questions regarding Northern Ireland and abortion in this period were not from key political players, nor were they asked with any level of regularity, which suggests that this was never a pressing topic for either government or opposition.

Similarly, members of successive Westminster governments were keen to stress that they did not wish to change the law and that they were conscious of what they perceived to be differing public sentiment around the issue in Northern Ireland. Asked in 1986 of the potential for an extension, the then Under-secretary of State for Northern Ireland said that "the legalisation of abortion in Northern Ireland was last reviewed in 1985. At that time it was concluded that any change in the law would be opposed by an overwhelming majority of the population. I believe that remains the case" (HC Deb 12 November 1987 vol. 122 cc537–8 537). In 1994, then Secretary of State for Northern Ireland, Michael Ancram, said "the Government have consistently held to the view that legislation should not be introduced to reform Northern Ireland abortion laws unless this is likely to command broad support within the Province" (HC Deb 25 May 1994 vol. 244 c200W). For the duration of this period, successive governments, Conservative and Labour alike, appeared highly reticent to take the lead on any change of legislation, using public opinion as a justification for a lack of action. Moreover, when Northern Irish MPs specifically did talk about abortion in Westminster, they were quick to point out the perception that there was no support in Northern Ireland itself for any change from the status quo. Speaking during the debate around the Abortion (Amendment) Bill in 1988, the Reverend Martyn Smyth MP said "I take this opportunity to repeat that, by and large, the bulk of people in Northern Ireland, irrespective of their religious outlook or political convictions, have no desire to see the 1967 Act extended to Northern Ireland" (HC Deb 5 July 1984 vol. 63 cc253–4W).

The dominant portrait painted at Westminster was one of a Northern Irish population who were happy to accept this legislative difference. Indeed, the anti-choice lobbying voice was loud in Westminster, whereas pro-choice beliefs did not appear able to find a voice in representatives at the national level. In 1984, then Secretary of State for Northern Ireland Douglas Hurd MP confirmed that "Since January 1981, representations have been received from eight district or borough councils, the Association of Local Authorities (NI), LIFE (NI), the 1982 Annual General Assembly of the Presbyterian Church, a Free Presbyterian Church and one private individual" (HC Deb 22 October 1984 vol. 65 c461W 461W). Similarly, in 1993, then Secretary of State for Northern Ireland Michael Ancram MP confirmed that "in the past 12 months, five representations have been received indicating that a majority of people in the Province would support the extension of the Abortion Act 1967 to Northern Ireland. Twenty-one representations have been received indicating that a majority of people would be opposed to such an extension and one that a majority of the medical profession would likewise be opposed" (HC Deb 25 May 1994 vol. 244 c200). This was similarly represented in the actions of Northern Irish MPs: in 1995, the Secretary of State confirmed that "In the last three years, no Northern Ireland Member has made representations supporting the extension of the Abortion Act 1967 to Northern Ireland. Seven Northern Ireland Members have made representations to Ministers expressing their opposition to the extension of the Act" (HC Deb 25 May 1995 vol. 260 c749W). In 1995, an all-party delegation met the Prime Minister John Major to express distaste for any attempt to extend the legislation to Northern Ireland (HC Deb 2 May 1996 vol. 276 cc1281–2). This cross-party group meeting the Prime Minister with an anti-liberalisation message reflects the broader message of support for the status quo which was reaching Westminster from Northern Ireland. The pro-choice voice was either not organised enough to target Westminster with its lobbying, or could not find supportive voices to champion its cause in Parliament. The capacity for pro-choice activists to "venue-shop" (Vickers *et al.* 2010) and force the issue onto central government's agenda appeared weak. From the suspension of Stormont in 1972 until 1998, there was no formal devolved structure in the province. As a result, if Westminster didn't appear to be listening, pro-choice advocacy had few alternative options by which they might try to get the issue onto the formal political agenda.

"A Special Case": Devolution and Abortion at Westminster

With a landslide Labour victory in the UK in 1997, major constitutional reform in the UK appeared inevitable. Devolution had been a key electoral promise of New Labour's, and the creation of new political institutions in Belfast, Edinburgh and Cardiff was proposed. With electorates in Wales and Scotland voting positively for devolution in 1997, and the Good Friday Agreement gaining the support of the Northern Irish population in 1998, the road was paved to begin working out the process of devolution from Westminster.

During debates around the devolution of power to the Scottish Parliament and the Welsh and Northern Irish Assemblies at Westminster, the issue of abortion was raised briefly in a debate in March 1998. An amendment was tabled by Dr. Liam Fox, Conservative MP, in an attempt to devolve power regarding abortion to Edinburgh and not to have it as a "reserved" power at Westminster as was intended. He was criticised by other Members for his apparent bid to stoke up Catholic sentiment within Labour's Scottish support base and complicate the referendum vote. Fox's argument centred on the apparent contradiction between what was and was not being devolved to Scotland in terms of ethical issues. Whilst abortion was being left with Westminster, "the death penalty – a major ethical issue – can be decided in the Scottish Parliament. Euthanasia is another major ethical issue. It, too, can be decided in the Scottish Parliament. Bizarrely, human transplantation can also be decided in the Scottish Parliament" (HC Deb 31 March 1998 vol. 309 c1095).

The British Government, however, was happy for abortion to remain at Westminster, making the argument, as then Secretary of State for Scotland Donald Dewar MP did, that, "Throughout the United Kingdom, common criteria and common conditions must be met before a termination can take place" (HC Deb 31 March 1998 vol. 309 c1109). Abortion was presented by the Labour government as something which was important enough that it had to be uniformly regulated from central government. MPs were quick to point out the inconsistency regarding Northern Ireland in this regard. In the words of Maria Fyfe, MP for Glasgow Maryhill: "I wonder whether any hon. Member is defending what happens in Northern Ireland. It is impossible to know how many hundreds of thousands of women are forced to make the journey to mainland Britain" (HC Deb 31 March 1998 vol. 309 c1099). Dewar's response to the Northern Irish exception was that the province was "different":

> It is perfectly proper for hon. Members to say "What about Northern Ireland?" I do not want to plunge into the *sad history of events* in Northern Ireland, but it is clear that we have made a distinction between Northern Ireland and the rest of the United Kingdom for a multiplicity of pressing political *and other reasons*. There is no case for saying that, because Northern Ireland is *different*, we should countenance the possibility of differences between the law on abortion in England and Scotland. (HC Deb 31 March 1998 vol. 309 c1108, emphasis added)

Dewar evokes the bloody recent history of Northern Ireland ("the sad history of events") but the logic of his argument does not elaborate on how this past relates to abortion rights. Northern Ireland is "different" because of this tragic past, but precisely how this difference corresponds to separate abortion legislation appears confused. When pushed further on this point by the leader of the Scottish National Party, Alex Salmond MP, Dewar declared that "The law in Northern Ireland is very *different*, because it is *a special case* ... The *special* social and political situation in Northern Ireland is not a reason for contemplating further differences in the United Kingdom in this sensitive area" (HC Deb 31 March 1998 vol. 309 c1109, emphasis added). In the wake of devolution therefore, a somewhat bizarre constitutional picture emerged regarding termination of pregnancy. Abortion was deemed too important, and an issue which required national uniform standards, to be devolved to Scotland. Simultaneously, Northern Ireland was "different," "special" and a unique case such that it could continue to remain an anomaly in terms of its legislation. Abortion was not a medical issue in this context, as it had been in the discourse of 1967, but an issue of separate cultural tastes and reservations. During the discourse on devolution, a picture emerges of a government which viewed Northern Ireland as different and which was happy to accommodate this difference with regard to specific (and controversial) issues. The "newness" of the devolved institution was very much "nested" (Chappell 2014a; Mackay 2014) within an older Westminster perspective of Northern Irish society and politics.

Furthermore, in the wake of devolution, the government appeared at times confused about where the responsibility for abortion really lay. In 1998, the Secretary of State for Northern Ireland responded to a question about when abortion powers would be devolved with the answer that "the law on abortion is currently classified as part of the criminal law and is therefore a 'reserved' matter. This means that it can be legislated upon either at Westminster, or, with the approval of the Secretary of State and Parliament, by the new Northern Ireland Assembly" (HC Deb 21 July 1998 vol. 316 c441). However, two years later, when asked about "access to abortion and contraceptive services for women in Northern Ireland," the reply was that "Responsibility for this matter has been devolved to the Northern Ireland Assembly and is therefore no longer a matter for the Secretary of State for Northern Ireland" (HC Deb 19 July 2000 vol. 354 c196). On both occasions, given that they were long prior to the 2010 devolution of policing and justice powers, the correct answer was the first that either Westminster or Stormont, with the Secretary of State's approval, could move on it. This inaccuracy betrays the lack of importance or thought given to this issue from a Westminster perspective.

"A Dirty Deal": 2008 at Westminster

As the scarcity of references to abortion in Northern Ireland at Westminster detailed above suggests, British political activism around abortion has been relatively minimal compared to other Western countries, most notably the USA. Halfmann (2011) argues that this is because whilst in America the Supreme Court decision legalising terminations rests on the right to privacy,[10] Britain has constructed abortion as a medical rather than a social issue. With the inherent legitimacy gained from seeing abortion as a medical concern, abortion activism from either the pro-choice or the pro-life community has never been as fervent or vocal at Westminster as it has in Washington. Building momentum for what is often viewed as a battle that has already been won can therefore be difficult. As one senior reproductive rights practitioner acknowledged, "there is no parliamentary party that sees the issue of abortion as anything other than a monumental pain in the arse … this is a small issue in the overall scheme of things."[11] None of the main British parties adopts a strong line on abortion, nor do they whip votes on the issue.

In spite of this, in 2008 a serious attempt was made at Westminster for the first time to extend the 1967 Act to Northern Ireland. The Human Fertilisation and Embryology (HFE) Bill was then passing through parliament. In 1990, this Act had been used to lower the abortion limit from 28 to 24 weeks, meaning that abortion amendments could also be tabled. Several liberalising measures related to abortion were proposed. Amendments were tabled which would have allowed for the requirement of two doctors' signature for abortions before 24 weeks to be replaced by only one, permitted nurses and other suitable medical practitioners to perform terminations, permitted abortions to take place at the primary care level (GP surgeries) and allowed women to have early medical abortions at home (via use of the "abortion pill") (Sheldon 2009, 3). Doing so via a bill intended originally to deal with controlling the issue of HFE research presented a "rather clumsy and convoluted mass of legislation" (Fox 2009, 334) and suggests again how toxic the issue of abortion was deemed to be politically. Unable to be discussed on its own terms, it had to be quietly inserted into a bigger bill which was only tenuously related to termination of pregnancy. Additionally, an amendment proposing that the 1967 Abortion Act be extended to Northern Ireland was also included.

Interviews conducted for this research found that activists in Northern Ireland had placed a lot of emphasis on the amendment related to the region passing and seemed confident of a positive outcome. They were especially hopeful as this was the last time that Westminster could intervene on this issue, given the (ultimately correct) supposition that further police and justice powers were to be devolved to the province,[12] thus leaving abortion as an issue for Stormont's jurisdiction. As a spokesperson for Alliance for Choice, Goretti Horgan wrote in the *Irish Times*, this did not suggest a positive future for liberalisation of the laws in Northern Ireland: "saying 'Leave abortion to the Northern Ireland Assembly' is like saying 'Leave it to the Taliban to sort out women's rights.'"[13] A renewed sense of vigour therefore accompanied activism and organising at this moment in Northern Ireland. As one Belfast-based activist described events at the time:

> There was a stall in Belfast city centre and they [pro-choice activists] were gathering signatures for the petition and someone else was in charge for writing to all the MPs … some of the other trade unionists then went over and delivered the petition to Downing Street … around the time that the bill was being debated, and I think at that stage people were really wishing that something might happen and hopeful that the amendment might go ahead.[14]

Emily Thornberry MP fronted the amendment regarding Northern Ireland but dropped it on the morning of the debate. Diane Abbott MP then took up the amendment. In spite of it retaining a visible presence via Abbott, a long-established and well-known parliamentarian, the amendment was pushed down the running order, thus rendering it essentially impossible to be discussed. As the *Guardian* editorial described it, "today a small, courageous band of pro-choice public figures in Northern Ireland claim that Downing Street is prepared to yield to the anti-abortion lobby, and use parliamentary chicanery to push any motion aimed at extending the '67 act so far down the agenda that it will disappear."[15] As a result, it was not debated and did not pass.

Speaking during the broader debate on the HFE Bill, Diane Abbott MP said that she had been "roundly abused by male politicians from Northern Ireland" for tabling the motion, and framed her interest in the issue as based on equal rights:

> If I go to Belfast and break a leg, I can have an operation on the national health service, but because of the manoeuvrings of politicians down the years, poor women have to find the money [for an abortion] … The question is whether this United Kingdom Parliament is *content to keep a group of women as second class citizens on this important issue of liberty and rights.* (HC Deb 22 October 2008 vol. 482 c328, emphasis added)

Northern Irish MPs argued against the amendment however and viewed this as a matter which was now under Stormont's remit. As Jeffrey Donaldson DUP MP argued:

> The implementation of the 1967 Act, if it were to be extended to Northern Ireland, would fall largely to the Northern Ireland Assembly. It would therefore be *entirely wrong for this House to legislate against the wishes of the parties in the Assembly*, as those parties would be required to implement a law with which they did not agree. (HC Deb 22 October 2008 vol. 481 c331, emphasis added)

Donaldson went on to berate Abbott for tabling the amendment, given that "the hon. Member for Hackney North and Stoke Newington has not set foot in Northern Ireland to talk to people about this issue" (HC Deb 22 October 2008 vol. 481 c332). Leaders of the Democratic Unionist Party, the Ulster Unionist Party, Sinn Féin and the Social Democratic and Labour Party, the four main Northern Irish parties, showing a rare instance of solidarity, wrote to every member of the House of Commons, declaring that "this sensitive matter should be dealt with by the Assembly and not by this Parliament" (HC Deb 22 October 2008 vol. 481 col. 332).

In the brief moments in which the amendment was discussed in the House of Commons, the way in which the issue was discussed had fundamentally changed. Whilst the 1967 Act could, at least at the lobbying level, discuss a wide range of possible ways to frame abortion legislation, by 2008 abortion in Northern Ireland had boiled down to one of two definitions. For Abbott and the broader pro-choice movement, it was a question of equal rights, the equivalent of breaking a leg and requiring the same safe, legal, taxpayer-funded treatment across all four nations of the UK. For the Northern Irish MPs, it was the "wishes of the parties in the Assembly" which must be respected. This was, they claim, an issue of acknowledging the boundaries of the Northern Irish Assembly and allowing the regional democratic will of the Northern Irish people to be respected. The discourse around abortion has therefore become more limited in a contemporary setting. Abortion in Northern Ireland is a polarised topic, an issue either of female equality and rights, or of devolved power and regional discretion.

The way in which Westminster was persuaded to drop the amendment suggested to Northern Irish activists that they could no longer focus their efforts at Westminster. It was widely perceived both by activists interviewed for this project, and in news reports at the time,[16] that the DUP had received assurances the previous month that were they to vote for the government's proposed 42-day detention limit for terror suspects, then no attempt would be made by the Labour government to extend the Abortion Act to Northern Ireland. Dr. Margaret Ward, then Director of the Women's Resource and Development Agency in Belfast, one of the key organisations in the Northern Irish women's sector, explicitly made this accusation in a speech in 2009, in which she described this as an example of "women's needs traded on the pretext of maintaining a 'peace process' in which women have become increasingly marginalised."[17] Indeed, Diane Abbott made this allegation directly in a Westminster Hall debate on abortion and Northern Ireland the following July: "I believe that the Government colluded in that [pushing the amendment down the debating list], because they knew that, had it got to the Floor of the House, there was a very good chance that it would have got through, because there is a pro-choice majority on both sides of the House" (HC Deb 15 July 2009 vol. 496 c89WH). This "dirty deal" was lamented by activists at the time:

> I didn't go to London but she [another Northern Irish based activist] had texted me basically along the lines of the amendment has been withdrawn, they've done a dirty deal and it's not going to go ahead … There was a general despondency then and I suppose anger too towards the Labour party and the likes of Harriet Harman who was supposed to be this very strong feminist … and we had heard that she had been involved then in all the manoeuvring that had happened. So there was … a lot of anger and frustration, particularly against the Labour party because there had been, from what I understand, these promises from the Labour government, [when they] came into power that one of the things they were going to do was bring in the Abortion Act here … that was one of the opportunities, the Embryology Bill, and they basically just pulled a rug from beneath the ground on that.[18]

Aware that this had been the last chance for change from central government, activists were bitterly disappointed by what they perceived to be a cynical political deal. The activity of 2008 appears to have signalled to Northern Irish activists that they could no longer count on support or help from Westminster.

Furthermore, activists in Northern Ireland were deeply scornful of the idea, apparently used by both Northern Irish MPs to stop action from the government, and by the government to stop the amendment being tabled by rogue backbenchers, that any attempt to extend abortion legislation would derail the peace process. Activists appeared aware of the perceived ignorance that is shown of Northern Ireland in Westminster and the ways in which this was manipulated by the pro-life community and politicians:

> British ministers being what they are, and MPs being what they are, this [Northern Ireland] is known as a quirky little place and people don't really understand it so they kind of want to leave us well alone. So if you tell them something like abortion could put the peace process in jeopardy then they're inclined to probably believe them … the anti-choice proponents tried to sell [it] to the British government, as Northern Ireland as a unique wee place where Catholics and Protestants, we are so morally just that we really don't want abortion and that's the line that Westminster was sold on the 2008 legislation.[19]

> … the MPs there were told it would jeopardise the peace process if this went through in Northern Ireland which was a load of rubbish. It was peddled in Westminster, if you rock the boat and force this through … the peace process may fail and that parties would be at each other's throats or whatever, so – total nonsense.[20]

Following on from Donald Dewar MP's similar language at the advent of devolution, British MPs appeared willing to sign up to a simplistic understanding of contemporary Northern Ireland. This uncomplicated rendering of the province and its politics could be exploited by pro-life elements and political parties eager to avoid a controversial issue. Furthermore, events of 2008 illustrate how the discourse around the "peace process" took on an almost hallowed air in political proceedings. The "peace process" is to be protected and saved at all costs, even if British MPs appear unsure of what this means. At this point, following the 2007 St. Andrew's Agreement, the entering into a joint Executive of Sinn Féin and the DUP, and the resumption of the Northern Irish Assembly, the province's politics were arguably the most stable they had been since the Good Friday Agreement. The "inactions" (Chappell 2014a, b, 2015) of the national government on abortion are thus significant. The failed amendment signalled a clear hierarchy of political importance—the peace process is paramount, with women's rights being relegated to second place.

Westminster–Stormont Relations and Abortion: Contemporary Tensions

With two very differing viewpoints emerging on this issue (a slightly more liberal Westminster, who would probably extend abortion rights if it could but wants to respect Northern Ireland's "difference," and a more conservative Northern Irish body who see this as an issue for Stormont and the Northern Irish electorate alone), tensions between the national and the devolved institutions can be seen.

Whilst the Good Friday Agreement brought a more established and institutionalised relationship between the centre and the devolved regions, Northern Ireland retains distinctive "peculiarities" (Birrell 2012, 282). Northern Irish parties retain no real links to parties on the British mainland. The Northern Irish Executive operates a unique five-party Coalition. Northern Irish politicians have long practised "double-jobbing"[21] (operating as both MLA and MP), although this was scheduled to be phased out by the 2016 Assembly election. Furthermore, parties differ in their attitudes to their relationships with Westminster and the Irish Daíl based on their own position on the constitutional question—until 2009 for example, MPs and MLAs from both Unionist parties refused to participate in the British–Irish parliamentary Forum (Birrell

2012, 273). Consideration of intergovernmental relations in a Northern Irish context has tended to focus on elite-level relations between Stormont, Westminster and the Irish Daíl. Westminster–Stormont relations alone tend to be viewed in terms of relations between the Prime Minister/Secretary of State and the OFMDFM (e.g. Birrell 2012). As a result, the work of MPs at Westminster and their specific place in the national institution has been little considered.

Whether abortion in Northern Ireland is an issue for Westminster or not is contentious. According to the UK's ratification of the Convention on the Elimination of All Forms of Discrimination Against Women (CEDAW), and certain European jurisprudence, the case for clarification of existing legislation or legislative change may rest at the national as opposed to the devolved level (Thomson 2017). Yet Northern Irish MPs appeared aware that Westminster was unwilling to act on abortion:

> I just think that there has been … a sense here [Westminster] that where there is a fairly strong consensus coming from parties in Northern Ireland around the '67 Act that people … said 'well then we'll not impose it just because we can'.[22]

Indeed, most MPs and MLAs were steadfast in their assurance that the issue of abortion was one that could now solely be considered at Stormont: "The decision on the abortion lies with the Assembly. … I'm glad that they don't get the last say in Northern Ireland. Because the people of Northern Ireland decide."[23] This belief was also echoed in a 2009 Westminster Hall debate on the subject. Many MPs who spoke in this debate, from both Northern Ireland and the broader UK, understood that the devolved Assembly gave the province alone the ability to decide on this issue. As Laurence Robertson, MP for Tewkesbury in England, argued, "For us [in Westminster] to take legislative steps that not only undermined the role of the Assembly but went against everything that all the political parties in Northern Ireland are saying would be wrong and somewhat anti-democratic" (HC Deb 15 July 2009 vol. 496 c92WH). There is therefore a broad appreciation at Westminster that abortion is an issue that must be left for Stormont to consider.

However, whilst most MPs interviewed understood abortion as a devolved issue, many also suggested that it was more complicated. Speaking with regard to the 2004 court ruling that stipulated guidelines on termination must be provided by the Department of Health in Northern Ireland, one MP said:

> … if Northern Ireland under its devolved capacity … doesn't discharge coherent guidance for the purposes which the court has required, [can] Westminster then say 'well look, we've given you all the scope and space that you want, if you're not even able to deliver within that ambit … then we have to step in'? … There's a risk that in resisting any form of guidance [at the Assembly level] … then you will maybe create the excuse for more dramatic overriding legislation from somewhere else.[24]

Another MP argued that although abortion was devolved, the situation was complex:

> … it is entirely a devolved matter, so the Northern Irish situation would not be discussed in Westminster virtually at all … isn't something that's discussed in terms of Northern Ireland and our policy, it is entirely devolved and my experience here is that *if people can hide behind devolution even where it isn't technically devolved*, they will.[25] (emphasis added)

This was reflected in a widely held belief on the part of Northern Irish activists and politicians that whilst Westminster, throughout successive governments, could have acted, it was afraid to provoke Northern Ireland on certain topics:

> … [what] I get angry with Westminster about is that they hide from it [abortion legislation] all the time and that they use it as a political tool to get other things.[26]
>
> Westminster in my view has just totally failed … I mean every opportunity that the government had to just say we are not treating women in Northern Ireland like 2nd class citizens they've always capitulated to the threats from the DUP.[27]
>
> I just don't think they [Westminster] would dare to even meddle in that type of politics over here. There's certain things that in this country that people have very strong opinions on and those are the things that really Westminster haven't come in as big brother and said we're pushing this through whether you like it or not 'cos there is strong opinion on it.[28]

This interview data suggested that devolution and inter-institutional relations between Westminster and Stormont are a process of continuous negotiation with no clear boundaries as to where decisions lie on controversial issues. Indeed, one MP was especially proud of his ability to "negotiate" on the part of Northern Ireland for exceptions on gendered issues: with reference to the 2013 Marriage (Same Sex couples) Bill, he declared that he "got a concession for Northern Ireland out of it."[29] Devolved powers appear as a movable point rather than a solid boundary: "a dynamic process, rather than an event" (Bache and Flinders 2005, 93). The exact boundaries of what is and is not for Stormont or Westminster to define appear fluid.

Yet, in 2017, Westminster did choose to intervene on this issue. The General Election of June 2017 unexpectedly returned a Conservative minority government. As a result, the Conservatives turned to the DUP, who had returned 10 MPs, to form a "confidence-and-supply" arrangement under which the DUP would provide the necessary votes to pass the Queen's Speech. Such an arrangement was the closest that any Northern Irish political party had been to the heart of British politics at Westminster for many years. The deal excited much media attention from the British press, largely devoted to the DUP's stance on abortion and LGBT issues, and the divergence between their attitudes and those of mainstream British political parties. Ruth Davidson, leader of the Scottish Conservative party, and engaged to marry a woman, publicly gained a promise from Theresa May that LGBT rights would not be at risk in the UK as a result of this deal.

In late June 2017, Labour MP Stella Creasy declared that she would seek an amendment to the Queen's Speech that would see NHS England cover the cost of terminations sought by Northern Irish women. This was particularly pressing given that the Supreme Court in London ruled earlier in the same month that women from Northern Ireland were not legally entitled to have abortions which they underwent in the rest of the UK paid for by the state. Before Creasy's amendment could be debated, the government, aware of the cross-bench support that it had, announced via the Department for Women and Equalities that:

> Following discussions with the Department of Health, we will ensure these payments will be funded through the Government Equalities Office with additional funding. This will mean no English health service user is disadvantaged as a result of this change.

The letter went on to say that, whilst the "Supreme Court judgment made clear that we have the power to make these arrangements":

> None of this changes the fundamental position that *this is a devolved issue in Northern Ireland*. It is for the Northern Ireland Executive and the Northern Ireland Assembly to decide on their policy going forward. This announcement does not change that position. (emphasis added)[30]

The government were thus very keen to emphasise that this change in funding did not in any way affect the legislative framework in Northern Ireland. The explanation they give here still frames abortion as an issue for devolved policy-makers first and foremost and not something which national government aims to tackle in a more fundamental manner. Northern Irish abortions remain ultimately for Northern Ireland to decide upon.

Prior to this announcement by government, the proposed amendment was briefly discussed in the House of Commons. Creasy framed the proposed change as a way in which political decisions in Northern Ireland had undue influence on health policy and practice in England:

> It is women from Northern Ireland who will pay the price for the coalition deal that the Government have made unless we in this House speak up. The ruling in June this year was very clear that those women were being discriminated against as UK taxpayers in their access to abortion rights. The Secretary of State, whatever his personal views on the matter, has the ability to provide the funding to enable those women to access services here. *Thousands of women have to travel from Northern Ireland, and I do not understand why a decision made in Belfast should influence what happens in my hospital in Walthamstow or in other hospitals across this country.* (HC Deb 28 June 2017 vol. 626 c676, emphasis added)

In response, Ian Paisley Jr., DUP MP for North Antrim, said:

> I respect the hon. Lady's genuine interest in this subject, but it is important for the House to recognise that *this is not a matter for Belfast; it is a matter for NHS England.* (HC Deb 28 June 2017 vol. 626 c676, emphasis added)

Again, as in 2008, this was framed as an issue for regional discretion, not something for national government to address. Across both the government's announcement and the brief debate the issue received in the Commons, abortion is understood as something which Stormont holds primacy over. Any further actions on the part of Westminster beyond this funding decision thus appear unlikely.

Multi-level governance at work in the UK with regard to Northern Ireland clearly has very gendered implications. In contrast to the years preceding the Troubles, since devolution in 1998 Westminster has been heavily involved in certain aspects of Northern Irish governance: as one of the key players in the evolving peace process, from the Good Friday Agreement, to the St. Andrew's Agreement, to the more recent Stormont House and "Fresh Start" agreements; shaping economic policy; and, indeed, suspending the devolved institutions entirely from 2002 to 2007 and re-enacting Direct Rule. Yet successive British governments have avoided intervening in tricky policy areas to do with gender and sexuality in the province; whilst the rest of the UK has liberalised laws around gay men donating blood, Northern Irish law remains unchanged, and the Westminster Health Secretary has refused to influence regional policy.[31] Central government has also been notably silent on the province's continued refusal to introduce same-sex marriage legislation. Gendered issues become regional, local issues, not topics for national government intervention. Devolution, and the understanding that Stormont rules supreme on these issues, often provides Westminster with a means by which it can sidestep controversy.

Conclusion

This chapter has illustrated the marginal place that abortion legislation in Northern Ireland has had at Westminster since the original 1967 Act which legalised abortion in the majority of the UK. The province was all but completely ignored during initial activism and the drafting of the Act and received scant, irregular attention from parliamentarians in the period following the Act until devolution. Although the construction of the new institutions in Cardiff, Edinburgh and Belfast did potentially allow for change, the dominant narrative was of Northern Ireland's "difference" and that the province must be allowed to continue with its separate legislative framework. To the frustration of Northern Irish activists, British MPs appear willing to sign up to this simple narrative of the province's "difference." Westminster–Northern Ireland relations post-devolution suffer from a "nested newness" (Chappell 2014a; Mackay 2014), in which understandings of the province as "different" and "unique" in relation to its past continue to perpetuate a logic which allows for differential treatment around the issue of abortion.

Furthermore, the issue of abortion in Northern Ireland at Westminster in a contemporary setting allows for two distinct interpretations: Diane Abbott MP's 2008 portrayal of the issue as one of equal medical rights across the four territories of the UK, and the opposing Northern Irish MPs' view that this was a reserved matter for the people and politicians of Northern Ireland. There are now two starkly different ways of understanding the Northern Irish abortion issue—is this an issue of regional determination and the boundaries of Stormont's powers? Or is this an issue of fundamental women's rights which cuts across devolved borders? As was seen most blatantly in 2008, abortion has been firmly segmented in the national government's mind as an issue first and foremost for the Northern Irish Assembly, before any broader appreciation of women's or human rights. Time and again from 1967 onwards, even in the 2017 decision to cover Northern Irish women's costs on the English NHS, abortion in the region has been defined as a Northern Irish issue first and as a women's issue second. Whether categorised as devolution or the continually evolving "peace process," the Northern Irish institutional forces have repeatedly been given greater priority than women's rights. As a result, instead of offering an additional arena for activists (Vickers *et al.* 2010, 237), central government has largely been silent. Nothing has been done by Westminster to change the restrictive legal framework which remains in Northern Ireland.

This chapter brings Northern Ireland into the broader conversation around the gendered effects of the multi-level governance structure which now exists following devolution. It suggests that there is a territorialisation of gendered rights where devolved governance and regional political sensibilities carry more weight than nationwide practice or long-existent policy. Northern Ireland has been a key part of domestic, security and governance policy for successive governments since the re-establishment of the Assembly in 1998, up to and including the arguably more distant approach taken by the Conservative-led Coalition of 2010–2015 and the Conservative government of 2015 onwards. Through the process of devolution, and the increasingly complex multi-level governance set-up of the devolved UK, Northern Irish governance has become more firmly enmeshed with that of the broader country. Yet abortion (and other gendered issues) has largely been off limits as far as Westminster has been concerned. The empirical evidence illustrated here shows that feminist institutionalism can conceptualise not only new institutions, but also relations between different institutions in complex political arrangements. A gendered "logic of appropriateness" (Chappell 2006) facilitates institutional relationships between Northern Ireland and Westminster, where certain subjects are clearly seen as appropriate for interventions by central government, and other (gendered) issues are not. This chapter argues for feminist institutionalism to widen its conceptual framework to consider how inter-institutional relations between national, sub-national and international bodies might be gendered and the effects this may have on policy formation and actions (not) taken.

Why then, if Westminster is not a vehicle for change, have liberalising moves not been possible from the regional based institution? The following chapters turn to consider the devolved institutions.

Notes

1. Professor David Paintin. Private interview with the author, October 2013. Professor Paintin is emeritus professor in obstetrics and gynaecology at St. Mary's Hospital, London, and former chairman of the Birth Control Trust. He was taught by Sir Dugald Baird at the University of Aberdeen and advised Sir David Steel during the passage of the 1967 Abortion Act.
2. Professor David Paintin. Private interview with the author, October 2013.
3. Professor David Paintin. Private interview with the author, October 2013.
4. Lord Steel. Private correspondence with the author, November 2013.
5. Vera Houghton once personally tackled the sitting Prime Minister Harold Wilson at a private event about his perspective on abortion reform: "I said 'I didn't see you having anything to say about abortion', and he replied 'And you won't'" (quoted in Furedi and Hume 1997, 31). She was also first made aware via her presence at a House of Lords tea party that the original ALRA wording of the Bill would be unpalatable to government and that it should be framed instead in terms of the medical opinion of the Doctor (Francome 2004, 59). Personal, elite links were key to ALRA's success as an organisation.
6. The Lane Committee was set up shortly after the 1967 Abortion Act, to investigate the workings of the Bill and largely reported in favour of the Act in 1974. James White's private member bill in 1975 tried to limit access to terminations and to greater control private clinics, which was

rejected, but another committee was then established to analyse the workings of the Act. This committee reported in largely anti-abortion terms. John Corrie's Bill of 1979 was an attempt to greatly restrict the circumstances in which abortion was legal—the necessity for pregnancy to pose a 'grave' risk to a woman's health for example (McBride 2001, Chapter 7).

7. Professor Wendy Savage. Private interview with the author, October 2013.
8. Indeed, this "peculiarity" (Birrell 2012, 282) of Northern Irish politics continues to this day, with only one of the main UK parties (the Conservatives) fielding candidates in the province.
9. This is not an infrequent occurrence in Northern Irish politics today either. Several contemporary examples include: Mark Durkan former SDLP MP and his nephew Mark Durkan SDLP MLA, Nigel Dodds DUP MP and his wife Diane Dodds DUP MEP, Roy Beggs and Sandra Overend UUP MLAs who both followed fathers into politics, and the former First Minister Peter Robinson DUP MLA and his wife Iris Robinson DUP MLA, prior to her dramatic exit from formal politics in 2009.
10. *Roe vs. Wade*, argued before the USA Supreme Court and decided upon in 1973. It ruled that under the 14th Amendment to the US constitution, the right to privacy allows for legal terminations up to the third trimester of pregnancy.
11. Private interview with the author, December 2013.
12. Policing and justice powers were devolved to Northern Ireland in the wake of the 2010 Hillsborough Agreement.
13. "Northern Irish abortion campaigners lobby British MPs," *Irish Times* (8 October 2008).
14. Pro-choice activist. Private interview with the author, February 2014.
15. https://www.theguardian.com/commentisfree/2008/oct/19/legalise-abortion-northernireland-labour. Accessed 30 January 2018.
16. "Legalise Abortion in Northern Ireland," Editorial, *The Guardian*, 19 October 2008. http://www.theguardian.com/commentisfree/2008/oct/19/legalise-abortion-northernireland-labour. Accessed 30 January 2018. R. Prince and M. Beckford, "Abortion Plans for Northern Ireland Abandoned Due to Peace Process," *Daily Telegraph* (15 October 2008). See also Northern Ireland Devolution Monitoring Report 2009, UCL Constitution Unit. http://www.ucl.ac.uk/constitution-unit/research/research-archive/ni09.pdf. Accessed 30 January 2018.
17. Address by Margaret Ward at the roundtable on gender and security: "Involving Women: A Key Issue in Security and Peace Reconstruction".

Vienna, 11 March 2009, Organisation for Security and Co-operation in Europe. http://www.osce.org/gender/36863. Accessed 30 January 2018.

18. Pro-choice activist. Private interview with the author, Belfast, February 2014.
19. Pro-choice activist. Private interview with the author, Belfast, March 2014.
20. Non-aligned MLA. Private interview with the author, Belfast, February 2014.
21. After the general election of 2005 16 out of 18 Northern Irish MPs were also MLAs (Birrell 2012, 278).
22. Northern Irish nationalist MP. Private interview with the author, London, November 2013.
23. Northern Irish unionist MP. Private interview with the author, November 2013.
24. Northern Irish nationalist MP. Private interview with the author, London, November 2013.
25. Northern Irish MP. Private interview with the author, London, November 2013.
26. Northern Irish Green Party representative. Private interview with the author, Belfast, February 2014.
27. Former NIWC activist. Private interview with the author, Skype, May 2014.
28. Unionist MLA. Private interview with the author, Belfast, February 2014.
29. Northern Irish unionist MP. Private interview with the author, November 2013.
30. https://www.gov.uk/government/uploads/system/uploads/attachment_data/file/623669/Letter_from_Justine_Greening_on_Abortion_in_England.pdf. Accessed 30 January 2018.
31. Gay men have been able to donate blood in England, Scotland and Wales since 2011. However, then Health Secretary in the Northern Irish Executive, Edwin Poots, opted to keep the ban in place. A court ruled in 2013 that this decision should rest with the Health Secretary at Westminster, not Stormont. Health Secretary Jeremy Hunt elected to challenge this decision, saying that the decision should rest at the Northern Irish level. As with the issue of abortion, debates were very two-sided, with the issue seen as either one of equality or of devolved powers. http://www.bbc.co.uk/news/uk-northern-ireland-26872539. Accessed 30 September 2014.

Bibliography

Bache, Ian, and Matthew Flinders. 2005. Multi-level Governance and British Politics. In *Multi-level Governance*, ed. Ian Bache and Matthew Flinders. Oxford: Oxford University Press.

Birrell, Derek. 2012. Intergovernmental Relations and Political Parties in Northern Ireland. *British Journal of Politics and International Relations* 14: 270–284.

Bogdanor, Vernon. 2001. *Devolution in the United Kingdom*. Oxford: Oxford University Press.

Chappell, Louise. 2006. Comparing Political Institutions: Revealing the Gendered "Logic of Appropriateness". *Politics and Gender* 2 (2): 232–235.

———. 2014a. 'New', 'Old', and 'Nested' Institutions and Gender Justice Outcomes: A View from the International Criminal Court. *Politics and Gender* 10(4): 572–594.

———. 2014b. Conflicting Institutions and the Search for Gender Justice at the International Criminal Court. *Political Research Quarterly* 67 (1): 183–196.

———. 2015. *The Politics of Gender Justice at the International Criminal Court: Legacies and Legitimacy*. Oxford: Oxford University Press.

Fox, Marie. 2009. The Human Fertilisation and Embryology Act 2008: Tinkering at the Margins. *Feminist Legal Studies* 17 (3): 333–344.

Francome, Colin. 2004. *Abortion in the USA and the UK*. London: Ashgate.

Furedi, Anne, and Mark Hume (eds.). 1997. *Abortion Law Reformers: Pioneers of Change—Interviews with the People Who Made the 1967 Abortion Act Possible*. BPAS. http://www.abortionreview.org/images/uploads/Abortion_Pioneers_(1).pdf. Accessed 30 January 2018.

Halfmann, Drew. 2011. *Doctors and Demonstrators: How Political Institutions Shape Abortion Law in the United States, Britain and Canada*. Chicago: University of Chicago Press.

Jackson, Alvin. 2011. 'Tame Tory Hacks'? The Ulster Party at Westminster, 1922–1972. *The Historical Journal* 54 (2): 453–475.

Keown, John. 1988. *Abortion, Doctors and the Law: Some Aspects of the Legal Regulation of Abortion in England from 1803 to 1902*. Cambridge: Cambridge University Press.

Mackay, Fiona. 2014. Nested Newness, Institutional Innovation, and the Gendered Limits of Change. *Politics and Gender* 10: 549–571.

McBride, Dorothy Stetson (ed.). 2001. *Abortion Politics, Women's Movements, and the Democratic State: A Comparative Study of State Feminism*. Oxford: Oxford University Press.

Rush, Michael. 2001. *The Role of the Member of Parliament Since 1868: From Gentlemen to Players*. Oxford: Oxford University Press.

Sheldon, Sally. 1997. *Beyond Control: Medical Power and Abortion Law*. London: Pluto Press.

———. 2009. A Missed Opportunity to Reform an Outdated Law (Guest Editorial). *Clinical Ethics* 4: 3–5.

Thomson, Jennifer. 2017. Thinking Globally, Acting Locally? The Women's Sector, International Human Rights Mechanisms and Politics in Northern Ireland. *Politics* 37 (2): 82–96.

Vickers, Jill, Melissa Haussman, and Marian Sawer. 2010. Conclusion. In *Federalism, Feminism and Multilevel Governance*, ed. Melissa Haussman, Marian Sawer, and Jill Vickers. London: Ashgate.

CHAPTER 5

Creating the Devolved Institution: The Peace Process

Whilst Chapter 4 considered Westminster's impact on the issue of abortion in Northern Ireland, the remaining chapters turn to the institutions in the region itself. Much recent academic work on Northern Ireland has been concerned with surveying the movement from "the Armalite to the ballot box."[1] The twenty years leading up to the Good Friday Agreement and the roots of the movement from paramilitary violence to democratic politics have been given much consideration, most notably with regard to the republican movement (Bean 2007; Frampton 2008; Maillot 2005). The majority of work on this period, and the dominant narrative which has emerged, has tended to focus on the elite level of political leadership (Blair 2010; Powell 2009; Thatcher 1993), and paramilitary operation (English 2012; Moloney 2003), with the story of civil society organisations' work for peace (Campbell 2008) in the province not really registering on the historical consciousness.

This focus carries gendered implications. Whilst women have had a low profile in the formal peace process and party politics, their involvement in grass-roots politics has been strong (Pierson and Thomson 2018). Women were behind the first civil rights protests in the 1960s which eventually led to the Northern Irish Civil Rights Association (NICRA), but this key element of Northern Irish history is rarely referred to. Because women were not especially prominent in paramilitary violence,[2] or the political elite, their experiences have not formed part of the mainstream history and understanding of the conflict.

J. Thomson, *Abortion Law and Political Institutions*, Gender and Politics, https://doi.org/10.1007/978-3-319-96169-9_5

Likewise, any understanding of the gendered nature of the conflict in the province (e.g. the overwhelmingly male-perpetuated violence) has only recently begun to be given consideration (Ashe 2006, 2007, 2008; Zalewski 2005).

This chapter explores how the processes and institutions that were formed in the movement towards the Good Friday Agreement were gendered and the ways in which this influenced the type of political institutions that were eventually created. It shows how "informal norms and practices as well as formal rules and structures impacted the processes and constrained outcomes in gendered ways" (Waylen 2014b, 497). This chapter focuses not only on women's organisations but also on "gender (and other) actors *within* these processes" (ibid.). It contends that despite efforts at the time to ensure a diverse range of voices were present at the table, the movement towards peace which culminated in the ratification of the Good Friday Agreement at the ballot box in 1998 was elite-driven. That elite was predominantly male and had a fixed conception of the problems facing Northern Ireland, in its understanding of the centrality of the constitutional question to the detriment of all else. As a result, a gendered perspective had little role to play in either defining the conflict of the past thirty years or suggesting means by which a post-conflict society might be governed.

Organising in an "Armed Patriarchy"[3]: The Women's Movement and Abortion in the Movement Towards the Good Friday Agreement

As Racioppi and See point out, civil society can be a more welcome environment than formal politics for gendered issues, and informal politics present a "wider array of associations and possibilities for cross-communal and gender mobilization" (2006, 192). Nonetheless, in a divided society, in which "primacy [was] attributed to 'The Cause', always male, on whichever side" (Smyth 1995, 196), it remained difficult for women to organise as women in the divided world of Northern Ireland during the Troubles. "The crisis of the early sixties and late seventies [in the province] left little energy for consideration of the re-emergence of feminism" (Evason 1991, 14) occurring elsewhere in the world.

Nonetheless, Northern Ireland maintained throughout this period a disparate and wide-reaching women's activism. In the 1970s, "accidental activism" (McWilliams 1995, 21) occurred around specific events which encouraged women to organise as women for the first time. The Falls Road Curfew of 1970, the Mothers of Belfast campaign around the cessation of free milk in schools in 1971 and the Relatives' Action Committee of 1976 all brought women together in political activism as women. However, these early beginnings were also fraught with sectarian and wider tensions. The Mothers of Belfast campaign was seen by many Protestant women as a Catholic anti-British state protest, "arguing the sectarian line that Catholics had more children and so stood to gain more from the state provision of free school milk" (McWilliams 1995, 22; Evason 1991, 11).[4] Similarly, the group Women Against Imperialism was viewed by Protestant women as a subversive Catholic nationalist grouping (Evason 1991, 28). The break-up of the Peace People, a Derry-based peace group established by two women, was also largely triggered by sectarian division. "Transversal" (Yuval-Davis 1997) feminist politics were difficult to maintain in a fractured social environment. The prescience of the national question often damaged feminist solidarity. The Northern Ireland Women's Rights Movement (NIWRM) was criticised by the Socialist Women's Group, for example, for its "non-position" on the constitutional question (Roulston 1989, 226). Women Against Imperialism struggled to get broad backing for their supportive position of the female hunger strikers in Armagh jail (ibid., 230). Other, more classic tensions also gripped the women's movement at this point with divisions between socialist feminists and others of more or less radical political persuasions emerging (Evason 1991, 24–26; Roulston 1989).

Moving into the 1980s, the women's movement in Northern Ireland gained a more concrete, formal existence. Several organisations were established which still exist today: the Belfast Rape Crisis Centre and the Women's Resource and Development Agency, alongside several key women's centres, the Shankill and the Falls Women's Centres amongst them. Funding appeared a continual difficulty (Evason 1991, 41, 52–53), but they grew in size and influence, and ultimately endured.

Hence, feminist politics in Northern Ireland were multifaceted and complex (Connolly 1999). Yet the formal political reach of the women's movement was still severely limited. The inability of the formal political sphere to take women's issues and concerns seriously is typified in an incident from the autumn of 1985. A cross-community group of Protestant and Catholic women travelled to Westminster to lobby their MPs about the Social Security Bill then passing through the Commons which would have restricted claims for welfare benefits. Having travelled overnight, "they were appalled to find that their own political representatives refused to meet with them because the parliamentarians were more interested in opposing the recent Anglo-Irish Agreement" (McWilliams 1995, 31). Women's concerns were still far from the main thrust of Northern Irish politics.

Within the women's movement, abortion was a particularly controversial issue. In the 1970s, the level of taboo surrounding it made it an "unmentionable and unmanageable subject in Northern Ireland. Many groups tried to bury it lest it bury them" (Evason 1991, 27). NIWRM struggled to adopt a coherent policy on the issue and eventually included it under a general subset of issues calling for a demand for parity with English women's rights (Connolly 1999, 147; Evason 1991, 21; Roulston 1989, 227). The Ulster Pregnancy Advisory Association continued to "quietly" work away sending women to England for terminations, but it was the establishment of the Northern Irish Abortion Campaign (NIAC) which really challenged the silence around the issue (Evason 1991, 21). They conducted general lobbying and educational work and "secured substantial media coverage when 600 coat hangers were sent to the House of Commons. Each had a facsimile of a British Airways ticket attached and a message to MPs which read 'These are the two ways in which Northern Ireland women get abortions'" (ibid.). By 1984, NIAC had all but disbanded, but a new iteration of the Northern Ireland Abortion League Reform Association (NIALRA) emerged (ibid.; NIALRA 1989, 17–20). From the mid-1980s onwards, abortion appeared to have greater visibility within the women's movement. NIALRA undertook surveys of the various political parties' policies on abortion, as well as the wider medical profession. They also organised a two-day conference in 1987 to coincide with the 20th anniversary of the 1967 Act, "in order to systematically present the evidence of the consequences for women of the continuing exclusion of Northern Ireland from the terms of the 1967 Abortion Act" (NIALRA 1989, 5). The core of the conference was an international tribunal consisting of 9 members, drawing from medical, legal and women's sector specialism. It also heard from anonymous women sharing their stories of the difficulties in accessing terminations either in Northern Ireland or privately in England. Though the conference programme was thorough and the tribunal impressive in their international range, the local media gave the event little attention, which, in the words of one of the organisers, "served to underline the fact that the media's laziness is part of the continuing conspiracy of silence in Northern Ireland in relation to abortion" (NIALRA 1989, 7).

The broader influence the conference may have had on public opinion and knowledge of the legality of abortion did not appear strong.

In 1995, a further one-day symposium on abortion was co-sponsored by the Family Planning Association (FPA) in Northern Ireland and the International Planned Parenthood Federation. This conference was decidedly more focussed on human rights and the law than the previous 1987 event, as the title of the succeeding booklet produced suggests: "The Abortion Law in Northern Ireland: Human rights and reproductive choice." Two contributions were included from Professor Simon Lee, then of the Law faculty at Queen's University, Belfast, who decried abortion law in Northern Ireland as "so uncertain that it violates the standards of international human rights law" (Lee 1995, 16). The focus of this symposium was an attempt to flag up the "twilight zone" (Lee 1995) of the situation of abortion law in Northern Ireland prior to the extensive legal and constitutional changes which were, at this point, clearly in the process of beginning. However, the elite nature of this gathering seems to have resulted in women's and voluntary groups being more distanced from the event, and, in terms of its legal focus, it had little impact on the successive peace negotiations and formal politics.

In a sign that societal attitudes towards sex and family structure were liberalising, the FPA and Brook (an NGO which provides sexual health advice to young people) both opened in Belfast in the early 1990s. Although this was a step forwards for both women's issues and sexual health within the province through the formal introduction of specific sexual and reproductive health services, the welcome that these organisations received illustrates the broader vehemence towards abortion that existed from certain sections of society. Even though Brook did not offer abortion provision or advice (indeed, it was specifically prohibited from discussing abortion and had to send young people wanting information on terminations to the FPA or to their GP[5]), it was still picketed vigorously upon its arrival. Initially, this was by separate Protestant and Catholic groups[6] until the advent of the group Precious Life in the province in the late 1990s. A former employee described how Brook at this point:

> …came under huge pressure from Precious Life … they had placards outside of our building saying that we murdered babies, so they named both myself and our senior doctor as murdering babies[7]

Brook was picketed every Friday afternoon by a free Presbyterian Minister from 1992 until 2011 when they moved to new premises.[8] That an organisation which did not discuss, let alone offer the possibility of terminations, could be protested so vigorously illustrates the controversy which continued to dog the issue.

In spite of successes, women's organising in this period remained at a remove from formal politics and found difficulties in gaining voice and recognition at that level. As Elizabeth Porter writes of Northern Ireland in the mid-1990s "the context for women [was] one of activism in communities and of absence from formal political structures" (1997, 83). Because of this informality, and a lack of women's voices within formal politics, gender equality has had a "lower public profile" (ibid., 92) in the province. Furthermore, within women's politics, abortion was a continually divisive and controversial issue, difficult at times to gain consensus around. Although clearer movements were made around the issue of abortion in the late 1980s and the 1990s, the events organised were still small ripples in public, and formal political, consciousness. In a broader societal context where abortion was viewed with such hostility (as the picketing of the Brook clinic shows), any progressive movement on the issue seemed impossible.

"If It Damages Our Struggle, Then It Will Have to Wait": Abortion in Republican Politics and the 1986 Ard Fheis

Whilst women's issues struggled to gain legitimacy within Northern Ireland's fractured politics, within the republican movement, there was a more visible discussion of women's issues than other parties. Of the main four parties, Sinn Féin have been the clearest to move on the issue of women's inclusion, both substantive and descriptive, in their politics.[9] They established a Women's Department in 1981 in an appreciation of "a growing grassroots demand for equality and a recognition that emancipation had to encompass the struggle for gender equality" (Maillot 2005, 108). At the 1983 Ard Fheis (AGM), it was decided that a quota of 8 women were to sit on the Ard Chomairle (National Executive) at all times (Frampton 2008, 36). Part of Sinn Féin's establishment as a credible political force involved a progressive position on women and equality.

However, Sinn Féin's success at involving women and women's concerns within the party framework was a tactical political move, their attitude more of a "proto-feminist agenda" (Frampton 2008, 36). The dominant ideology of Sinn Féin at this point hinged on a tension between "a traditionalist and probably even patriarchal tendency within the movement … which coexisted, on the other end of the spectrum, with a radical voice which was seeking change and recognition" (Maillot 2005, 111). As one activist from this period put it, "We gradually found that this [discussion of abortion rights] was damaging the overall struggle, which was more important … If it damages our struggle, then it will have to wait" (quoted in Maillot 2005, 114). Just as this period was about the movement from "the Armalite to the ballot box" for the party, it was also about reconciling these two extremes (the more radical left on the one hand, the conservative Catholic element on the other) to a position where issues such as abortion could find common ground.

Sinn Féin's leanings towards a descriptive and substantive representation of women during this period thus have to be seen within this deeply pragmatic context. This contrast between left-leaning ideology and pragmatic nationalist desires is most especially typified in how abortion was discussed (or not discussed). Sinn Féin's position on abortion in this period was decidedly woolly. In 1980, the Ard Fheis directed the Department of Women's Affairs to "investigate the alternatives to abortion." Their ensuing report discusses the statistics regarding women undergoing terminations in Northern Ireland and the Republic and outlines the various groups working around the issue. It concludes that:

> The reasoning behind this report is to show that abortion is an issue in Ireland and will not end with a solitary sentence in a policy document.
>
> Any one of these statistics could be your wife, your sister or your daughter.
>
> We believe that those who are "totally opposed" to abortion and those who see it as a tragedy and an indictment against society must work to improve conditions for and attitudes towards pregnant women.[10]

The document typifies Sinn Féin's attitude to abortion from this period onwards. Women must not be stigmatised or criminalised, and some sort of positive action must be taken—but quite what exactly is never suggested.

This Janus-faced approach to the issue was brought to a head at the 1985 Ard Fheis. The Ard Fheis passed the motion that "Women have the right to choose," but not without controversy: "The debate raised a high level of discomfort and discontent," and the eventual success of the motion "was ascribed by some to the fact that the vote had taken place at the end of the conference, when a sizeable number of delegates, some of whom were from rural areas, had already left" (Maillot 2005, 113). There is the sense that this liberalising motion on abortion was only possible due to the fact that it had been debated at the very end of the three-day event, in the section specifically relating to women's concerns, and was therefore off the radar for the majority of conference attendees.

At the following year's Ard Fheis, the success of the motion on abortion had clearly had time to filter to all levels of party membership and had caused much consternation. The section on motions concerned with women was moved to the most central point of the conference, immediately before the break for lunch on the second day. Out of a total of 17 motions within the remit of women's issues, 13 of those were concerned with abortion. 7 of those encouraged deletion of the previous year's amendment, or a stricter Sinn Féin policy on abortion, whilst only two encouraged a retention or strengthening of the amendment. The remaining 4 motions encouraged a return to the ambiguous wording of the 1980 policy document or for abortion in limited cases: where the woman's life was endangered, or in cases of rape or incest. 30 delegates made contributions to the debate, "mostly in support of motions 83 and 88" (Sinn Féin 1986, 42). Motion 83 advocated deleting the 1985 wording entirely, whereas motion 88 proposed the establishment of a "secular state" and "the individual's right to make a conscientious decision for or against abortion without coercion from any other individual or group" (Sinn Féin 1986, 49). Several key figures within the party spoke "in favour of the deletion of the pro-choice wording" (Frampton 2008, 39), including Máirtín Ó Muilleoir and Francie Molloy,[11] who claimed that he and fellow Sinn Féin canvassers had been physically assaulted at doors because of the change in position (Sinn Féin 1986, 42). Sinn Féin president Gerry Adams spoke in favour of motion 83, saying that the Ard Chomairle in 1985 had been opposed to the change:

> … not because we are anti-feminist, not because we think women should not have control over their own fertility or bodies or their own sexuality, but because the phrase is synonymous with the abortion on demand campaign. It makes a nonsense of what precedes it and reduces policy on abortion to a fudge. (ibid., 43)

Adams appears wary of appearing overly liberal on the issue and of the party's policy becoming understood as aligned with that of the vaguely defined "abortion on demand campaign." The number of key Sinn Féin figures speaking on this motion (at an Ard Fheis which also saw the party voting to remove its policy of abstention at the Daíl Éireann, a fundamentally new direction for Sinn Féin) illustrates how controversial and how important this matter was. As Maillot notes, "even among some who had spoken forcefully in favour of the proposal" there was the sense that "the previous year's vote had been a hasty decision which did not serve the interests of the movement, as it was too divisive, too controversial and, ultimately, too damaging" (Maillot 2005, 114). Sharrock and Devenport go further, arguing that there was a deliberate behind-the-scenes manoeuvring to force those at the top to change the policy: "promises [were] made [by the Sinn Féin leadership] to drop the women's right to choose their position on the abortion issue to placate the conservatives" (quoted in Conrad 2004, 113). Instead of the all-out support for a woman's right to choose, there was instead a return to the ambiguous wording of previous policy documents. The decision of the 1986 Ard Fheis now read that "we are opposed to the attitudes and forces that compel women to have abortions. We are opposed to abortion as a means of birth control but we accept the need for abortion where the woman's life is at risk or in grave danger, for example ectopic pregnancy and all forms of cancer" (Sinn Féin, 43). This policy remained until the party voted to allow abortion in specific cases (largely for health, fatal foetal abnormality, rape and incest) at the 2017 Ard Fheis.[12]

A further 1992 policy document on abortion, produced because of the November referendum on the X case in the Republic,[13] reiterates the party's ambiguous position. It concludes, in a similar manner to the 1986 Ard Fheis decision, that:

> Sinn Féin is opposed to the attitudes and forces in society that compel women to have abortions and criminalise those who do make this decision. We accept the need for abortion where a women's life is at risk or in grave danger (e.g. all forms of cancer) and in cases of rape or child sexual abuse.[14]

This is supported with reference to 13 leading obstetricians and gynaecologists who released a statement, anchoring the party policy in medical validation. The document also expresses Sinn Féin's strong support for contraception and comprehensive sex education. Like the 1980 document, it carries an incredibly vague conclusion and stops far short of coming out in support of abortion rights:

> Sinn Féin is advocating a new vision of society, where women who decide to have children have access to adequate health care, where couples can avail of free, safe, contraception, where there is childcare and education for all, where every child is a wanted child.
>
> Sinn Féin has consistently argues (sic) for progressive changes to benefit the lives of women in the 26 Counties. We have produced a document on the reality of women's lives in this state and will continue to defend women's rights to freedom and equality, not just in the forthcoming referendum but in all areas of women's lives.[15]

Whilst presenting a liberal vision of equality between the sexes and a progressive approach to contraception, the party delicately sidesteps the issue of abortion. Termination of pregnancy does not feature in this picture of sexual health that Sinn Féin presents here.

The documents of this period and the proceedings of the 1985 and 1986 Ard Fheiseanna suggest a strong degree of discomfort with the notion of abortion from Sinn Féin. Whilst outright support for terminations may be present in some of the more secular and feminist factions of the party, this does not carry enough weight across the party to be adopted as policy. More general disgust at the "attitudes and forces in society" that compel women to have abortions can, however, be shown. Mindful of the potential to tap into the SDLP voter pool, and of the more Catholic leaning of that segment of Northern Irish society, Sinn Féin kept one eye on the ballot box when it came to the issue of abortion. Their policy on this issue goes to the heart of who Sinn Féin were as a party—trying to balance their conservative, Catholic vote on one side, with the radical, secular, left-leaning tendencies on the other.

Sinn Féin's debate here is indeed the only recorded moment in which a party consciously considered its stance on abortion prior to devolution. The fact that they were the sole party to have an open, recorded discussion on the issue speaks to their radical tendencies. To consider Sinn Féin in depth is not to suggest that this was an issue only of interest to republican women or republican politics: yet it does illustrate the difficulties a political party faced when trying to reach consensus on the issue, even when that party was arguably the most left wing in Northern Ireland. If Sinn Féin could not adopt a coherent pro-choice position, it is highly unlikely that any other party in Northern Ireland would.

Gendering the Good Friday Agreement Negotiations

With the Downing Street Declaration and the paramilitary ceasefires of 1994,[16] a settled peace seemed to be a growing prospect for Northern Ireland. In this section, the gendered nature of the peace process in the 1990s is considered. Like Waylen, it is argued that "presence at the table may be necessary but it is not sufficient" (2014b, 517) when it comes to acting on gender, and hence, the focus here is on gender "actors" as opposed to just the presence of women. Mainstream thinking on Northern Ireland and the peace process has had less to say about negotiations outside of the main political parties or actors.[17] There was, however, a vibrant civil society focused on peace, much of which was fuelled by women's organisations working at the community and voluntary level (Campbell 2008; Donaghy 2002, 85).

Following Waylen (2014b), this period is considered by using the framework of three distinct phases to the negotiations process—pre-negotiations, the establishment of the Northern Ireland Women's Coalition (NIWC) and the multiparty talks that finally led to the Good Friday Agreement.

Pre-negotiations

Following the cease-fires and the 1994 Downing Street declarations, it became apparent that Northern Ireland was beginning to formally move towards peace. In the face of the distinctly masculine make-up of Northern Irish politics, women's civil society organisations began to consider how women were going to figure in the negotiations. The Northern Ireland Women's European Platform (NIWEP) and the National Women's Council of Ireland (NWCI) issued a joint response to the Downing Street Declaration, requesting that both governments explain how women would figure in the peace process (Hinds 1999, 114). Several conferences around the issue of women and political participation were held in the mid-1990s, in Dublin in 1994 and in Draperstown, Northern Ireland, in 1995, bringing together key actors from civil society around the issue of how to bring more women into formal politics. These gatherings helped to focus attention around women's exclusion from formal politics and encouraged a sense that independent action would need to be taken (Fearon and McWilliams 2001, 119).

Some of this activism came from within the traditionally divided sectarian communities. In 1994, a republican feminist conference was held in Belfast, organised by a group named Clár na mBan. The group brought together women from over 25 voluntary and community organisations and eight women's centres, "in a context of uncertainty about the meaning of 'peace'" (Connolly 1999, 119). Of key concern was the worry that nationalist and republican women would, once again, in the words of one speaker, "be asked to bury our demands [as women], this time in the common purpose of achieving peace" (ibid., 120). As a result of this conference, the group submitted a document to the Ireland Forum for Peace and Reconciliation to ensure that "women's voices will be heard this time round" (ibid., 126). Other actions by women's groups were far more transversal, such as that of the Women's Support Network in Belfast (Mulholland 2005, 172) which worked across the sectarian divide to lobby policy-makers about women's needs within the community. It also worked with trade unions to gain funding and deliver programmes under the European Special Support Programme for Peace and Reconciliation (ibid., 174). Women in civil society in the build-up to the peace process were thus clearly organised as women. Attempts were being made to ensure that women's voices and a gendered perspective had a chance of inclusion at the talks table.

Yet, as the more formal process gained ground, few women were included. The Framework Agreement, published in 1995 jointly by the British and Irish governments, advocated a power-sharing government in Belfast with cross-border cooperation. The Forum set up in Dublin by the Irish government had a female chair, but only 13 of the 64 delegates were women. These movements regarding gender concerns were therefore small and largely conducted outside of the main political parties. As Waylen points out, the peace process at this point was "small-scale informal (i.e. not public or formally rule-bound)" (2014b, 502) and heavily dominated by men. Feminist intervention at this point was key, but was still only making minor, if any, incursions into the formal process.

The Northern Ireland Women's Coalition and the Build-Up to Formal Negotiations

In what was largely viewed as the British government's acquiescence to unionist concerns (an "expensive white elephant" (Fearon 1999, 52) in one commentator's words),[18] an elected Forum for Political

Dialogue was facilitated in Belfast alongside the peace talks. A joint communiqué was issued by the Irish and British government on 28 February 1996, inviting parties to give their views on the electoral system and proposing that elections be held for the Forum (Fearon and McWilliams 2001, 119; Galligan 2006, 207). In spite of the vibrancy of the civil society groups outlined above, these actions had little impact on the formal process. Ideas about how to make this more gender-friendly had already been floated by NIWEP—gender-proofing party lists, childcare allowances and family friendly hours were amongst their suggestions (Hinds 1999, 122). With a lack of movement on any of these suggestions by the formal parties involved, there was a "dawning awareness that women would be left out, combined with the realisation that there was no effective option other than a 'women's party'" (Hinds 1999, 122). NIWEP urged the Northern Ireland Office to include a women's group on the list of official parties. When a final list of 30 parties was produced, a women's party was included (Galligan 2006, 208).

Thus, the NIWC was formed. The founders were motivated by a belief that women were not being heard in existing political parties and that "since political parties were not going to ensure that a woman's voice would be heard, the women who had navigated and negotiated grassroots politics for many years would go ahead and do it themselves" (Fearon 1999, 9). Working from the principles of inclusion, accommodation, human rights and equality (Hinds 1999, 124), based on several of the members' involvement in the Fourth World Conference on Women in Beijing in 1995, the Coalition also took no decision on the constitutional question. In the space of seven short weeks between the decision to form the Coalition and the elections, seventy candidates were fielded. Their development was rapid, with a "make do" attitude: the former press officer describes being given her role, where she was present at a meeting and "the campaign director of the NIWC … was kind of going around, and she just said – so and so will stand in this ward, and then she said…and [you] will be press officer, and I said 'what?!'"[19]

The appearance of a consciously non-community specific party in Northern Irish politics was rare. As Hinds notes, "what passes for politics in Northern Ireland is limited" (1999, 113), not only in that politics often means a discussion of the constitutional question alone (Murtagh 2008, 52), but also in the dominance of formal institutional politics (Connolly 1999, 152). As discussed above, women had long been active socially and politically in the province, but due to the rigid parameters of how politics was understood, had rarely been part of elite formal political structures.[20] The NIWC worked across the sectarian divide (one of only three parties to do so—the others being the Alliance Party and the Labour Coalition), and the two women elected to the Forum talks (Monica McWilliams and Pearl Sagar) were Catholic/Middle class and Protestant/Working class, respectively. This decision to operate along transversal feminist lines (Yuval-Davis 1997) went strongly against the grain of the ways in which the conflict had been understood and the way political reconciliation had previously been attempted (most especially the Sunningdale Agreement of 1974 and the reformed and ultimately abortive Assembly of 1982–1986).

The NIWC was far from a rallying point for all women within Northern Irish politics. Dawn Purvis, later leader of the PUP (and Director of the Belfast Marie Stopes clinic), said that she "wouldn't be comfortable in the Women's Coalition for the very reason that I would feel my unionism was being compromised. I'm a Unionist first, yes, I'm a woman, but I'm a Unionist first" (Ward 2006, 67). The NIWC delegates experienced little solidarity from other women in the talks—overt criticism of the NIWC "provided other women with a chance to show that they were 'one of the boys', able to denigrate the NIWC with the best of them" (Fearon 1999, 68). Furthermore, the agenda of the NIWC was far from radical. There was no mention of LGBT rights in their manifesto, and they did not feel "pressured to have a strong liberal-leaning policy" (Fearon 1999, 27) on abortion. The rapid way in which the Coalition had come together meant that it did not actually have a formal policy on abortion until four years after it formed.[21] As the former press office of the NIWC described it, getting agreement around abortion from members to formulate a policy position was not easy—"not everybody was happy with it … there was ambivalence with some people." As she also points out:

> It wasn't really central to the negotiations … ultimately it's a small thing in the big picture – but we were really given a hard time [from the media about not having a clear position on abortion] … we didn't have the position but we couldn't take a position without the agreement of the party. I mean it wasn't the way we worked.[22]

The NIWC was therefore not a voice for a radical rethinking of norms in a socially conservative society, but its presence did help to address the sex imbalance in representatives and present a more gendered perspective to proceedings.

The Forum for Political Dialogue and the Multiparty Talks

The Forum for Political Dialogue was set up in 1996 and was active alongside the multiparty talks which led to the Good Friday Agreement. The Forum elections were designed to ensure that a wide range of parties were represented through the top-up system (Elliott 1997). Despite only gaining 1% of the overall vote, this was enough for the NIWC to get two seats from the regional list. Once there, they found little female company. Only 15 (13.6%) of the delegates were female, with Sinn Féin performing best out of the major parties in returning 29% female delegates (Waylen 2014b, 513).

The NIWC delegates often failed to be taken seriously by their colleagues from different parties. Other political figures used highly gendered language to describe the NIWC, suggesting that they could not cut it with the "boys." Future First Minister Peter Robinson declared that "they [the women of the NIWC] haven't been at the forefront of the battle when shots were being fired or when the constitution of Northern Ireland was in peril" (quoted in Fearon 1999, 14). Then Deputy Leader of the SDLP, Seamus Mallon, said, in relation to the NIWC, that the peace negotiations "won't be about setting differences aside, this will be about facing differences that we have in this community, facing them full-frontal and dealing with those differences. What we must realize is that these negotiations which are going to take place are going to be very hard-nosed and they are going to be real" (quoted in Fearon 1999, 17). The highly gendered language of both politicians here suggests the disparagement with which male members of other parties held the NIWC. Mallon argues that these negotiations are going to be "real" in the sense that they are going to be work for "real" men, and that the women of the NIWC will not be able to cope with the difficult work of "facing differences." Likewise, Robinson transplants the male violence of the Troubles onto the party political sphere with the inference that if women were not present in one, then they should not be present in the other. Underpinning these beliefs is an understanding that at this point in Northern Ireland, politics meant the conflict, and the conflict meant politics. For Mallon in the above quote, what is "real" is the constitutional question and ethno-national division. If the talks won't be "about setting differences aside," then they will be about debating these differences instead. In this context, the Coalition found it difficult to forge the cross-party alliances that a small party needed, and that was foundational to its ideology.

Further to comments such as those from Mallon and Robinson above, the women faced repeated sexist abuse during Forum meetings, with the Belfast Telegraph claiming that the women were "treated with derision" and the *Irish Times* describing the behaviour towards them in the Forum as "quite appalling" (Fearon 1999, 56). McWilliams was once interrupted seven times during one speech, "including a well-publicised 'moo, moo' from Ian Paisley Jr." (Fearon 1999, 62). There was also a concern that the women might slip into traditional, essentialist roles as "housekeeper" given their ability to mediate across sectarian boundaries and their role as "watchdog" in ensuring that the Forum abide by its own rules (ibid., 56). There was a further danger that the remit of the party was too small, in that it was too essentially defined as a woman's party without a more radical outlook. As Little writes, "underpinning this narrow definition of diversity [in Northern Ireland] lies a strong essentialism which implies that male politicians have let the province down and that the participation of women would improve dialogue" (Little 2002, 7). This essentialism was seen in how the Coalition defined its policies (see below) but equally appeared in what others expected of the NIWC: "the amount of pressure that was put on the Women's Coalition, they were just expected to ensure that the peace was made! They were meant to ensure that it was completely gender-proofed in the face of some of our politicians" (Ashe *et al.* 2016).

Whilst the language and behaviour of the Forum and talks created an exclusionary atmosphere for the NIWC, they were also able to use informal processes to their advantage. They met with Sinn Féin when the party was banned from proceedings, in pubs and cars (Waylen 2014b, 515). They conducted discussions informally, "hanging round corridors, talking to people, dispersing information among different actors and developing back channels" (ibid.). In order to include the all-important clause on the right of women to political participation, Pearl Sagar, one of the two elected officials from the NIWC to the negotiations, managed to discuss this inclusion with Mo Mowlam by hanging around her office, and persuading the Secretary of State to discuss the wording in a shared toilet cubicle, away from prying ears (Fearon 1999, 106). The presence of the NIWC helped to expand the notion of what politics meant in the context of Northern Ireland, inserting a cross-community women's party into the negotiations. The party did not just illustrate the gender gap in Northern Irish political representation: it also acted to highlight the "gulf between community leadership and the narrow exclusive world of party politics in Northern Ireland" (Roulston 1989, 4).

What type of peace was being envisioned, and what type of conflict was being defined, in the movement towards the Good Friday Agreement (Bell and O'Rourke 2007)? At one level, peace talks in Northern Ireland in the run up to the Good Friday Agreement were incredibly inclusive. As noted above, the NIWC worked from politics at a grass-roots and community level to bring female voices into the discussion. Within the Forum for Political Dialogue, multiple small parties were represented, especially on the Unionist side: representatives from 24 separate parties vied for election. Furthermore, the outcome of the peace process saw a huge amount of public support, as evidenced in the huge turnout to vote on the Good Friday Agreement referendum across the island of Ireland. There was 81.1% turnout in Northern Ireland and 55.6% in the Republic. The referendum passed with 71.1% support in Northern Ireland and 94.4% in the Republic.[23] The Good Friday Agreement mobilised many small political parties, encouraging the creation of entirely new bodies such as the NIWC, and produced a concluding agreement that had great all-Ireland support.[24]

Yet it is debatable how much of these broad-based negotiations were a genuine attempt to solicit multiple viewpoints and how much was a tokenistic inclusion of minor parties. The negotiations—or the "real stuff" of the negotiations—often appears to have been happening at the elite political level. Various political biographies, both around the time of the Good Friday Agreement (Mowlam 2002) and in successive negotiations (Powell 2009), portray a picture of an elite, at times highly secretive process, which focussed much more on individual personalities than the broader remit of political parties and Northern Irish society. The abuse experienced by the NIWC, outlined above, details not only the sexism explicit in Northern Irish politics, but also the extent to which newcomers were deemed "outsiders" and not welcome in formal politics. There remains the widespread perception that the Forum was a talking shop, designed solely to please Unionists (reflected in the fact that Sinn Féin declined to take their seats, and the SDLP withdrew after three weeks of attendance).

Where Was Abortion in the Movement Towards the Good Friday Agreement?

With regard to women's issues specifically, the inclusion of the NIWC within the peace talks was clearly an important addition. It was only the presence of the NIWC (and some very subtle manoeuvring on their part) that an explicitly gendered perspective was inserted into the Good Friday Agreement. They decided that, based on the principles of the Beijing conference which had underpinned so much of the NIWC's ideology, a sentence declaring "the right of women to full and equal political participation" should be included. Women are mentioned explicitly within the text of the Good Friday Agreement twice, both in the section regarding "Rights, Safeguards and Equality of Opportunity": with the support of Mowlam, the "right of women to full and equal political participation" is included, as is "the advancement of women in public life."[25] Yet these small inclusions, both referencing only women's role in public affairs, go nowhere in terms of recognising women's specific circumstances during the Troubles, nor advocating for a more equitable and just form of peace.

The NIWC's presence was important, but not enough to radically rethink the nature of the peace process. The celebrated Peace Studies scholar Johan Galtung argues for an understanding of the difference between two types of peace: "negative peace which is the absence of violence, absence of war - and positive peace which is the integration of human society" (Galtung 1964, 2). A negative peace, feminist scholars have argued, often creates peace at the expense of thinking about the broader and more invisible gendered injustices in society. Gendering peace agreements and the processes that lead up to them is about not just adding women into proceedings but also asking more fundamentally what type of peace is being envisioned. What is the negative "before" that peace negotiations want to move from and the positive "after" that they are trying to construct? Who creates and employs these definitions? Feminist thinking on transitional justice and peace agreements argues that a broader conception of peace (a "larger dream" [Bell and O'Rourke 2010, 38]) is necessary for a fully just and equitable society, and that this is rarely present in peace negotiations. However, in both Northern Ireland and elsewhere, "negotiations are often premised on the imperative of ending intra-male public violence" (Rooney and Ní Aoláin 2007, 343), rather than on thinking in a broader fashion about any of the more ingrained or invisible injustices in society.

Within this narrow picture of the peace agreement, where women's rights were added as little more than an afterthought, abortion was, in the words of one activist, "a small thing in the big picture."[26] Even the Women's Coalition did not have a policy on abortion until the early days of the newly formed Assembly. The narrow prescriptions of the Good Friday Agreement meant that a more inclusive peace, one which included a gendered appreciation of Northern Irish society, and which may within that have considered reproductive rights, was not possible. In the words of one NIWC representative: "What we were going into at that stage was the peace talks, where, to be honest, abortion wasn't going to be a paragraph in the agreement ... There's a time and a place for that issue as well, but the peace talks wasn't really that" (Avila Kilmurray, quoted in O'Rourke 2013, 205). As O'Rourke notes, "the narrow gendered terms within which peace processes tend to unfold are apparent in this quote" (2013, 205). Because of the dominant ethno-national underpinnings of the Good Friday Agreement, and the relative absence of positive gender actors, discussion was too specifically focussed to consider abortion rights.

Conclusion

When considering the "hidden life" (Waylen 2014a, 213) of the processes and organisations which led to the Good Friday Agreement, gender has been especially obscured. In mainstream accounts of the Northern Irish Troubles, a lack of consideration has been given to women's activism, and both the implicit male dominance of formal politics and the prominence of the ethno-national question have been tacitly accepted.

Looking at both formal politics and the more informal processes which led up to the Good Friday Agreement helps to understand the "actions not undertaken" (Chappell 2014, 193) around the issue of abortion in Northern Ireland in this time period. Abortion was a difficult topic for the women's movement to tackle, and feminist activism itself was often fractured and transient, beset by wider sectarian and ideological tensions. Abortion proved deeply controversial for republican politics in the 1980s, dividing Sinn Féin and having to be carefully managed to ensure a tactful (if benign) compromise on the issue. Equally, as the move towards peace became more established, the parameters on which a political settlement were established reveal a particular "gendered logic of appropriateness" (Chappell 2006). Peace was envisioned as the cessation of physical violence and governance as primarily involving competing communal identities. An acceptance of the dominance of ethno-national identity and the primacy of the constitutional question underpinned negotiations.

Feminist scholars of transitional justice ask "Whose justice – and for whom? What is the transition to?" (Buckley-Zistel and Solkos 2011, 2). The justice envisioned in Northern Ireland at this point was narrowly defined along ethno-national paradigms and a cessation of (male-dominated) physical violence. As a result, any place for gender as a political identity, or gendered policy issues, was limited. Discussion of abortion in this framework, let alone policy formulation or legislative action, was especially difficult. The hope that the political institutional element of the peace settlement would be sensitive to gendered concerns was thus weak; the next chapter turns to consider this.

Notes

1. At the 1981 Sinn Féin Ard Fheis, Danny Morrison, then editor of Republican newsletter *An Phoblacht*, addressed the convention regarding the party's potential future in political elections: "Who here really believes we can win the war through the ballot box? But will anyone here object if, with a ballot paper in one hand and the Armalite in the other, we take power in Ireland?" (http://cain.ulst.ac.uk/othelem/chron/ch81.htm. Accessed 5 March 2018). The "Armalite and the ballot box" is often used to refer to the republican movement's strategy from this point onwards.
2. Although there were several key female paramilitaries, most notably in the republican movement—Mairead Farrell and the Price sisters being perhaps the most well-known. O'Keefe (2013) argues that women's involvement, and feminist thinking, was highly important to the republican movement and that women actively resisted and reinterpreted patriarchal understandings of Irish nationalism. The presence of female loyalist paramilitaries was less obvious, although McEvoy (2010) argues that they played a key role in the various loyalist groupings.
3. Derry civil rights activist, Cathy Harkin, described Northern Irish society during the Troubles in this way. Quoted in Fearon (1999, 106).
4. Activism such as this often referred to women's roles in terms of "their responsibilities in and for the family rather than by appealing to their interests as individuals" (Roulston 1989, 222). As such, it may be viewed as less "purely" driven by feminist or female concerns. Indeed, women's roles as mothers and guardians of the family/community were often exacerbated in communities where men were imprisoned (Galligan 2006, 206).

5. Former employee of Brook Northern Ireland. Private interview with the author. Belfast, March 2014.
6. In the words of the former employee, the key Presbyterian minister involved in the protests "would not be seen dead with the Catholics," suggesting that even when there was a shared perspective on this issue, religious divisions still trumped anti-abortion sentiment.
7. Former employee of Brook Northern Ireland. Private interview with the author. Belfast, March 2014.
8. As the former Brook employee said (with a large degree of humour), she viewed this as quite an accomplishment: "I wanted to do something for him when he finished, I thought he deserved something for that!" Private interview. Belfast, March 2014.
9. To argue this, and to focus on Sinn Féin in this section, is not a suggestion that it is the only party to adopt positive strategies on women's rights, nor is it to suggest that the republican movement is alone in developing a more progressive politics. On the unionist side of the electoral spectrum, the Progressive Unionist Party (the PUP) have been a continuous left-wing presence (Edwards 2010) and have adopted a pro-choice position. The former leader, Dawn Purvis, was director of the Marie Stopes clinic in Belfast from 2012 to 2015. Furthermore, as Chapters 6 and 7 show, Sinn Féin's policy on abortion has been far from coherent in terms of its practical implications.
10. "Abortion Ireland," the Sinn Féin Department of Women's Affairs, Linen Hall Library Political Collection, Linen Hall Library, Belfast.
11. Ó Muilleoir was Lord Mayor of Belfast from 2013 to 2014. Molloy has been as MLA since 1998 and an MP since 2013.
12. See greater discussion of contemporary policy positions in Chapters 6 and 7.
13. See footnote 12, Chapter 1.
14. "Defend a woman's right to travel, to know, to live," Sinn Féin, Linen Hall Library Political Collection, Linen Hall Library, Belfast.
15. "Defend a woman's right to travel, to know, to live," Sinn Féin, Linen Hall Library Political Collection, Linen Hall Library, Belfast.
16. The Downing Street Declaration, formally known as the Joint Declaration on Peace, was issued on the 15 December 1993 by the British Prime Minister, John Major, and Irish Taoiseach, Albert Reynolds. It stated that peace must involve the ending of paramilitary violence, and that both governments "will seek, along with the Northern Ireland constitutional parties through a process of political dialogue, to create institutions and structures which, while respecting the diversity of the people of Ireland, would enable them to work together in all areas of common interest" (Article 9, Joint Declaration on Peace. http://cain.ulst.ac.uk/events/peace/docs/dsd151293.htm. Accessed 26 January 2018.) In August of 1994, the

PIRA announced cessation of paramilitary operations. In October, the Combined Loyalist Military Command announced a similar ceasefire.

17. Exceptions to this include Campbell (2008) and Fearon (1999).
18. Such was the desire to please all and ensure cooperation that seating in the building had to be rearranged, and "even the Tipperary brand [a company from the Republic] water dispensers had to be replaced with River Rock [a Northern Irish brand] before many of the unionist delegates would partake" (Fearon 1999, 52).
19. Former NIWC activist. Private interview with the author, Skype. May 2014.
20. This was acknowledged too by Marjorie "Mo" Mowlam, the first female Secretary of State for Northern Ireland. Writing in her autobiography several years later, she said that whilst "impossible to quantify … the contribution of individual women and women's groups to the cause of peace in Northern Ireland is immense. Across all communities, the links and relationships that women forge and the work that they do – usually away from the public gaze – has been invaluable in keeping the social fabric of Northern Ireland together, especially in the most troubled times" (Mowlam 2002, 233).
21. Former NIWC activist. Private interview with the author. May 2014.
22. Former NIWC activist. Private interview with the author. May 2014.
23. http://www.ark.ac.uk/elections/ff96.htm. Accessed 17 April 2015.
24. However, these high percentages mask the split between the two ethno-national communities. Some estimates put the Catholic "Yes" vote at as high as 97%, and the Protestant "Yes" vote as low as 51–53%.
25. https://www.gov.uk/government/uploads/system/uploads/attachment_data/file/136652/agreement.pdf. Accessed 26 January 2018. The document is referred to as the Belfast Agreement on the main government website, but as the "Agreement Reached in the Multi-Party Negotiations" on the first page of the document itself. It is referred to in the text here as the Good Friday Agreement—although unofficial, this is generally how it is addressed in academia and journalism alike.
26. Private interview with the author. May 2014.

Bibliography

Ashe, F. 2006. The McCartney Sisters' Search for Justice: Gender and Political Protest in Northern Ireland. *Politics* 26 (3): 161–170.

———. 2007. Gendering Ethno-Nationalist Politics in Northern Ireland. *Ethnic and Racial Studies* 30 (5): 766–786.

———. 2008. Gender and Ethno-Nationalist Politics in Northern Ireland. In *Northern Ireland After the Troubles*, ed. Colin Coulter and Michael Murray, 45–60. Manchester: Manchester University Press.

Ashe, Fidelma, Gorana Mlinarevic, Claire Pierson, and Jennifer Thomson. 2016. Gendering Research in Divided Societies: A Conversation. *International Feminist Journal of Politics* 18 (4): 606–613.

Bean, Kevin. 2007. *The New Politics of Sinn Féin*. Liverpool: Liverpool University Press.

Bell, Christine, and Catherine O'Rourke. 2007. Does Feminism Need a Theory of Transitional Justice? An Introductory Essay. *International Journal of Transitional Justice* 1 (1): 23–44.

———. 2010. Peace Agreements or Pieces of Paper? The Impact of UNSC Resolution 1325 on Peace Processes and their Agreements. *International and Comparative Law Quarterly* 59 (10): 941–980.

Blair, Tony. 2010. *A Journey*. Farnham: Arrow.

Buckley-Zistel, S., and M. Zolkos. 2011. Introduction: Gender in Transitional Justice. In *Gender in Transitional Justice*, ed. Susanne Buckley-Zistel and Ruth Stanley. Basingstoke: Palgrave Macmillan.

Campbell, Beatrix. 2008. *Agreement! The State, Conflict and Change in Northern Ireland*. London: Lawrence and Wishart.

Chappell, Louise. 2006. Comparing Political Institutions: Revealing the Gendered "Logic of Appropriateness". *Politics and Gender* 2 (2): 232–235.

———. 2014. Conflicting Institutions and the Search for Gender Justice at the International Criminal Court. *Political Research Quarterly* 67 (1): 183–196.

Connolly, Linda. 1999. Feminist Politics and the Peace Process. *Capital and Class* 23: 145–159.

Conrad, Kathryn. 2004. *Locked in the Family Cell: Gender, Security and Political Agency in Irish National Discourse*. Madison: University of Wisconsin Press.

Donaghy, Tahnya Barnett. 2002. Women's Contributions to the Northern Ireland Peace Agreement. *Canadian Women's Studies* 22 (2): 83–87.

Edwards, Aaron. 2010. The Progressive Unionist Party of Northern Ireland: A Left-Wing Voice in an Ethnically Divided Society. *British Journal of Politics and International Relations* 12 (4): 590–614.

Elliott, Sydney. 1997. The Northern Ireland Forum/Entry to Negotiations Elections, 1996. *Irish Political Studies* 12 (1): 111–122.

English, Richard. 2012. *Armed Struggle: The History of the IRA*. London: Pan.

Evason, Eileen. 1991. *Against the Grain: Contemporary Women's Movement in Northern Ireland*. Dublin: Attic Press; Cork: University College Cork.

Fearon, Kate. 1999. *Women's Work: The Story of the Northern Ireland Women's Coalition*. Belfast: Blackstaff Press.

Fearon, Kate, and Monica McWilliams. 2001. Swimming Against the Mainstream: The Northern Ireland Women's Coalition. In *Gender, Democracy and Inclusion in Northern Ireland*, ed. Carmel Roulston and Celia Davies. New York: Palgrave.

Frampton, Martyn. 2008. *The Long March: The Political Strategy of Sinn Féin, 1981–2007*. London: Palgrave Macmillan.

Galligan, Yvonne. 2006. Women in Northern Ireland's Politics: Feminizing an 'Armed Patriarchy'. In *Representing Women in Parliament: A Comparative Study*, ed. Marian Sawer, Manon Tremblay, and Linda Trimble. Abingdon: Routledge.

Galtung, Johan. 1964. An Editorial. *Journal of Peace Research* 1 (1): 1–4.

Hinds, Bronagh. 1999. Women Working for Peace in Northern Ireland. In *Contesting Politics: Women in Ireland, North and South*, ed. Yvonne Galligan, Ellis Ward, and Rick Wilford. Boulder, CO: Westview.

Lee, Simon. 1995. An A to K to Z of Abortion Law in Northern Ireland: Abortion on Remand. In *The Abortion Law in Northern Ireland: Human Rights and Reproductive Choice*, ed. Anne Furedi. Belfast: Family Planning Association Northern Ireland.

Little, Adrian. 2002. Feminism and the Politics of Difference in Northern Ireland. *Journal of Political Ideologies* 7 (2): 163–177.

Maillot, Agnes. 2005. *New Sinn Féin: Irish Republicanism in the Twenty-First Century*. Abingdon: Routledge.

McEvoy, Sandra. 2010. Loyalist Women Paramilitaries in Northern Ireland: Beginning a Feminist Conversation About Conflict Resolution. In *Gender and International Security: Feminist Perspectives*, ed. Laura Sjoberg. Abingdon: Routledge.

McWilliams, Monica. 1995. Struggling for Peace and Justice: Reflections on Women's Activism in Northern Ireland. *Journal of Women's History* 6 (4): 13–39.

Moloney, Ed. 2003. *A Secret History of the IRA*. London: Penguin.

Mowlam, Mo. 2002. *Momentum: The Struggle for Peace, Politics and the People*. London: Coronet.

Mulholland, Marie. 2005. The Challenge to Inequality: Women, Discrimination and Decision-Making in Northern Ireland. In *Victims, Perpetrators or Actors: Gender, Armed Conflict and Political Violence*, ed. Caroline O.N. Mosher and Fiona C. Clark. London: Zed Books.

Murtagh, Cera. 2008. A Transient Transition: The Cultural and Institutional Obstacles Impeding the Northern Ireland Women's Coalition in Its Progression from Informal to Formal Politics. *Irish Political Studies* 23 (1): 21–40.

NIALRA. 1989. *Abortion in Northern Ireland: The Report of an International Tribunal*. Belfast: Beyond the Pale Publications.

O'Keefe, Theresa. 2013. *Feminist Identity Development and Activism in Revolutionary Movements*. Abingdon: Palgrave Macmillan.

O'Rourke, Catherine. 2013. *Gender Politics in Transitional Justice*. Abingdon: Routledge.

Pierson, Claire, and Jennifer Thomson. 2018. Allies or Opponents? Power Sharing, Civil Society and Gender. *Nationalism and Ethnic Politics* 24 (1): 100–115.

Porter, Elisabeth. 1997. Diversity and Commonality: Women, Politics, and Northern Ireland. *The European Journal of Women's Studies* 4 (1): 83–100.

Powell, Jonathan. 2009. *Great Hatred, Little Room: Making Peace in Northern Ireland*. London: Vintage.

Racioppi, L., and K.O. See. 2000. Ulstermen and Loyalist Ladies on Parade: Gendering Unionism in Northern Ireland. *International Feminist Journal of Politics* 2 (1): 1–29.

———. 2006. Engendering Democratic Transition from Conflict: Women's inclusion in Northern Ireland's Peace Process. *Comparative Politics* 38 (2): 189–208.

Rooney, Eilish, and Fionnula Ní Aoláin. 2007. Underenforcement and Intersectionality: Gendered Aspects of Transition. *International Journal of Transitional Justice* 1: 338–354.

Roulston, Carmel. 1989. Women on the Margin: The Women's Movement in Northern Ireland, 1973–1988. *Science and Society* 53 (2): 219–236.

Sinn Féin. 1986. *The Politics of Revolution: The Main Speeches from the 1986 Ard-Fheis, Including the Presidential Address of Gerry Adams*. Dublin: Sinn Féin.

Smyth, Ailbhe. 1995. Paying Our Disrespects to the Bloody States We're In: Women, Violence, Culture and the State. *Journal of Women's History* 6 (4): 190–215.

Thatcher, Margaret. 1993. *The Downing Street Years*. New York: HarperCollins.

Ward, Rachel. 2006. *Women, Unionism and Loyalism in Northern Ireland: From 'Tea-Makers' to Political Activists*. Dublin: Irish Academic Press.

Waylen, Georgina. 2014a. Informal Institutions, Institutional Change and Gender Equality. *Political Research Quarterly* 67 (1): 212–223.

———. 2014b. A Seat at the Table—Is It Enough? Gender, Multiparty Negotiations, and Institutional Design in South African and Northern Ireland. *Politics and Gender* 10: 495–523.

Yuval-Davis, Nira. 1997. *Gender and Nation*. London: Sage.

Zalewski, M. 2005. Gender Ghosts in McGarry and O'Leary and Representations of the Conflict in Northern Ireland. *Political Studies* 53 (1): 201–221.

CHAPTER 6

The Devolved Institution: Power-Sharing

Feminist institutionalism has highlighted the ways in which gendered concerns and issues might be more readily incorporated into new, as opposed to already existing, institutions. As Waylen writes, "the creation of new institutions can offer opportunities for gender concerns to be incorporated more easily and fundamentally at the outset of an institution's life than it is to 'add them in' at a later stage" (2008, 273). As Chapter 5 illustrated, however, gendered concerns played a limited role in the negotiations which led to the Good Friday Agreement and the (re-) establishment of devolved institutions in the province. This chapter considers how gendered issues, and abortion specifically, were addressed in the implementation of the Good Friday Agreement and the institutional design of the new Northern Irish Assembly.

This chapter argues that the power-sharing consociational basis of the post-Good Friday Agreement institutions creates a hierarchy which privileges ethno-national identity and issues, and makes it difficult for gender to exist as a political identity. As a result, both women and positive

---

This chapter draws on Claire Pierson, Ronan Kennedy and Jennifer Thomson. 2016. Challenging Identity Hierarchies: Consociational Power-Sharing and Gendered Political Representation. *British Journal of Politics and International Relations* 18 (3): 618–633.

J. Thomson, *Abortion Law and Political Institutions*, Gender and Politics, https://doi.org/10.1007/978-3-319-96169-9_6

gender actors have been a marginal force in the new Assembly. This has led to a lack of movement around gendered issues such as abortion, and a general disillusionment with politics within the community of pro-choice activists.

Consociationalism and Gender

As Edwards points out, consociationalism dominates the debate on Northern Ireland "to such an extent that it can rarely be avoided by students of Northern Irish politics" (Edwards 2007). Power-sharing of various ilks was implicit to both the Sunningdale Agreement of 1973 and the short-lived Assembly of the 1980s, but had little impact on the conflict at these points. An understanding of consociational power-sharing was fundamental in movements towards peace in the 1990s. The Northern Ireland Assembly as conceived of in the Good Friday Agreement was based on the principles of consociationalism as initially outlined by Arend Lijphart in consideration of his native Netherlands (Lijphart 1977). According to his definition, consociationalist democracies can vary, but follow four basic principles:

1. *Executive power-sharing* (*EPS*). Each of the main communities shares power, in an executive chosen in accordance with the principles of representative government.
2. *Autonomy or Self-government.* Each enjoys some distinct measure of autonomy, particularly self-government in matters of cultural concern.
3. *Proportionality.* Each is represented proportionally in key public institutions and is a proportional beneficiary of public resources and expenditures.
4. *Veto rights.* Each is able to prevent changes that adversely affect their vital interests (Lijphart 1977).

In the words of John McGarry and Brendan O'Leary, the main academic proponents of this theory for Northern Ireland, "consociationalist theory has been a central part of Northern Ireland's 'meta-conflict', that is, the intellectual conflict about the nature of the conflict and the appropriate prescriptions to tackle it" (McGarry and O'Leary 2004). McGarry and O'Leary remain the intellectual heavyweights behind the justification for this framework of the new iteration of devolved governance at

Stormont, based on their now "most Orthodox explanation of the Northern Ireland conflict" (Edwards 2007), a belief in the bi-nationalism of Northern Irish society (see variously McGarry and O'Leary 1995, 2004, 2009). Their work remains as adamant now as it did over twenty years ago that, given that "Northern Ireland is best understood as a bi-national place" (McGarry and O'Leary 2009, 25), consociationalism is the only practical means possible for Northern Irish governance.[1]

McGarry and O'Leary build upon Lijphart's original ideas, in the sense that they consider themselves "critical supporters rather than slavish disciples" (McGarry and O'Leary 2004, 2) of his work. In their consideration of Northern Ireland, they diverge from Lijphart's original model in significant ways. They view the Northern Irish conflict, and the societal divisions that remain, as fundamentally *ethno-national* in scope (McGarry and O'Leary 1995). They argue that, thus far, consociationalism has largely viewed power-sharing in terms of ethnic or religious groupings. It has largely neglected the way that power-sharing might emerge in pluri-nationalist settings such as Northern Ireland. Lijphart's original model was largely based on Western liberal democracies (Switzerland, Belgium, the Netherlands) in which McGarry and O'Leary argue there was an overarching nationalism amongst the differing ethnic and linguistic groupings. They add to his model by proposing that opposing nationalisms can also be accommodated within consociational settings.

They further argue that "classic" consociational thinking has treated political systems as though they were "sealed entities, immune from exogenous factors" (McGarry and O'Leary 2009, 37). Lijphart believed that if a state's differing communities were aware of an external threat, they would be more likely to find an internal settlement (ibid.). McGarry and O'Leary argue that external actors have helped to bring about consociationalism in the Northern Irish case, due largely to the actions and interventions of London and Dublin, but also the developing role of the USA, particularly in the 1990s.

They argue finally that in traditional consociationalist views, there has been too strong an emphasis placed on political settlements and the design of institutional governance, at the expense of considering larger problems facing societies transitioning from periods of conflict to peace. Important for a broader picture of consociationalist governance is a consideration of, variously: the design of the security forces, treatment of displaced peoples or refugees, the demilitarisation of state and paramilitary forces, how to integrate former paramilitaries into society, processes such as truth commissions or newly formed human rights bodies and economic reconstruction (McGarry and O'Leary 2009, 45). In Northern Ireland, considerations of security—especially policing and the decommissioning of weapons—were central to consociational power-sharing as it was understood in the Good Friday Agreement and peace talks. Likewise, bodies such as the Parades Commission (Walsh 2014) and the Northern Irish Human Rights Commission have been important to the devolved institutions. McGarry and O'Leary's contribution to consociational theory as it is understood in the Northern Irish context has therefore been to broaden and contextualise its framework. Their model in Northern Ireland is one of "complex power-sharing" based on liberal consociational principles, as opposed to those defined more rigidly by Lijphart (Wolff 2003, 2011).

Consociationalism in the Northern Irish Model

Consociational power-sharing, as envisioned in the Good Friday Agreement and put to work in the Northern Irish institutions, largely follows Lijphart's outline described above, although with key adaptations which echo McGarry and O'Leary's concerns. The following are the key features of the post-Good Friday Agreement political institutional framework (adapted from O'Leary 2004):

- *Executive power-sharing*
  The Good Friday Agreement provides for a First Minister and Deputy First Minister of the Northern Irish Assembly. Until the St. Andrew's Agreement, both were elected by Assembly Members with successful candidates requiring at least 50% of Nationalist and Unionist members' votes, in addition to a majority of the Assembly as a whole. As O'Leary argues (2004, 263), an incentive was provided to ensure the parties nominate a candidate who is likely to have the support of a majority of the opposing camp. From 2007, they are now nominated by the two largest parties in the Nationalist and Unionist segments, respectively. Furthermore, in spite of the difference in names "both posts have identical symbolic and external representation functions … [and] identical powers" (O'Leary 2004, 264).
- *Proportionality*
  Members are elected to the Assembly through use of the single transferable vote (STV) system. Ministerial positions are divided up according to the D'Hondt formula, meaning that parties nominate Ministers

according to the strength of their position within the Assembly. Proportionality is also extended in the Good Friday Agreement to cover the promotion of equal employment within the public sector and the police force.

- *Communal autonomy and equality*
  "The compulsory integration of peoples" (O'Leary 2004, 270) is avoided in the Good Friday Agreement. Provision is made for equal funding and support for Protestant, Catholic and integrated schools. The Good Friday Agreement carries a strong human rights provision, with support for a Bill of Rights for Northern Ireland to be created. This has, however, yet to come to pass.
- *Minority veto rights*
  Minority rights are further protected in the institutional design of Northern Irish governance by allowing for a minority veto. MLAs must designate as Nationalist, Unionist or Other upon being elected to the Assembly. The veto is largely enshrined through the petition of concern in the Assembly. A petition can be brought by thirty members of the Assembly. Cross-community voting rules are then brought into effect, meaning that a weighted majority of MLAs must vote in favour (an overall majority of MLAs must support the vote, including a majority of both Nationalist and Unionist members present). MLAs who designate as "Other" cannot file a petition meaning that they are "less protected in the Assembly" (O'Leary 2004, 271).

The nature of consociationalism in the Good Friday Agreement therefore largely follows Lijphart's original description but also allows for a more holistic approach to post-conflict management as argued for by McGarry and O'Leary. It is noticeable, however, that certain aspects of the Agreement have endured (notably those more related to the formal political institution such as the petition of concern) whilst others have not (such as the Northern Irish Bill of Rights, which has never been implemented.) Consociationalism has become entrenched in Northern Ireland's political structures but has had less influence on the legal or policy aspects that the Good Friday Agreement provided for.

Critiques of Consociationalism

Of the "new wave"[2] of consociationalist democracies, Northern Ireland "shines as the brightest star in the consociationalist universe" (Taylor 2009, 7). It has become a "model for export" (Wilson 2010), influencing other peace agreements around the world. Consociational institutional design was a fundamental part of reconstruction in both post-war Iraq and Bosnia–Herzegovina (McGarry and O'Leary 2007) and has been discussed as a means of governance in South Sudan, Syria and Cyprus.

Consociationalism as a basis for government does not go unquestioned, however, by a growing body of academics working in the field of Northern Irish politics or post-conflict governance. They view consociationalism as an essentialist understanding of human identity, in that it creates a system where people are defined by their ethnic identity and that alone (Oberschall and Palmer 2005). Critiques of consociationalism argue that it solidifies identity around ethnic categories: reducing "cultural practices and political attitudes to taken-for-granted ethno-national 'communities'" (Wilson 2009, 223; see also Wilford and Wilson 2006). By requiring MLAs to designate as Unionist, Nationalist or Other within the Assembly, these identities are concretised in the new political institution. Indeed, by requiring those who do not identify as Unionist or Nationalist to be designated with the title "Other," not a name of their choosing, they are distanced from Northern Irish politics, with "Other" suggesting a grouping at a significant removal from the mainstream. Further, Wilson argues that in the Northern Irish situation it cements the equation of religious and national identity (Wilson 2010, 189) and thus fails to allow for a real transformation to the conflict. Because identities have been fixed within the political system, a form of "mental partition" (Wilson 2009, 224) occurs in which there is no way for them to be transcended and for common ground to be established. Furthermore, as Tonge acknowledges in the context of a largely pro-consociational argument, "consociationalists are vague over the precise means and timetable for reintegration" (Tonge 2014, 46). Hence, as a structure for governance, consociationalism merely provides a temporary halt to violence (a "benign apartheid" [Nagle and Clancy 2010]) rather than a means to permanently overcome the identity issues at the conflict's base.

Indeed, the anti-consociationalists' belief that consociational governance will further cement the division between the two communities appears to be reflected in voting figures following the Good Friday Agreement. As is discussed in more detail in Chapter 7, the years following the Good Friday Agreement have seen a move "towards more authoritarian political options within each community" (Wilford and

Wilson 2006, 12). Following anti-consociational logic, the new institutions, have created a system based on separate identites and are now seeing the results of this in the make-up of the new Assembly. Not only does McGarry and O'Leary's belief that "it is best to leave consociations to decay organically" (McGarry and O'Leary 2009, 69) not appear to be bearing any immediate fruit in the province, but anti-consociationalists argue that it is the consociational design itself which is impeding identity change.

Perhaps, the most lasting critique of the Good Friday Agreement made by anti-consociationalists is that it has not done what it was supposed to do: reconcile division between the bi-nationalism of Northern Irish life and politics. "Why has the agreement not proved to be a force for reconciliation?" (Wilford and Wilson 2006, 10). As Taylor describes, whilst it has signalled a period of reduced paramilitary violence and political accommodation, "the Agreement has not marked the birth of a 'post-conflict', non-sectarian era" (Taylor 2009, 320). This is played out in empirical evidence from contemporary Northern Ireland. The Department of Justice in Northern Ireland reports that there are 47 "peace" walls[3] in Belfast (Gormley-Heenan and Byrne 2014, 447), whilst the Belfast Interface Project records 97 "security barriers" in the city.[4] Since the Good Friday Agreement, an additional 21 "security barriers" have been built and 18 already in existence have been rebuilt or extended (Gormley-Heenan *et al.* 2013). Less than 7% of schoolchildren attended integrated schooling in 2015–2016 (Wilson 2016). According to the British government, the security threat from paramilitaries in Northern Ireland remains "severe" (Wilson 2016, 46).[5] It is on these facts, anti-consociationalists argue, that the Good Friday Agreement and the consociationalism it brought about should be judged. If it has not acted to end political and social division, then it should not be worthy of the success story reputation that it so widely enjoys in an international setting (Wilson 2010).

McGarry and O'Leary have countered the majority of these claims in their work. Their main riposte to critics is primarily that, in terms of human lives lost, no one can argue that the Agreement is not working: "the Agreement … is clearly causally associated with a highly significant reduction in political violence" (McGarry and O'Leary 2009, 51). Moreover, they argue that the growing influence of Sinn Féin and the DUP is not indicative of a rise in support for "extremist" parties as anti-consociationalists might argue. The Good Friday Agreement, they believe, has brought once "extreme" parties into the fold and helped to facilitate their development into the political mainstream[6]: "There is significant evidence that the policy differences between Sinn Féin and the SDLP have narrowed considerably since the Peace Process began, and since the Agreement" (McGarry and O'Leary 2009, 55). Primarily, however, they argue that the pragmatism of a consociationalist arrangement cannot be bettered. Their advocacy of consociationalism remains grounded in a "concrete analysis of concrete situations" (McGarry and O'Leary 1995, 167). Consociational democracy is realistic because it is based on identities which continue to have resilience in Northern Ireland. In the 2016 Northern Ireland Life and Times Survey, 24% of respondents said that they were "Irish not British" and 21% said that they were "British not Irish" (NILT 2016).[7] As they write, "we believe that the charge of wishful thinking is more accurately directed at integrationists" (McGarry and O'Leary 2004, 19). Furthermore, the liberal features of consociationalism in the Northern Irish example mean that political categories are not prescribed, but freely chosen, with the additional potential of defining as "Other." Consociationalism can adapt to changing identities and also provide for those who subscribe to neither. Consociational government remains therefore, in its proponents' view, best placed to provide stable and representative institutions.

How Is Consociationalism Gendered?

The pro- and anti-consociational argument has largely become entrenched along the above lines. Over twenty years after McGarry and O'Leary's seminal *Explaining Northern Ireland* (1995), the merits versus disadvantages of the consociational framework remain the dominant academic argument about Northern Irish political institutions. Because of the centrality of this debate, there has been less consideration of the various elements of consociation as they have played out in practical terms in Northern Ireland. As a result, consociationalism, both as it has been conceptualised and as it is practised in the region, has under-theorised and under-considered its effect on the "Others."

The emphasis on ethno-national groups as the standard bearers for democratic representation makes it difficult to talk about any other institutional provision for representation via any other political identity (gender, class, etc.) within the remit of consociational thinking.

McGarry and O'Leary's answer to the critique that consociationalism sections off broader debate on political representation is quite simple: there is no evidence to suggest public support for greater inclusion by gender or class, so it does not warrant further inquiry:

> As for the suggestion that consociational politics promotes a superficial ethno-national politics at the expense of more popular questions of class or gender, we submit that there is no evidence, either from public opinion data or from elections, that the latter questions are more popular. If they were, why do people not vote for parties that put such questions at the top of their agenda? (McGarry and O'Leary 2009, 82)

Such a belief portrays an unsophisticated understanding of gender. Looking for evidence of gender disparity through voter preference is markedly ineffective and obscures the more subtle, "barely visible" (Mackay *et al.* 2010, 583) ways in which gender works. McGarry and O'Leary's stipulation here also shows the importance which consociational theory places on party politics. Party politics is only one way in which citizens' opinions can be gleaned. To conflate party preference with interest in gender or class-based issues ignores the broader institutional framework of formal politics, which may be structurally biased against such concerns. McGarry and O'Leary's stipulation that there is no "evidence" for a societal appreciation of gendered issues also reflects an epistemological mismatch between consociational thinking and gender politics: there is plenty of "evidence" to suggest that the public are aware of gendered issues (and want change: see Tables 3.10 and 3.11 in Chapter 3 regarding public opinion on abortion). Consociational theorists may simply not be looking in the right places.

Consociationalism, in both theory and practice, has thus been especially gender blind.[8] In later writing, consociational theory gives slightly greater consideration to gender and how inclusion of women in formal politics might be encouraged, primarily via the use of electoral quotas:

> For some, supporting women's political quotas might, indeed, appear to be the antithesis of consociationalism, but in what sense are ethnic identities less 'progressive' than those based on gender? Why are gender quotas apparently less challenging to equality than consociation? Why are some 'essences' better than others? (McCrudden and O'Leary 2013, 11)

This discussion is, however, brief, appearing only in a footnote in the original text, and has generated little further thinking on gender from key consociationalist thinkers. The gendered implications of ethno-national power-sharing have largely gone unconsidered.

As a result of this, consociational theory ignores the vast amount of research which has illustrated both the gendered effects of conflict and the inordinate effect that conflict has on women. Indeed, feminist research often presents a broader account of conflict than mainstream literature allows for. As Bell and O'Rourke note, "While feminists acknowledge that 'the' conflict is significant, and may indeed be at the vanguard of movements to end the conflict, they also tend to ask questions about the nature of political conflicts: whether there is one conflict or many and how levels of public and private conflict intertwine in women's lives" (2007, 38). Conflict can entail a range of offences which may not be immediately understood as part of the violence it brings, but which can have devastating effects for the female population—rape, sexual abuse and domestic violence. There can also be a strong "gendered division of labour" (Racioppi and See 2006, 190) in conflict, where men mobilise externally, leaving women relegated to the domestic and private realm. Equally, although conflict can sometimes disrupt social relations and bring women into the public sphere (as in the UK in the First World War, for example) women's contributions are regularly marginalised in the aftermath of conflict (Enloe 1993; Meintjes *et al.* 2001; Ni Aolain *et al.* 2011). The space opened up for women's political liberation can disappear following warfare, as social relations revert to old practices.

Furthermore, a significant amount of literature has addressed Northern Ireland specifically regarding the gendered nature of the conflict and post-conflict era. Sales (1997a, b), Ward (2002, 2006), and Racioppi and See (2000, 2001) have detailed the ways in which unionist politics was, and continues to be, part of an "ethno-gendered" order in Northern Ireland. Racioppi and See argue that gender and ethnicity are mutually reinforcing in the Northern Irish context, across both nationalist and unionist communities: "gender identities and roles are crucial in sustaining the ethnic loyalties and boundaries that harden during protracted conflict, and ethnicity infuses gender identities and interests" (2006, 190). This belief underpins the vast majority of feminist literature on Northern Ireland, so that an understanding of gender cannot be separated from an understanding of the conflict more broadly. Ashe (2006, 2007, 2009a, b, 2012, 2014) has continued this into a post-conflict setting, looking at the ways in which gendered language and discourse continues to reinforce Northern Irish politics and society. She argues that men and men's experiences have continued to define both the historical understanding of the conflict and the post-conflict environment, to the detriment of a wider understanding of the effect that the Troubles had on women (2014). This is further reflected in literature which illustrates the difficulties women have had in establishing themselves in post-conflict politics and society, as Northern Ireland establishes peace. In addition to the well-established literature considering women and formal politics in Northern Ireland (Braniff and Whiting 2015; Cowell-Meyers 2003, 2011; Galligan 2006, 2013; Matthews 2014; Murtagh 2008), Gilmartin (2015), also argues that republican women who held active, combat roles have struggled to be included politically following the Good Friday Agreement (see also McEvoy 2010). As McLeod notes, there is a "long held feminist awareness that wars don't just end" (2015, 147) and that the gendered effects of conflict reach into society long after fighting has ceased. Northern Ireland is a key example of this. The gendered nature of the region's contemporary social and political history underpinned both the conflict and the post-conflict situations, even if this is largely unacknowledged by the mainstream literature.

Although the institutional relationship to these gendered issues is under-theorised, a growing body of work in the social sciences has begun to emphasise the gap that exists around gender issues and the manner in which consociational political structures inhibit discussion (Byrne and McCulloch 2012; Hayes and McAllister 2013; Hoewer 2013; Kennedy *et al.* 2016), in addition to the ways in which specific features of the consociational framework are used to avoid gendered issues (such as the use of the petition of concern to repeatedly avoid legislating on same-sex marriage: Thomson 2015). Academic work has also emphasised the difference that exists between men and women's perception of the consociational institutions in Northern Ireland (Hayes and McAllister 2013), with women displaying a greater lack of trust and support for these bodies, and this gendered difference growing since the Good Friday Agreement.

Yet, with ethno-national identity dominating the framework of post-Good Friday Agreement institutions there is little space for any other understanding of identity or difference (Racioppi and See 2006). Equality of representation and the legitimacy of political institutions has become framed solely around the ethno-national paradigm. Attempting to politicise cross-community issues around gender is difficult. A "gendered logic of appropriateness" (Chappell 2006) exists within the formal political institution where cross-cutting gendered issues fall behind ethno-national ones in terms of importance. Conceptually, therefore, the consociational model in Northern Ireland can be found wanting in terms of its ability to address gendered issues and equal political representation. The prescription for post-conflict governance (power-sharing between nationalists and unionists) was inadequate, because the diagnosis of the fault lines of conflict was incomplete (it did not pay enough attention to gendered concerns [Kennedy *et al.* 2016]). The rest of this chapter considers how the gendered implications of consociationalism played out in practice in the new Assembly, with especial regard to abortion.

Gender Actors in the New Assembly

In the post-Good Friday Agreement landscape "a commitment to gendered equality of outcomes is far from realised" (Wilford and Galligan 1999, 182) by the major political actors. Whilst the literature on women's descriptive representation in post-Good Friday Agreement Northern Ireland is well-developed (Galligan 2006, 2013; Matthews 2014), there has been less consideration of "gender actors" (Waylen 2014, 297) in the processes of post-conflict governance in Northern Ireland. In this section, firstly, women's descriptive representation in the new Northern Irish assembly is considered, and secondly, their role as "gender actors" (ibid.) within the assembly is discussed.

"A Very Strange Job for a Female": Where Are the Women?[9]

Women have, since the advent of the new Assembly, been a minority (see Table 2.1). They have also not been an especially distinct group, with early research into female and male MLAs' voting interests illustrating no great gendered distinction (Cowell-Meyers 2003). Unsurprisingly perhaps, differences emerged only in the MLAs' perception of gender discrimination, with women more conscious than men of its existence, and women more liberal on social gender roles (Galligan 2006, 217). Furthermore, from the beginning of the new Assembly, it appears that it has been difficult to facilitate any kind of community amongst female MLAs. The Alliance MLA Eileen Bell formed a cross-party caucus in the first administration but Unionist women were reticent to join when Sinn Féin were present (Galligan 2006, 215). Some female MLAs also reported "resentment" at the presence of the "Janey-come-latelys" (Cowell-Meyers 2003, 8) of the NIWC and the way that their emergence potentially overshadowed women in the established political parties. In interviews conducted in 2003 by Cowell-Meyers, female MLAs seemed pessimistic about the possibility of a cross-coalition women's group forming in the first Assembly: "At this stage, it doesn't have a big enough priority or a big impact to be of any specific use" (Cowell-Meyers 2003, 8). However, some women seemed to think that as the Assembly evolves, women would reach out across the political divide and that a women's caucus might be more probable in the future. Cowell-Meyers seemed confident enough to suggest in 2003 that, "over time, these experiences may encourage women to become comfortable in informal cross-party coalitions around common interests and thus, may sow the seeds of further and more extensive collective action" (ibid., 10).

Interview data from contemporary MLAs strongly refutes this however. When asked if there was any community of women MLAs from across parties, one MLA responded that:

> … it never happens because first and foremost you're a member of a political party before you're a female. You got elected as a member of a political party not as yourself … First and foremost we're members of political parties and if you have a problem you go to your party, if you have an idea you go to someone in your party … I want to bring a motion forward to do with actually sexual health, in a couple of weeks' time. Instead of going to other female members or going to other members of the APG on sexual health, I'd go to my party and say 'ok I'm going to do this, what way am I going to word it.'[10]

From her experience, party remains the clearest organisational body in the new Assembly. Another female MLA concurred, but linked the notion of a women's caucus to certain All-Party Groups (APGs)[11] in the Assembly:

> Not really. Ok, there are all party groups, there is an APG on, can't remember what they're called - 13? Sexual health? And the other is – I don't know, I can't even remember what it's called, how bad is that.[12]

The MLA's response to this question suggests that certain groups, particularly those more closely associated with "women's issues," such as sexual health and UNSCR 1325, formed an informal women's caucus. Yet the gender make-up of both these groups is mixed—50/50 on the All-Party Group on Sexual Health and 60/40 on the All-Party Group on 1325. From 2016 there is now a Northern Ireland Women's Caucus within the Assembly which draws members from across the major political parties. This, however, has been instigated by an NGO as part of a broader package of programmes around women in public life, not by the institution itself nor any of the parties, suggesting that change is more easily encouraged by extra-institutional bodies.[13]

Furthermore, there has been a consistent sense across the literature on women in the Northern Ireland Assembly that they occupy positions within the government that are of lesser importance. Interviews in 2000 suggested that many female MLAs felt that sexist stereotypes were at play in parties' decision regarding what committees women should sit on: "People don't see women as real politicians" (Cowell-Meyers 2003). Regarding the Health Committee, one female MLA despaired, "Were women put on that committee by their parties because they think that nurse, health, you know, women? Are we going to be wipers of noses and cleaners of bottoms?" (Cowell-Meyers 2003, 7) Bríd Rogers, Agriculture Minister in the first Assembly, declared that "When they were giving out the ministerial portfolios at the Assembly, the two [SDLP] women were given the two that nobody else wanted" (Galligan 2006, 215).

Indeed, this was reflected in worries that present-day female MLAs expressed about their role. Several contemporary female MLAs raised the concern that if they spoke out on gender issues specifically, they would be labelled as "female" politicians and taken less seriously by male colleagues.

> So sometimes when you're trying to put issues forwards … [you] just think are they gonna be "here she goes again, here she goes again", and then you get frightened of getting pigeon holed. That was another fear I had, because at the beginning they [her party] were like "we want you to go on the sexual health APG, we want you to go on the 1325 APG, we want you to do this" - but I don't know about these issues. I know about lots of other issues … Why am I being pushed forward into these female issues?[14]

> [on not attending either the APG on sexual health or UNSCR 1325] I don't want particularly to be labelled … I might have a view but I don't want to be put up on a pedestal as an example of something or other, I suppose I prefer to work on the ground and to talk to individuals rather than to stand up and preach. So I suppose that's just my way of working.[15]

Women MLAs therefore remain very aware of their status as *women* representatives, worried that they will be "pigeon-holed" if they act in a way that might draw attention to this. Although the stereotyping that MLAs describe is not unique to Northern Ireland there appears little effort to tackle it from within the institution itself, nor from political parties. The formal structure is doing little to address the issue of gendered representation from the inside, with the main measure taken to tackle it so far (the Women's Caucus) the work of an exogenous entity. Women's representation has not been seen as a key issue which the Assembly itself needs to address.

"You Might as Well Be a Man": Are/Were Women Good Gender Actors?

The limited number of women who have been elected to the Northern Irish Assembly makes it difficult to come to any conclusions about whether or not they have had a positive impact on gender issues. Women, as gender actors, do seem to have had some limited impact on issues of gender. The NIWC spearheaded efforts to ensure a family-friendly timetable in the new Assembly (Fegan and Rebouche 2006, 291; Galligan 2006, 215) and were keen to support the creation of a children's commissioner in Northern Ireland (Fearon 1999, 138). They also provided a different perspective in debates. In 2002, a Bill was introduced to adopt adultery in Northern Irish law as acceptable grounds for divorce and to reduce the period of separation necessary to prove irretrievable breakdown from 5 to 3 years (Fegan and Rebouche 2006, 291). In her contribution to the debate, NIWC MLA Monica McWilliams' speech "focused much more on the practicalities involved in relationship breakdown than any philosophical discursive on the social role and sanctity of marriage" as other Members had been wont to do (ibid., 292).

Contemporary female MLAs interviewed for this research often stressed the different perspective that they brought to formal politics, largely in terms of their differing career paths to their male counterparts.

One MLA related her pro-choice stance directly to her previous work as the Director of an NGO which had been involved in helping young people access services through the FPA and sometimes providing translation services in both Northern Ireland and, if necessary, for young women seeking abortions in England.[16] Another said that originally public office "wasn't something I ever – ever, ever - thought I would be or do in my lifetime, never interested me, politics actually really didn't interest me" but that, "if it all ended tomorrow I'd go back to my old life [previous career] and I would enjoy that every bit as much." She went on to say that:

> I think that's good, that gives a different quality and a different – you have to have that because some of the things we discuss in here especially like welfare reform and things like that you look at it in a different way. I do certainly, and say 'hey you know I remember what it was like to be a single mum with two kids you know, [if] we bring that rule in, it's going to really hit hard with females' [sic]. So there's been loads of things that's happened because we have females here in the assembly, a few more would be good.[17]

There is therefore a sense from some female representatives that they approach their role with a feminist sense of acting for other women and speaking out on issues which inadvertently affect the female population.

Yet the limited number of women in the Assembly and the minimal movement on abortion legislation which has happened means that it is difficult to extrapolate on how influential women have been on debates around the issue. With party loyalty appearing to trump any gendered identity, in the words of one pro-choice activist, women MLAs "do look like token women and when they are privately telling you that they're pro-choice but they have to toe the party line because they're told what to do, how to do it and what to say then what's the point – you might as well be a man."[18] Indeed, the little *positive* movement on abortion at all, and over a relatively long period of time, added to the relative dearth of female representatives, means that it is difficult to judge. Whilst the majority of the most vocal pro-life MLAs are male, Iris Robinson DUP MLA was loudly pro-life and the key figure in overturning the 2007 guidelines (see Chapter 7). Similarly, of the two MLAs in the 2011–2016 administration who called for the extension of the 1967 Act, one was male (Stephen Agnew, Green MLA) and one female (Anna Lo, Alliance MLA).

Liberal voices around abortion have not been solely associated with female politicians. Within the institution, actors are still encouraged to "toe the party line" on the issue which, given the ethno-national dominance of the party structure, inhibits a cross-cutting sense of women as a political community unto themselves.

"They're Not Even Pretending to Make This Place Function": Disillusionment with Formal Politics and Pro-choice Activism

As a result of the general absence of positive gender actors, the pro-choice message has had difficulty in finding a voice in the new Assembly, whilst the pro-life equivalent is firmly established within the institution. An All-Party Pro-Life Group was established in the early 2000s and was active until mid-2015. The pro-life organisation Precious Life provided the secretariat for the group. As of early 2015, its population was all-male. All-party groups (APGs) "provide a forum by which MLAs and outside organisations and individuals can meet to discuss shared interests in a particular cause or subject."[19] They have no legislative or consultative powers and instead provide a sounding board for cross-party interests and the facilitation of information from NGOs and civil society organisations. Attendance is not as consistent compared to Committees. In the words of one member of the APG on Sexual Health, "we only ever have 2 members turn up, sometimes 3 … nobody turns up for them, so you can't go by the membership of it, you go by the attendance of it."[20] Yet interview data suggested that the APG on pro-life enjoyed a relatively high level and consistency of attendance compared to other groups.[21] According to one MLA, it was "one of the more useful and one of the more active groups."[22] The social conservative leanings of the major political parties mean that this provides a rare area in which cross-communal work is possible.

Yet this appears much more difficult to foster with regard to pro-choice activists. Whilst an All-party group on Sexual Health has also been established, and for which the Secretariat is provided by the FPA Northern Ireland, abortion is clearly "off-topic." The group does not seem to enjoy as consistent attendance and support when compared to the All-Party Pro-life Group.[23] When asked if abortion was ever discussed at the Sexual Health APG, one MLA who regularly attends said:

> Never. Rarely. I don't think we've ever discussed it so long as I've been on the committee. I don't think it's been on the agenda, it's been more to do with the promotion of sexual health.[24]

Similarly, the Director of the FPA declared that abortion was off limits, and even setting up a group around the issue of sexual health had been difficult:

> We don't do abortion on it. ... You have to have 12 cross party MLAs. It took us a year to recruit 12 MLAs. And the only reason I was able to do that, [was that] this [the APG] was just on sexual health ... So we're very clear about the boundaries there. So the sexual health [APG] is not about reproductive health as such so abortion is not on the agenda for it. *If abortion had been on the agenda we would never have got it off the ground but whereas because we've got it off the ground sexual health is seen as a public health area.* (emphasis added)[25]

Discussion of abortion has largely only been possible from a pro-life perspective, even in the context of APGs, which act more as a sounding board for presentations from civil society and informal cross-party policy discussion, rather than having any real legislative power.

Activists from Alliance for Choice, the main lobbying group around abortion in the province, also reported difficulties and frustrations in trying to connect with Stormont over this issue. Interviews continually threw up the sentiment felt by activists that they had no "in" to formal politics in the province and that it only presented them with a dead end:

> We cannot get in, we have no voice up there ... We have exhausted the influence of the political end.[26]

> [re: trying to organise and promote discussion with MLAs at Stormont] I think you can only bang your head off the brick wall for so long.[27]

Activists were frustrated by the make-up of Stormont in terms of the backgrounds and interests of its Members:

> [Stormont is made up of] rich councillors and farmers and public figures. It's not people who are interested in government because of community work and evidence based social policy or anything like that, and that's the problem I think.[28]

Continuing, the activist linked this to the wider problem of Northern Irish institutions and the way in which they function:

> … *the structure's so badly set up in the first place, the political system is so malfunctioning*, that you can't reform anything cos it's almost impossible.[29] (emphasis added)

The activist went on to describe how difficult it was to mobilise the Assembly around gendered or women's issues:

> … our [political] representation ignores any other kind of community, whether it's community of place or community of interest. So women's interests in general, social justice issues in general, have been ignored cos it's more about this notion of achieving parity [between ethno-national communities] and that's the top level of importance. So before peace, there's 'oh we can't talk about anything else because we need to sort out peace' and then once whatever version we have of peace now, it's 'oh we can't talk about anything else because we don't wanna upset the status quo'.[30]

In this activist's experience, ethno-national communal concerns take priority as a political concern. Women's issues face a difficulty in being heard by formal politics, especially given the inference that they might "upset the status quo" and damage an already fragile peace. Pro-choice activists thus find little hope in the political structures and parties of Northern Ireland. Formal politics inspires neither hope nor trust in the members of pro-choice groups, nor does it appear to offer the mechanisms by which such perspectives might be heard.

Conclusion

Political structures matter (Htun 2003) in that the shape they take limits the scope of discussion. This chapter has illustrated how, following the devolution of substantial powers to Northern Ireland in 1998, the consociational make-up of the new Northern Irish Assembly affects formal political discussion of abortion. There is a "gendered logic of appropriateness" (Chappell 2006) to post-Good Friday Agreement politics in Northern Ireland in that the consociational structure renders it difficult to move beyond ethno-national issues and to address concerns which cut across both communities. Northern Irish contemporary politics remain "nested" (Chappell 2014; Mackay 2014) in a two-community model of the province which acts to disincentivise "other" political identities and concerns. The formal "rules of the game" (Krook and Mackay 2011, 1) are thus structured so that a hierarchy of identity exists, in which ethno-national identities dominate.

Due to this emphasis on the politics of communal identity, politicising gendered issues has been difficult. As Waylen writes, "it helps if gender issues are framed strategically in ways that resonate in that political climate" (Waylen 2009, 251). Due to the cross-cutting nature of women's concerns and political identity, this has proven difficult in the Northern Irish political institutions as they struggle to resonate in the ethnonational framework. Women's representation has remained small, with little institutional attempt to address the lack of female politicians, and a general absence of action around gendered issues from representatives. Furthermore, this also influences the type of citizen and civil society involvement which is possible. The pro-choice community has struggled to engage formal politics in its campaign, and there has been little influence from the pro-choice message on formal politics.

The pro- vs. anti-consociational debate within the literature on Northern Ireland and beyond is now firmly cemented within thinking on power-sharing. For consociational adherents, "good fences make good neighbours" (McGarry and O'Leary 1993, 16): for those of the anti-consociational persuasion, "high fences do not make good, but rather mistrustful neighbours" (Wilson 2009, 235). The debate has rarely moved beyond these stark lines in the sand. In spite of the largely critical tone used to address consociationalism in this chapter, this book does not take a position on either side of this debate. Instead, it argues for a different direction in consociational thinking, forwarding a consideration of the gendered implications of consociational power-sharing. Gender is all but completely ignored in consociational arguments (McGarry and O'Leary 1995; Taylor 2009; Tonge 2014) yet, as this chapter showed, as a framework for governance it carries distinct gender blind-spots. As a result, there are structural, institutional difficulties in mobilising around political gender issues.

Moving on from the structural, macro focus of this chapter, the following chapter addresses the more micro-level of Northern Irish formal politics, by looking at how debates within the Assembly have discussed the issue of abortion.

Notes

1. Their work on consociationalism has also led to an involvement in the promotion of consociational power-sharing as a response to further global conflict, including post-war Iraq. Both have been advisors to key international bodies including the United Nations, the United Kingdom Department for International Development and the Kurdistan National Assembly (For one such example see McGarry *et al.* 2006).
2. Taylor defines the following countries as the "new wave" of "strong consociational cases": Bosnia–Herzegovina, Burundi, Macedonia, Afghanistan, Iraq, Kenya and Northern Ireland (Taylor 2009, 6).
3. Walls which separate communities of largely one ethno-national make-up from the other.
4. https://www.belfastinterfaceproject.org/sites/default/files/publications/Interfaces%20PDF.pdf. Accessed 8 February 2016. The difference between these two figures is explained by the fact that the DOJ only recognises a peace wall if it is erected by statutory bodies (Nolan 2014, 70).
5. In the 2010s, there have been several high-profile murders by dissident Republicans: prison officer David Black was shot on his way to work in 2012; in 2009 two off-duty soldiers were killed, and two other soldiers and two delivery men injured in an attack on the Massereene army barracks for which the Real IRA claimed responsibility; and in 2016 a prison officer was killed following a bomb planted under his car.
6. Also echoed in Mitchell *et al.*, who argue that, in spite of the electoral turn to "extremes" in Northern Ireland post-GFA, the structure of the parliament necessitates a pragmatism on both sides and creates "centripetal dynamics that inhibit outbidding" (2009, 397).
7. See Table 3.8, p. 66.
8. This is reflected not only in the normative underpinnings of the theory itself, but also the makeup of those academics discussing it. The edited collection by Taylor, *Consociational Theory* (2009), for example, brings together scholars working on this issue all over the world yet contains not one essay by a woman.
9. This phrase is consciously adopted from Cynthia Enloe's *Beaches and Bases: making feminist sense of international relations* (1990, 133).
10. Unionist MLA. Private interview with the author, Belfast. February 2014.
11. All-party groups provide forums for MLAs from various parties to meet to discuss policy issues. They cannot produce legislation. Discussed in more detail on p. 178.
12. It is assumed that the MLA was incorrectly referring to the All-Party Group on UNSCR1325. Unionist MLA. Private interview with the author, Belfast. March 2014.

13. The Caucus was brought about by Politics Plus, a Belfast based NGO. http://politicsplus.com/news-item/northern-ireland-womens-caucus/. Accessed 8 February 2018.
14. Unionist MLA. Private interview with the author, Belfast. February 2014.
15. Unionist MLA. Private interview with the author, Belfast. March 2014.
16. Non-designated MLA. Private interview with the author, Belfast. February 2014.
17. Unionist MLA. Private interview with the author, Belfast. February 2014.
18. Pro-choice activist. Private interview with the author, Belfast. March 2014.
19. http://www.niassembly.gov.uk/your-mlas/all-party-groups/. Accessed 18 May 2018.
20. Unionist MLA. Private interview with the author, Belfast. February 2014.
21. Nationalist MLA, Belfast, March 2014, Unionist MLA, Belfast, March 2014, Unionist MLA, Belfast, March 2014.
22. Unionist MLA. Private interview with the author, Belfast. March 2014.
23. Unionist MLA. Private interview with the author, Belfast. February 2014.
24. The absence of abortion as a topic for discussion on the APG on Sexual Health was also reiterated in an interview with an Administrative Director for an MLA affiliated to the group. Belfast, February 2014.
25. Director of the FPA Northern Ireland. Private interview with the author, Belfast. March 2014.
26. Pro-choice activist. Private interview with the author, Belfast. March 2014.
27. Pro-choice activist. Private interview with the author, Belfast. March 2014.
28. Pro-choice activist. Private interview with the author, Belfast. March 2014.
29. Pro-choice activist. Private interview with the author, Belfast. March 2014.
30. Pro-choice activist. Private interview with the author, Belfast. March 2014.

Bibliography

Ashe, F. 2006. The McCartney Sisters' Search for Justice: Gender and Political Protest in Northern Ireland. *Politics* 26 (3): 161–170.

———. 2007. Gendering Ethno-Nationalist Politics in Northern Ireland. *Ethnic and Racial Studies* 30 (5): 766–786.

———. 2009a. Iris Robinson's Excitable Speech: Sexuality and Conflict Transformation in Northern Ireland. *Journal of Politics* 29 (1): 20–27.

———. 2009b. From Paramilitaries to Peacemakers: The Gender Dynamics of Community-Based Restorative Justice in Northern Ireland. *British Journal of Politics and International Relations* 11 (2): 298–314.

———. 2012. Gendering War and Peace: Militarized Masculinities in Northern Ireland. *Men and Masculinities* 15 (3): 230–248.

———. 2014. Gendering Demilitarisation and Justice in Northern Ireland. *British Journal of Politics and International Relations* 17 (4) (November): 665–680.

Bell, Christine, and Catherine O'Rourke. 2007. Does Feminism Need a Theory of Transitional Justice? An Introductory Essay. *International Journal of Transitional Justice* 1 (1): 23–44.

Braniff, Maire, and Sophie Whiting. 2015. There's Just No Point Having a Token Woman: Gender and Representation in the Democratic Unionist Party in Post-agreement Northern Ireland. *Parliamentary Affairs* 69 (1): 93–114.

Byrne, Siobhan, and Allison McCulloch. 2012. Gender, Representation and Power-Sharing in Post Conflict Institutions. *International Peacekeeping* 19 (5): 565–580.

Chappell, Louise. 2006. Comparing Political Institutions: Revealing the Gendered 'Logic of Appropriateness'. *Politics and Gender* 2 (2): 232–235.

———. 2014. 'New', 'Old' and 'Nested' Institutions and Gender Justice Outcomes: A View from the International Criminal Court. *Politics and Gender* 10 (4): 572–594.

Cowell-Meyers, Kimberley. 2003. Women Legislators in Northern Ireland: Gender and Politics in the New Legislative Assembly. http://www.qub.ac.uk/cawp/research/assembly.PDF. Accessed 21 April 2015.

———. 2011. A Collarette on a Donkey: The Northern Ireland Women's Coalition and the Limitations of Contagion Theory. *Political Studies* 59 (2): 411–431.

Edwards, A. 2007. Interpreting the Conflict in Northern Ireland. *Ethnopolitics* 6 (1): 137–144.

Enloe, Cnythia. 1990. *Beaches and Bases: Making Feminist Sense of International Relations.* Berkeley: University of California Press.

———. 1993. *The Morning After: Sexual politics at the End of the Cold War.* Berkeley: University of California Press.

Fearon, Kate. 1999. *Women's Work: The Story of the Northern Ireland Women's Coalition.* Belfast: Blackstaff Press.

Fegan, Eileen V., and Rachel Rebouche. 2006. What Happened to the Women? In *A Farewell to Arms.* Manchester: Manchester University Press.

Galligan, Yvonne. 2006. Women in Northern Ireland's Politics: Feminizing an 'Armed Patriarchy'. In *Representing Women in Parliament: A Comparative Study*, ed. Marian Sawer, Manon Tremblay, and Linda Trimble. Abingdon: Routledge.

———. 2013. Gender and Politics in Northern Ireland: The Representation Gap Revisited. *Irish Political Studies* 28 (3): 413–433.

Gilmartin, Niall. 2015. Negotiating New Roles. *International Feminist Journal of Politics* 17 (1): 58–76.

Gormley-Heenan, Cathy, and Jonny Byrne. 2014. Beyond the Walls: Dismantling Belfast's Conflict Architecture. *City: Analysis of Urban Trends, Culture, Theory, Policy, Action* 18 (4–5): 447–454.

Gormley-Heenan, Cathy, and Paula Devine. 2010. The 'Us' in Trust: Who Trusts Northern Ireland's Political Institutions and Actors? *Government and Opposition* 45 (2): 143–165.

Gormley-Heenan, Cathy, Jonny Byrne, and Gillian Robinson. 2013. The Berlin Walls of Belfast. *British Politics* 8 (3): 357–382.

Hayes, Bernadette, and Ian McAllister. 2013. Gender and Consociational Power-Sharing in Northern Ireland. *International Political Science Review* 343 (2): 123–139.

Hoewer, Melanie. 2013. UN Resolution 1325 in Ireland: Limitations and Opportunities of the International Framework on Women, Peace and Security. *Irish Political Studies* 28 (3): 450–468.

Htun, Mala. 2003. *Sex and the State: Abortion Divorce and the Family Under Latin American Dictatorships and Democracies.* Cambridge: Cambridge University Press.

Kennedy, Ronan, Claire Pierson, and Jennifer Thomson. 2016. Challenging Identity Hierarchies: Consociational Power-Sharing and Gendered Political Representation. *British Journal of Politics and International Relations* 18 (3): 618–633.

Krook, Mona Lena, and Fiona Mackay. 2011. Introduction: Gender, Politics and Institutions. In *Gender, Politics and Institutions: Towards a Feminist Institutionalism*. Basingstoke: Palgrave Macmillan.

Lijphart, Arend. 1977. *Democracy in Plural Societies: A Comparative Exploration.* New Haven: Yale University Press.

Mackay, Fiona. 2014. Nested Newness, Institutional Innovation, and the Gendered Limits of Change. *Politics and Gender* 10: 549–571.

Mackay, Fiona, Meryl Kenny, and Louise Chappell. 2010. New Institutionalism Through a Gender Lens: Towards a Feminist Institutionalism? *International Political Science Review* 31 (5): 573–588.

Matthews, Neil. 2014. Gendered Candidate Selection and the Representation of Women in Northern Ireland. *Parliamentary Affairs* 67 (3): 617–646.

McCrudden, Christopher, and Brendan O'Leary. 2013. *Courts and Consociations: Human Rights Versus Power-Sharing.* Oxford: Oxford University Press.

McEvoy, Sandra. 2010. Loyalist Women Paramilitaries in Northern Ireland: Beginning a Feminist Conversation About Conflict Resolution. In *Gender and International Security: Feminist Perspectives*, ed. Laura Sjoberg. Abingdon: Routledge.

McGarry, John (ed.). 2001. *Northern Ireland and the Divided World: The Northern Ireland Conflict and the Good Friday Agreement in Comparative Perspective.* Oxford: Oxford University Press.

———. 2007. Iraq's Constitution of 2005: Liberal Consociation as Political Prescription. *International Journal of Constitutional Law* 5 (4): 670–698.

McGarry, John, and Brendan O'Leary. 1993. Introduction: The Macro-Political Regulation of Ethnic Conflict. In *The Politics of Ethnic Conflict Regulation*, ed. John McGarry and Brendan O'Leary, 1–40. Abingdon: Routledge.

———. 1995. *Explaining Northern Ireland*. Edinburgh: Blackwell.

———. 1996. *The Politics of Antagonism: Understanding Northern Ireland*. London: Athlone Press.

———. 2004. *The Northern Ireland Conflict: Consociational* Engagements. Oxford: Oxford University Press.

———. 2009. Part 1. Argument. Power-Shared After the Deaths of Thousands. In *Consociational Theory: McGarry-O'Leary and the Northern Ireland Conflict*, ed. R. Taylor, 13–84. Abingdon: Routledge.

McGarry, John, Brendan O'Leary, and Khaled Salih (eds.). 2006. *The Future of Kurdistan in Iraq*. Philadelphia: University of Pennsylvania Press.

McLeod, Laura. 2015. *Gender Politics and Security Discourse: Personal-Political Imaginations and Feminism in 'Post-Conflict' Serbia*. London: Routledge.

Meintjes, Sheila, Anu Pillay, and Merdeth Turshen (eds.). 2001. *The Aftermath: Women in Post-conflict Transformation*. London: Zed.

Mitchell, P., G. Evans, and B. O'Leary. 2009. Extremist Outbidding in Ethnic Party Systems Is Not Inevitable: Tribune Parties in Northern Ireland. *Political Studies* 57 (2): 397–421.

Murtagh, Cera. 2008. A Transient Transition: The Cultural and Institutional Obstacles Impeding the Northern Ireland Women's Coalition in Its Progression from Informal to Formal Politics. *Irish Political Studies* 23 (1): 21–40.

Nagle, John, and Mary-Alice C. Clancy. 2010. *Shared Society or Benign Apartheid? Understanding Peace-Building in Divided Societies*. Basingstoke: Palgrave Macmillan.

Ní Aoláin, Fionnuala, Dina Francesca Haynes, and Naomi Cahn. 2011. *On the Frontlines: Gender, War and the Post-conflict Process*. Oxford: Oxford University Press.

NILT. 2016. Northern Ireland Life and Times Survey, Various Years. http://www.ark.ac.uk/nilt/. Accessed 11 January 16.

Nolan, Paul. 2014. *Northern Ireland Peace Monitoring Report*. Number Three. http://cain.ulst.ac.uk/events/peace/docs/nipmr_2014-03_1-Intro.pdf. Accessed 8 February 2018.

Oberschall, Anthony, and L. Kendall Palmer. 2005. The Failure of Moderate Politics: The Case of Northern Ireland. In *Powersharing: New Challenges for Divided Societies*, ed. Ian O'Flynn and David Russell. London: Pluto Press.

O'Leary, Brendan. 2004. The Nature of the Agreement. In *The Northern Ireland Conflict: Consociational Engagements*. Oxford: Oxford University Press.

Racioppi, L., and K.O. See. 2000. Ulstermen and Loyalist Ladies on Parade: Gendering Unionism in Northern Ireland. *International Feminist Journal of Politics* 2 (1): 1–29.

———. 2001. "This We Will Maintain": Gender, Ethno-Nationalism and the Politics of Unionism in Northern Ireland. *Nations and Nationalism* 7 (1): 93–112.

———. 2006. Engendering Democratic Transition from Conflict: Women's Inclusion in Northern Ireland's Peace Process. *Comparative Politics* 38 (2): 189–208.

Sales, Rosemary. 1997a. *Women Divided: Gender, Religion and Politics in Northern Ireland.* Abingdon: Routledge.

———. 1997b. Gender and Protestantism in Northern Ireland. In *Who are 'The People'?: Unionism, Protestantism and Loyalism in Northern Ireland*, ed. Peter Shirlow and Mark McGovern. London: Pluto Press.

Taylor, Rupert. 2006. The Belfast Agreement and the Politics of Consociationalism: A Critique. *The Political Quarterly* 77 (2): 217–226.

——— (ed.). 2009. *Consociational Theory: McGarry and O'Leary and the Northern Ireland Conflict.* Abingdon: Routledge.

Thomson, Jennifer. 2015. Abortion and Same-Sex Marriage: How Are Non-sectarian Controversial Issues Discussed in Northern Irish Politics? *Irish Political Studies.* https://doi.org/10.1080/07907184.2015.1103226.

Tonge, Jonathan. 2014. *Comparative Peace Processes.* Cambridge: Polity Press.

Walsh, Dawn. 2014. Northern Ireland and the Independent Parades Commission: Delegation and Legitimacy. *Irish Political Studies* 30 (1): 20–40.

Ward, Rachel. 2002. Invisible Women: The Political Roles of Unionist and Loyalist Women in Contemporary Northern Ireland. *Parliamentary Affairs* 55 (1): 167–178.

———. 2006. *Women, Unionism and Loyalism in Northern Ireland: From 'Tea-Makers' to Political Activists.* Dublin: Irish Academic Press.

Waylen, Georgina. 2008. Feminist Perspectives on Transforming Global Governance: Challenges and Opportunities. In *Global Governance: Feminist Perspectives*, ed. Shirin Rai and Georgina Waylen. London: Palgrave Macmillan.

———. 2009. What Can Historical Institutionalism Offer Feminist Institutionalists? *Politics and Gender* 5 (2): 245–253.

———. 2011. Gendered Institutional Analysis: Understanding Democratic Transitions. In *Gender, Politics and Institutions: Towards a Feminist Institutionalism*, ed. Mona Lena Krook and Fiona Mackay, 147–162. Basingstoke: Palgrave Macmillan.

———. 2014. A Seat at the Table—Is It Enough? Gender, Multiparty Negotiations, and Institutional Design in South African and Northern Ireland. *Politics and Gender* 10: 495–523.

Wilford, Rick, and Yvonne Galligan. 1999. Gender and Party Politics in Northern Ireland. In *Contesting Politics: Women in Ireland, North and South*, ed. Yvonne Galligan, Ellis Ward, and Rick Wilford. Boulder, CO: Westview.

Wilford, Rick, and Robin Wilson. 2006. *The Trouble with Northern Ireland: The Belfast Agreement and Democratic Governance*. Dublin: New Island.

Wilson, Robin. 2009. From Consociationalism to Inter-culturalism. In *Consociational Theory: McGarry and O'Leary in the Northern Ireland Conflict*, ed. R. Taylor. Abingdon: Routledge.

———. 2010. *The Northern Ireland Experience of Conflict and Agreement: A Model for Export?* Manchester: Manchester University Press.

———. 2016. *Northern Ireland Peace Monitoring Report*. https://www.community-relations.org.uk/sites/crc/files/media-files/NIPMR-Final-2016.pdf. Accessed 21 August 2018.

Wolff, Stefan. 2003. *Disputed Territories: The Transnational Dynamics of Ethnic Conflict Settlement*. Oxford: Bergahn Books.

———. 2011. Post-conflict State Building: The Debate on Institutional Choice. *Third World Quarterly* 32 (10): 1777–1802.

———. 2016. *Northern Ireland Peace Monitoring Report*. Number Four. https://www.community-relations.org.uk/sites/crc/files/media-files/NIPMR-Final-2016.pdf. Accessed 8 February 2016.

CHAPTER 7

The Devolved Institution: Stormont

Abortion has been a recurring issue in formal political discussion in the "new" Northern Irish politics post-devolution (Tonge 2005) (Table 7.1). Whilst there has been no substantial change around abortion legislation in the region since the 1945 Criminal Justice (Northern Ireland) Act, as an issue it has maintained a political profile. This chapter considers how abortion has been discussed in the formal political sphere in post-Good Friday Agreement Northern Ireland, following the devolution of substantial powers to the region as part of a UK-wide movement towards multi-level governance (MLG). This chapter looks at debates on abortion in the Northern Ireland Assembly from the year 2000. It then goes on to address the various attempts to produce guidelines on the procedure for medical professionals and the advent of the Marie Stopes clinic in Belfast in 2012 which reignited debate on the issue.

Whilst the previous chapter considered the conceptual basis of the new political arrangements, this chapter looks at the level of debates, language and actors. It draws upon discursive institutional ideas to focus on the agency and workings of individual political figures. As Schmidt writes, "the new institutionalists brought institutions 'back in' but they may have tipped it too far in the other direction … the institutions they have

---

This chapter replicates parts of, and expands upon, Thomson, Jennifer. 2018. Resisting Gendered Change: Feminist Institutionalism and Critical Actors. *International Political Science Review* 39 (2): 178–191.

J. Thomson, *Abortion Law and Political Institutions*, Gender and Politics, https://doi.org/10.1007/978-3-319-96169-9_7

Table 7.1 Timeline of events regarding abortion and the Northern Irish Assembly, 1998–2017

1998	June—Elections for the Northern Irish Assembly take place July—First meeting of the new Assembly
2000	June—The Assembly debate the motion "*That this Assembly is opposed to the extension of the Abortion Act to Northern Ireland.*" Passes by 43 votes to 15
2001	June—The FPA are granted leave by courts in Northern Ireland to seek a judicial review of medical practices relating to abortion and provision of abortion services in the region
2002	March—Judicial review brought by the FPA is heard in the High Court in Belfast October—The Assembly is suspended
2003	July—The FPA lose the judicial review
2004	July—The FPA succeed in their appeal against the judicial review judgement. The Court of Appeal instructs Health Minister Bairbre de Brún (Sinn Féin) to (a) inquire into the adequacy of termination of pregnancy services provided in Northern Ireland (including aftercare) and (b) following such inquiry and after appropriate consultation with concerned organisations, issue appropriate guidance
2007	May—Following the St. Andrew's Agreement, the Assembly is reinstated. Michael McGimpsey MLA (UUP) becomes Health Minister October—The Assembly debates the motion "*That this Assembly opposes the introduction of the proposed guidelines on the termination of pregnancy* in Northern Ireland; believes that the guidelines are flawed; and calls on the Minister of Health, Social Services and Public Safety to abandon any attempt to make abortion more widely available in Northern Ireland." An amendment urging the Health Minister to publish the guidance is also tabled. The motion passes and the guidance is revised as a result
2008	July—Draft guidance is issued for consultation October—The Health Committee convenes and considers the guidance
2009	March—Revised guidance is published June—SPUC seeks a judicial review claiming that the guidance document is illegal on seven counts and misinterprets the law November—Court rules that the guidelines correctly interpret the law. However, it also rules that the parts of the guidance considering non-directive counselling and conscientious objection failed to give clear guidance. As a result, the Court orders the immediate withdrawal of the document
2010	February—An interim document, with the two sections the Court took issue with removed, is released. SPUC initiate a second judicial review of this document February—Justice and policing powers devolved—abortion now part of Northern Irish law June—DHSSPS remove the guidance entirely

(continued)

Table 7.1 (continued)

2011	May—Edwin Poots MLA (DUP) becomes Health Minister
2012	October—A Marie Stopes clinic opens in central Belfast. It can perform terminations up to 9 weeks of pregnancy. Large protests greet its opening September—Having received no further word of when the guidance document was to be released, the FPA begin the process of initiating another Judicial Review
2013	January—On the morning when the Judicial Review was due to begin, DHSSPS concede and say that it will submit a draught of the guidance to the Executive within 14 days March—The Assembly debates an amendment (tabled by a combination of DUP, SDLP and UUP MLAs) to the Criminal Justice Bill which would have made terminations taking place outside of public facilities illegal and would thus have closed Marie Stopes. The amendment passes 53–40, but does not become law due to the use of the petition of concern, filed by Sinn Féin, Alliance and the Greens April—Another version of the guidance is circulated for a period of consultation to last until October October—DHSSPS release a summary on consultation responses to the draft guidance, which are generally critical. Sarah Ewart, pregnant with a fatal foetal abnormality, talks publicly to Northern Irish media about her situation. The case gains widespread media comment December—David Ford MLA, Minister for Justice (Alliance) announces that he will undertake a consultation on abortion with a view to change the law with regard to fatal foetal abnormality, rape and incest
2014	May—The High Court in London hears a case brought by a 17-year-old girl and her mother, arguing that the girl should have been allowed to receive a termination paid for by the state in England. The court rules against them. They appeal the decision September—Jim Wells MLA (DUP) becomes Health Minister
2015	February—The NIHRC is granted leave to seek a judicial review of abortion in Northern Ireland, with a particular view to change the law regarding fatal foetal abnormality, rape and incest May—Following comments he made regarding same-sex couples and child-rearing at a public event, Jim Wells resigns as Health Minister and is replaced by Simon Hamilton MLA (DUP) June—Another attempt to make abortions performed in private facilities illegal through Stormont fails. The Court of Appeal in London hears the case of the mother and daughter from 2014. The NIHRC judicial review is held in the High Court in Belfast. A Northern Irish woman is placed on trial in Belfast for helping her teenage daughter seek a termination via medication November—The High Court in Belfast rules that Northern Irish abortion law is incompatible with human rights law and the ECHR in particular. It recommends that the Assembly introduce legislation to amend the existing framework, especially with regard to fatal foetal abnormality and rape

(continued)

Table 7.1 (continued)

2016	January—The Northern Irish Attorney General, John Larkin, and Justice Minister, David Ford, both intimate that they will appeal the High Court's ruling February—Proposed amendments to allow for abortions in cases of fatal foetal abnormalities fail to pass in the Assembly March—A new iteration of guidance on termination of pregnancy is released by the Department of Health on Good Friday. They exact less controversy than the previous guidelines and have yet to be legally challenged March—A 21-year-old in Belfast is convicted of buying abortion pills on the internet and using them to procure a miscarriage June—The UK votes to leave the European Union in a nation-wide referendum
2017	January—The Assembly is suspended June—General Election. DUP enter into a "confidence-and-supply" arrangement in order to prop up the minority Conservative government June—The Supreme Court in London upholds the previous ruling that Northern Irish women seeking terminations are not entitled to receive free treatment in England June—The Northern Irish Court of Appeal, following a case made after the 2015 judgement, rules that it remains for the Assembly, and not the legal system, to change the law on abortion June—Following a proposed amendment to the Queen's Speech by Labour MP Stella Creasy, the government announce that NHS England will now pay for terminations for Northern Irish women who travel for abortions. The Scottish and Welsh governments quickly follow suit

defined have had a tendency to be overly 'sticky' and the agents (where they exist) have largely been fixated in terms of preferences or fixated in terms of norms" (Schmidt 2008, 313). As Chapter 2 outlined, the contributions that feminist institutionalism has made to the structure/agency debate have largely focused on positive examples—Chappell's (2002) consideration of the feminist movements in Canada and Australia, for example. But, as the previous chapter illustrated, pro-choice activists in Northern Ireland cannot get clear access to the state, either through the devolved consociational structures, or via the national parliament at Westminster. With activists having no "in," conservative actors are thus largely free to act and speak uninfluenced by liberal action. This allows for institutional resistance on abortion by key conservative figures.

This chapter works "from the inside" (Schmidt 2008, 2010) to illustrate how language and ideas about abortion within the new Assembly have developed over time. It employs feminist discourse analysis, most notably the method proposed by Carol Lee Bacchi in her "What's the problem?" approach (1999), as outlined in Chapter 2. This chapter argues that the way in which the 1967 Act has been discussed by politicians has seen it constructed as a problematic piece of legislation, which is overly permissive and allows for "abortion on demand." Furthermore, this chapter illustrates that although this issue has been discussed by a wide array of politicians, from different parties and across the political divide, it has been particularly important to a handful of individuals. Conservative "critical actors" have been key to obstructing action on this issue. It builds upon the previous chapter and links "the micro- to the macro-level" (Mackay and Krook 2011, 10), showing that it is not just the institutional makeup of the Assembly which shapes the conversation around abortion but also the actions of a key group of politicians.

"I Cannot Stop Them from Going to England, but I Can Stop Them from Receiving My Blessing to Murder Their Children": The 2000 Abortion Debate

Following the closure of the short-lived Assembly from 1982 to 1986, Northern Ireland did not have formal devolved governance until after the Good Friday Agreement. In June of 2000, the new Northern Irish Assembly, less than two years into its first term, debated the motion "*That this Assembly is opposed to the extension of the Abortion Act 1967 to Northern Ireland.*"[1] The motion was proposed by Jim Wells DUP MLA (and Stormont Health Secretary from late 2014 to Spring 2015[2]) in part because of Mo Mowlam's comments regarding her disappointment that she had not been able to extend the act to the province during her period as Secretary of State for Northern Ireland.[3] It was also instigated at the request of the pro-life group, Precious Life, who wished "to test the view of the Assembly."[4] Such influence illustrates the influence that pro-life groups, and Precious Life in particular, have had from the early days of the Assembly.

Throughout the debate, MLAs were clear that they saw this as an opportunity to send a signal to Westminster about how politicians in Northern Ireland felt about abortion. As one MLA put it, "by having this debate, we are putting down a marker" on the issue. Similarly, Jim Wells concluded the debate by noting that:

> At present there is pressure in Westminster to extend the 1967 Act to Northern Ireland and Dr Mowlam mentioned that. The last point Dr Mowlam made when she left Northern Ireland was that she wished she had found the time to extend the amended 1967 Abortion Act to Northern Ireland. *We must send out this evening a very clear, cross-community message – supported by different parties with different viewpoints – that the people of Northern Ireland totally resist any extension of the 1967 Abortion Act to this community.* (emphasis added)

Certain key politicians were thus eager to use this debate to emphasise that Northern Ireland had "clear, cross-community" feeling on the issue and should be left alone as regards abortion. Not only did this debate set the tone for political debate on abortion in the newly devolved governance in the province, it also sent a clear message to Westminster that it should not try to exert its influence on the issue.

The dominant portrayal of the 1967 Act in the 2000 debate was of a barbaric piece of legislation that had wreaked moral havoc in the rest of the UK:

> Wells (DUP): "Every 24 hours in hospitals in England, Scotland and Wales an average of 530 human beings are legally killed … Since the 1967 Act became law, 5.3 million abortions have been carried out in Great Britain – more than the populations of Northern Ireland and the Irish republic combined, and almost the same number as the number of Jews who were murdered in Hitler's death camps."

MLAs also displayed a widely held belief that the Abortion Act has created "abortion on demand." Their language suggested that the two go hand in hand:

> Wells (DUP): "What has happened under the Abortion Act 1967 in the rest of the UK has in effect been abortion on demand."
>
> Maginness (SDLP): "The Abortion Act of 1967 effectively created a climate of medical opinion and of legal opinion that made abortion on demand possible."

Cementing this feeling, MLAs across parties expressed the belief that the absence of the Act in Northern Ireland was to the betterment of the province:

> Birnie (UUP): "I have little doubt that if the provision of the 1967 Act applied in Northern Ireland, the 1600 abortions of Northern Irish origin would be multiplied by 2 or 3, with a consequent increase in human misery."
>
> Poots (DUP): "If we were to introduce the Abortion Act 1967 to Northern Ireland, the child's life would become of little or no consequence."

Indeed, even a desire for legal clarification was treated with great scepticism by some MLAs. Jim Wells declared that he was "deeply suspicious of those who demand clarification" of the current legal situation in Northern Ireland because those "demands are exactly the same as those that were made in 1966 by David Steel when he was pushing through his Act. His so-called clarification opened the floodgates to abortion on demand throughout Great Britain." Similarly, Danny O'Connor, SDLP MLA, said that "There is the potential for the situation to be abused … Clarification of the abortion law would mean permissive abortion in Northern Ireland." Any movement on the issue whatsoever is addressed as though it is the beginning of a slippery slope which will eventually lead to the Abortion Act and, by extension, "abortion on demand."

Throughout the debate, cross-communal sentiment on abortion was furthered as an argument against the 1967 Act: "an overwhelming majority of our community are opposed to the concept of abortion on demand and the current practice in Britain of the creative interpretation of sections of the existing legislation, which achieves the same outcome" (McLaughlin, Sinn Féin). The evocation of "our community" as opposed to "our *communities*" is rare in Northern Irish politics. This continued throughout the debate, and from members of different political parties:

> Boyd (UK Unionist Party): "I am confident that my view on abortion is one that is held by the vast majority of people in Northern Ireland."
>
> Wells (DUP): "…both communities are perhaps more united on this issue than on any other."

Northern Irish politicians, including many unionists, were happy to assert their unique situation on this issue. They continually evoked their difference from Britain on abortion. Even some of the most strident DUP members, who had campaigned for a "No" vote in the Good

Friday Agreement referendum, did not wish to replicate the rest of the UK on this issue. This debate went further, however, to assert that abortion was one of the few issues which brought communities in the province together. Equally, there is no suggestion in the debate that people in Great Britain might share their anti-abortion sentiments. Again, the understanding of Northern Ireland in this debate creates a picture of it being largely independent from the broader governance structure of the UK, rather than embedded within it.

Despite this dominant anti-abortion tone, the debate was not entirely one-note. The Press Officer for NIWC at the time of the debate had positive recollections of its outcome: "I remember thinking that the result wasn't as bad as it could have been … yes, there were the key people who were clearly never going to change their mind, but even among the MLAs there was a diversity of opinion expressed."[5] Monica McWilliams, one of the two NIWC MLAs who proposed an amendment that the issue of abortion be referred to the Health Committee, was part of the minority who spoke in opposition to the general tone of the debate, pointing out that "the situation in Northern Ireland is a mess and desperately needs to be reviewed." McWilliams' interventions gave greater nuance to the issue, setting it in a wider context of reproductive services and health issues, but it is notable that she did not advocate a clear-cut pro-choice position. Although less emotive and more eager to be guided by professional advice, the NIWC were not advocating the extension of the 1967 Act or a similar liberal legislative situation.

Contributions in favour of the amendment came from a variety of different parties beyond the NIWC. Joan Carson, a UUP MLA, was one of the few members to point out that, in fact, "the 1967 act does not give women carte blanche to obtain abortion on demand." She went on to highlight the hypocrisy of the present legal situation in the province:

> Abortion is here whether we agree with it or not. Abortions are already being carried out in Northern Ireland. … Almost 2000 women from Northern Ireland travel to GB every year to use abortion services.

Other MLAs (from several different parties) also highlighted the reality of abortion as it existed in Northern Ireland, in terms of the distances women had to travel to seek terminations, and which was largely ignored in pro-life accounts:

> McLaughlin (Sinn Féin): "The invisible multitudes of women who travel to other countries for abortions are prevented by our culture from discussing their experience."
>
> Ervine (PUP): "There is an awful stinking painful route that is travelled by people in our society – not just by women but by people. They are not women; they are people; they are equals; and, indeed, they are the majority."
>
> Bell (Alliance): "Are we really to believe that we are best serving their interests by keeping abortion largely illegal here? Because England is so close that it is easy for us to keep abortions both illegal and uncommon, but it does not stop abortions from happening, and neither will this motion. All it will do is keep consciences clean."

Whilst the dominant tone of the debate was strongly pro-life, centring around images of the "unborn child", a sense of dissent from this emerges. Although not overtly "pro-choice," and pointedly not calling for the extension of the 1967 Act, there was a range of opinion presented on the matter, which made an attempt to draw on an evidence base of legal uncertainty and the facts and figures of Northern Irish women travelling for terminations. This was not enough to pass the amendment that guidance be considered by the Health Committee, rather than dismissed outright. It was defeated by 43 votes to 15, a sizeable majority. The fact that over half of MLAs turned out to vote on the issue also illustrates the level of interest. Although there were no obvious attempts being made to extend the Act from Westminster at this point, MLAs were eager to express their view. The debate was a way through which any potential action on the part of Westminster could be dissuaded.

"The Law Won't Change, so the Best We Can Hope for Is Guidance": Guidelines on the Termination of Pregnancy, 2002–2007

The 2000 debate in the Assembly was a clear statement on where politicians, political parties and political discourse in the province stood on the 1967 Act. From the onset of devolution, it thus appeared unlikely that political action on this issue via the Assembly would be possible. Furthermore, there was no clear guidance for health professionals in

Northern Ireland regarding abortion—only a series of vague legal judgements compounded by sporadic case law. In the words of Breedagh Hughes, Director of the Royal College of Midwives in Northern Ireland, "there was already a degree of I'd say uncomfortableness with midwives working out there, because they were caring for women who were having their pregnancies terminated and the midwives were never quite clear whether these were lawful or not."[6] In the light of this uncertainty, in 2001 the Family Planning Association of Northern Ireland (the FPA)[7] initiated legal action against the Department of Health, Social Service and Public Safety (DHSSPS). The FPA "asked the courts to advise DHSSPS that it was failing in its statutory duty to ensure that all women had equal access to reproductive healthcare services."[8] The FPA were keen to stress that this legal challenge "wasn't about changing the law, it was about clarifying the law and producing guidelines."[9]

The FPA won the right to a judicial review of medical practices related to the provision of abortion services in Northern Ireland, which was held in March 2002. Justice Brian Kerr presided and presented his judgement in July 2003. Whilst the FPA failed in its bid to force DHSSPS to issue guidelines around termination of pregnancy, Justice Kerr's decision did include a clear legal judgement on when abortions were deemed legal in the province, the first time such a clear statement had been made. He ruled that abortions are legal in circumstances where to continue the pregnancy would have permanent or long-term physical or mental health effects.[10]

The FPA launched an appeal against the judgement later in July 2003. The appeal was held the following year in July 2004. The Court of Appeal in Belfast ruled that DHSSPS had failed to provide adequate guidance.[11] The Health Minister, then Bairbre de Brún (Sinn Féin), was instructed to conduct an inquiry into termination of pregnancy services offered in Northern Ireland, and whether or not they were adequate, and, following such an inquiry and a period of consultation with appropriate and interested parties, to issue guidance to medical professionals. Following a period of consultation, guidelines were released in 2007.

In October 2007, the Assembly debated the guidelines. Proposed by Iris Robinson, DUP MLA and then Chairperson of the Health, Social Services and Public Safety Committee, the motion "*That this Assembly opposes the introduction of the proposed guidelines on the termination of pregnancy in Northern Ireland; believes that the guidelines are flawed; and calls on the Minister of Health, Social Services and Public Safety to abandon any attempt to make abortion more widely available in Northern Ireland*"[12] was debated. A late amendment was also proposed by two members of the UUP, arguing that the Minister for Health should in fact bring forth the guidelines, "*as defined by the Offences Against the Person Act 1861, the Criminal Justice Act (Northern Ireland) 1945, and the Bourne Judgement case law, and in accordance with the ruling of the Courts.*" From the terms of the first motion alone, there was a blurring of a consideration of the guidance, with a broader discussion of abortion provision and legislation in the province. Although this debate was ostensibly about the guidelines, it was also a broader debate on the 1967 Act itself.

Certain members were eager to point out that the extension of the Act was not what was being discussed here:

> McAllister (UUP): "… whatever debate we might have at some stage on the 1967 Abortion Act, today is not the day for that debate."
>
> Lo (Alliance): "It is important that we are clear that the House is not debating whether abortion should be legalised in Northern Ireland."
>
> O'Dowd (Sinn Féin): "This debate is not about the Abortion Act 1967 … [it] is about ensuring that the Minister of Health, Social Services and Public Safety can meet his legal obligations and his ministerial responsibility."

Reflecting this, the Minister for Health had to reiterate that, with the introduction of the guidelines, he was not attempting to extend the Act:

> Minister: "…let me make it clear that I will not change, or do not propose to change, the law on abortion in Northern Ireland — nor could I, even if I wished to. The purpose of the guidance is not to make it easier or more difficult to obtain an abortion in Northern Ireland; the reason for producing the guidance is to clarify the existing law on abortion and to provide clinical and good practice guidance to health professionals. Those are actions that my Department has been directed to take by the Court of Appeal."

Further on in his speech to the Assembly, he reiterated again that the guidance "is in no way an attempt to introduce the provisions of the Abortion Act 1967 to Northern Ireland by the back door." Distancing himself in such a way from the 1967 Act illustrates how eager the Minister was to disassociate himself from this legislation.

Members who were supportive of the amendment to bring forth the guidelines also felt the need to distance themselves from the 1967 Act:

> McCallister (UUP): "Let me make it absolutely clear, as the proposer of the amendment, that I do not support the extension of the 1967 Act to Northern Ireland, nor do I support abortion on demand."
>
> Ní Chuilín (Sinn Féin): "Sinn Féin is not in favour of abortion. It is against the extension of the British Abortion Act 1967 to the North of Ireland."

This desire to distinguish one's position as being apart from the 1967 Act is due to the way that it is constructed in the language of MLAs: as an immoral piece of legislation which has led to "abortion on demand," as was its portrayal in the 2000 debate. Although the motion for debate, and the guidance more broadly, had little relevance to the 1967 Act, it was still evoked by many of the members who spoke. There was a repeated insinuation from multiple members that the 1967 Act was overly liberalising:

> Buchanan (DUP): "Many believed those carefully worded assurances, but it soon became clear that the Abortion Act 1967, amended by the Human Fertilisation and Embryology Act 1990, permitted abortion on demand."
>
> Easton (DUP): "The Act that permits abortion on demand does not apply here."
>
> Buchanan (DUP): "This Province has been spared from becoming home to such ungodly legislation, which legitimises the murder of the unborn child, on demand."

As in the 2000 debate, there was a widespread sentiment that the guidelines were the first step on the "slippery slope" to more liberal abortion laws. If any change is to occur, no matter how small, it is the equivalent of "the opening shots in a campaign to make abortion on demand freely available in the Province" (Easton, DUP), and it will "liberalise the law and … make abortion more likely in Northern Ireland" (Deeny, Independent). The "problem" (Bacchi 1999) that is constructed through this language is that any change is connected to the Abortion Act, which in turn is linked to an idea of immorality.

As with the 2000 debate, there was a sense that a strong statement was necessary from Stormont to dissuade Westminster from becoming involved in this debate. Jim Wells (DUP) asked one of the proposers of the amendment:

> Does the honourable Member realise that an amendment has been proposed in the House of Commons by a Liberal MP, almost as we speak, to extend the 1967 Act to Northern Ireland? Whereas my party's motion will send a clear message to Westminster that that is not acceptable, his amendment, if passed, will send it a very woolly motion that will mean nothing.

Later in the debate, Jeffery Donaldson, DUP MLA, raised the same issue, pointing to the fact that "a Liberal Democrat MP, Dr Evan Harris, proposes to table an amendment, the effect of which would be to extend the Abortion Act 1967 to Northern Ireland." Because of this, he argued, "what better time than now for the Assembly to send a clear signal that it is not in favour of liberalising the law on abortion?" Concluding, Donaldson said that "the Assembly must put down a clear marker on its position." As with the 2000 discussion, this debate was used as a way for Stormont to signal to Westminster that it did not want intervention on this issue.

Reflecting this, and as with the 2000 debate, a cross-community consensus was again given as justification for opposition to the amendment:

> Robinson (DUP): "Does the member also accept that the majority of people in Northern Ireland – from all faiths and one – would baulk if any Government or legislative assembly insisted on softening the 1967 Act?"
>
> McCrea (UUP): "Everyone in the Chamber would agree that abortion, and anything to do with it, is a tragedy."
>
> Kennedy (UUP): "Members on all sides of the House have clearly expressed their opposition to any extension of the Abortion Act 1967."

Again, cross-community language was used to argue against any change on abortion. This line of argument helped to reinforce the Assembly's "nested newness" (Mackay 2014) within the province's politics. Abortion is such an important issue, these MLAs argued, because it has the ability to unite opinion across the ethno-national divide. This evocation of the particular nature of divided politics in Northern Ireland acts to reinforce an idea of the province as "special" and "unique" due to its conflicted history. Northern Ireland's "difference" is stressed in the construction of abortion as a particular "cross-community" issue. It thus forms part of something that the rest of the UK, national government included, cannot fully understand and thus cannot be trusted to act upon.

Guidelines on Abortion Post-2007

Following the debate on the guidelines in the Assembly in 2007, draft guidance was finally issued for a period of consultation in July 2008. This closed in September 2008. The guidance was then released in March 2009 by Health Minister, Michael McGimpsey MLA (UUP). The document ("Guidance on the Termination of Pregnancy: The Law and Clinical Practice in Northern Ireland"[13]) set out the legal background to abortion in Northern Ireland and explained that abortion is only legal when "it is necessary to save the life of the woman, or where there is a risk of real and serious adverse effect on her physical or mental health, which is either long term or permanent," reflecting the 2004 court ruling. It is stressed that foetal abnormality is not grounds for termination. The guidelines adopt a largely neutral tone vis-à-vis the issue of abortion—"woman" and "foetus" are used throughout, not "mother" and "child."

A judicial review of the guidance was launched by the Society for the Protection of Unborn Children (SPUC) in October 2009. The Court ruled that the guidelines were "not an erroneous interpretation of the law" (FPA 2014) but took issue with the sections which dealt with non-directive counselling and conscientious objection. As a result, the immediate withdrawal of the guidance was ordered. In February 2010, interim guidance was then published with the sections which the Court had questioned removed. SPUC then began the process to initiate another judicial review on the basis that the document should not have been released at all, even without the sections the Court had taken issue with. In June 2010, the guidance was removed in its entirety.

In July, the contested sections were rewritten and the document was released for public consultation. The consultation closed in October 2010. At this point, the guidance document had run the gauntlet of several periods of public consultation and Court cases, and was largely accepted across legal, political and civil society arenas. In the words of the Director of the Royal College of Midwives, with the exception of the section on conscientious objection, "the rest of the guidance was fine! [It had been] through the Health Committee, the whole of the Assembly, the Executive at the Assembly and the Courts, and the vast majority of the guidance was found to be fit for purpose."[14] In May 2011, Edwin Poots MLA (DUP) took over as Health Minister. Following correspondence from the FPA to DHSSPS from his appointment until early 2012, no clear statement was made from the department as to when the guidance was going to be issued. Consequently, the FPA began the process to initiate another Judicial Review in September 2012. On the morning of the hearing, in January 2013, DHSSPS conceded, indicating that it was willing to publish the document and that a draft would be submitted to the Executive within 14 days. In April 2013, revised guidance was issued for consultation.

Yet the document produced in 2013 "bore no resemblance to the previous guidance at all." The tone of the 2013 guidelines is dramatically different from those produced in 2009. The title alone is indicative of the change—"The *Limited* Circumstances for a Lawful Termination of Pregnancy in Northern Ireland: A Guidance Document for Health and Social Care Professionals on Law and Clinical Practice"[15]—as is the opening statement: "The aim of the health and social care system must be *protection of both the life of the mother and her unborn child*" (emphasis added). "Mother" and "child" are used throughout the document, despite the highly emotive nature and the fact that such language lacks reference to any legal or medical context. This was also the first time that such language had been used in any iteration of the guidance.

The document goes to great lengths to stress that termination of pregnancy should remain "highly exceptional" and is only legal in "very limited circumstances." It also goes further than the 2009 guidelines in that it states that any health or social care professional who is aware of a potentially illegal termination taking place, but may not necessarily have assisted in the procedure themselves, must report such instances to the police. If they do not, "he or she may be liable, upon conviction, to a maximum penalty of ten years imprisonment." This claim has no legal basis in Northern Ireland nor the rest of the UK.

The public consultation around this version of the guidance closed in October 2013. The document received a largely critical reception during the consultation process. The Royal College of Nurse declared it to be "inadequately drafted"[16] and the Royal College of Midwives were equally strident, criticising the "tone and language" of the document.

They called it "intimidatory and threatening" and said that it "would appear to have been written in such a way as to create uncertainty and fear of possible criminal or legal repercussions amongst those working in this area of healthcare."[17] Multiple respondents to the consultation echoed these beliefs and critiqued the use of "inappropriate terminology,"[18] including the British Medical Association (the BMA), the FPA, the WRDA, Marie Stopes and Amnesty International.

The "chilling effect" that this had on health professionals impacted medical practice. Instead of creating greater clarity around termination of pregnancy, more confusion occurred. According to Professor Jim Dornan, "The mood is fear within the health care professionals because of these guidelines. … Some of the trusts went to their legal teams at that stage (March 2013) and were advised to stop … giving advice on what to do in these situations."[19] Similarly, Dr. Samina Dornan, Consultant Obstetrician at the Royal Maternity Hospital in Belfast, believed that the "atmosphere in hospitals … changed" with the 2013 guidelines and that they were "intimidatory"[20] for medical staff. This set of guidelines thus not only failed to provide greater clarity to medical professionals, but appeared to have further restricted an already very limited set of circumstances in which women can access terminations.

In late 2013, a group of key stakeholders was invited to Stormont, and a general concession appeared to be given from the department that the guidance was not fit for purpose.[21] Yet interviews in early to mid-2014 gave no clear indication of when a new version could be expected. In the words of a representative from the Royal College of Nurses in July 2014, "at the moment I don't know where we are. I really don't."[22]

In late 2014, a new Health Minister was appointed in the shape of Jim Wells, DUP MLA. Wells, who introduced the 2000 debate on the 1967 Act, has a long history of opposition to abortion and is on record as opposing the procedure even in cases of rape or incest. Under his Ministership, movement on the guidance seemed unlikely. However, following comments he made at a public hustings in the run-up to the 2015 General Election regarding same-sex couples and parenting,[23] Wells resigned from his position as Health Minister. Simon Hamilton replaced him as Health Minister and has a far quieter public record on the issue of abortion than either Wells or, preceding him, Poots. Under Hamilton's Ministry, on Good Friday 2016, a set of guidelines on termination of pregnancy was quietly released on the Department of Health's website. The guidelines contain none of the emotive language of the previous guidelines (there are no references to "mothers" or "babies"). They state clearly that abortions can "only be carried out with the intention of protecting the woman against physical or mental health issues that are 'real or serious' and 'permanent or long term.'"[24] They outline guidance for appropriate clinical assessment, counselling options and conscientious objection. Yet they also stress that the guidance "cannot, and does not, make any change to the law in Northern Ireland." The legal framework may not have changed, but there are now finally guidelines in frame for medical practice which have yet to be challenged in Court or via the Assembly.

Whilst the story of the guidelines provided here is largely legal and procedural, it outlines subtle but important changes that have occurred since devolution in how abortion is addressed by government in the province. As various iterations of the guidance have emerged, the discourse around abortion has changed dramatically. Whilst versions in the 2000s adopted largely neutral language ("foetus", "woman"), the 2013 version brought in the words "mother" and "child" for the first time, and went beyond its remit to make claims about prison terms with no legal precedent. The difficulties inherent in attempting to establish this guidance, and the (more than) decade-long proceedings which accompanied it, show how problematic it has become to make even small changes. Although guidelines cannot make any difference to the legal framework around abortion, the possibility of their existence was still interpreted by the Assembly and key figures in formal politics in the province as representing a slippery slope to the 1967 Act and "abortion on demand."[25]

The story of the guidance also illustrates the power that individual politicians have had to shape the political discourse around this issue. The Health Minister has had clear power and influence over the shape of the guidance. Under Edwin Poots, the guidance was rewritten entirely from the version overseen by Michael McGimpsey in the late 2000s, producing a version which was widely derided as being overly restrictive and confusing in its language, and which attempted to step beyond its limits and create new laws. Jim Wells, Health Minister from 2014 to 2015, has made clear his distaste for any liberalising moves around abortion, and no movement on the guidance happened under his Ministership. John Larkin, the Northern Irish Attorney General, is widely perceived as having a key influence on the tone of the 2013 guidance. The director of the FPA declared that "I think where we have been very unfortunate is who we have as the Attorney General that has been the unfortunate issue. If he hadn't have been appointed, we may not have been in the same situation that we're in now."[26] The Royal College of Midwives Director also stressed in an interview for this research the impact she felt that the Attorney General, and not the Chief Medical Officer, had on the 2013 version of the guidelines. Indeed, the guidelines that have finally been produced after nearly fifteen years of legal and political wrangling have been ushered in by the DUP Minister for Health, Simon Hamilton, who is decidedly less vocal on the issue of abortion than his two predecessors. With pro-choice voices struggling to be heard politically, conservative "critical actors" (Childs and Krook 2009) have been able to exert a strong influence, having huge impact on the shape and tone of the guidance, and, thus, the broader debate around abortion in Northern Ireland.

"Marie Stopes Is Operating Under a Cloud of Darkness": Marie Stopes Clinic and Private Abortion Care

In September 2012, Marie Stopes International opened a reproductive and sexual health services clinic in central Belfast. There was much surprise from the political community at its appearance. Dawn Purvis, Director of the Clinic from 2012 to 2015, expressed confusion at this and, outlining the long process of registering the clinic with the regulatory authority prior to its opening, said that "it's not that people didn't know, maybe it's just that the politicians didn't know."[27] The clinic was met with large protests on its opening, mostly from anti-abortion protesters. Media reports recorded "hundreds" of protesters carrying prolife material and only one pro-choice individual.[28]

As part of its facilities (which operate on a part-time basis of only two days per week), the clinic provides terminations up to a period of 9 weeks pregnancy under the strict legal remit which exists in Northern Ireland. Two attempts, in March 2013 and June 2015, have been made via the Assembly to amend the Criminal Justice Bill to limit terminations to public facilities. If passed, these would have made all provision of abortion procedures illegal outside NHS facilities, thus essentially evicting Marie Stopes from the province.[29] Abortion per se was not challenged through these moves, but rather a specific feature of abortion provision—that of the role of private healthcare. As Amery notes, this type of tactic is redolent of other anti-abortion mechanisms in the UK and beyond, where "those wishing to restrict access to abortion have identified weak points in the existing regulatory model" and have tried "to foster a climate of mistrust in abortion providers" (2014, 45). Both of these amendments were subject to petitions of concern,[30] for which Sinn Féin provided the majority of the necessary signatures. Both failed due to lack of nationalist support—25% of nationalist MLAs voted for the amendment in 2013, but only 21% in 2015.

As with the previous debates, cross-community opposition to any abortion liberalisation was stressed in Stormont's discussion. Indeed, the March 2013 amendment[31] was tabled by an unusual three-party alliance, which crossed the ethno-national divide (the DUP, the UUP and the SDLP). Paul Givan, DUP MLA, one of the three cross-party members proposing the motion, was keen to acknowledge cross-community support, not only in Northern Ireland, but also in the Republic:

> I have been humbled and immensely gratified by the support that it has received from across the political and religious spectrums in Northern Ireland and in the Republic of Ireland. The protection of vulnerable women and unborn children is an issue that *transcends normal politics and religious boundaries.* Although I and colleagues in the House have disagreed on other matters, *many of us have found unity of purpose on this issue.* That applies not just in this jurisdiction. Only last week, in the Dáil, I briefed TDs and Senators, including Fianna Fáil leader Michael Martin and his colleague Éamon Ó Cuiv and Fine Gael members about this matter. (emphasis added)

Further in the debate, he declared that "Across the island of Ireland, we share a common bond in seeking to protect and provide the best care for mothers and unborn children." Using the language of broader post-conflict politics in the province, Givan declared that this was an example of good practice: "People ask what *a shared future*[32] looks like, and I point to this moment of an SDLP, DUP and Ulster Unionist bringing forward proposed legislation related to the most basic of human rights; the right to life" (emphasis added). Givan emphasised that this was not only reflected in commonly shared values ("the values of our society, which is a society that upholds the sanctity of human life"), but also extended across theological positions, naming support he had received from various Christian denominations.

This was echoed by other members throughout the debate and by Alban Maginness, SDLP MLA and co-proposer of the amendment, who specifically attacked the use of the petition of concern:

> Given that it is a cross-community, cross-religious and cross-party amendment — it was all those things — it should have been supported, and, in particular, it was and is inappropriate for a petition of concern to be used. The petition of concern was envisaged to deal with broader political issues and issues that involve protecting communities … this is a gross misuse of the petition of concern.

Proposers of the amendment were thus keen to stress the cross-community support behind it and the perceived lack of respect for this by using a petition to stop the motion. Again, the specific nature of Northern Irish society and politics was enmeshed in the argument against abortion liberalisation. The language of community politics is used to describe abortion, rather than the language of women, their rights and needs.

Compared to any of the previous debates, the discourse of this debate carried a far greater sense of the tensions between the DUP and Sinn Féin. Arlene Foster, DUP Minister, declared that, in using a petition of concern to halt this debate, "we are today witnessing the ideological meltdown of Sinn Féin." DUP members in particular were keen to stress Sinn Féin's perceived pro-abortion position:

> Poots (DUP): "Sinn Féin is saying that it does not support the 1967 Abortion Act, but it is standing shoulder to shoulder with an organisation that wants to bring the 1967 Abortion Act to Northern Ireland."

Bell (DUP) went on to argue that members should "not be led by the nose by Caitríona Ruane." Sinn Féin were thus particularly attacked by the DUP for their stance in this debate, with this occasion showing greater partisanship than previous debates.

As a result of this DUP attack, members talking against the amendment were largely on the defensive:

> Ruane (Sinn Féin): "Sinn Féin is not in favour of abortion. We opposed and voted against the extension of the 1967 Act to the North of Ireland when it was proposed in the Assembly. That remains our position. … It is not necessarily the case that I believe that we should extend the 1967 Abortion Act to Northern Ireland. Northern Ireland needs to have its own legislation on abortion."

Again, as in previous debates discussed in the last chapter, the Abortion Act was deemed so toxic that there was a need for those who spoke against the amendment to stress that this did not indicate support for the 1967 legislation.

In spite of this evocation of the 1967 Act, and as with the 2007 debate on the guidelines, the 2013 debate was incredibly narrow and largely boiled down to the issue of private service provision. Throughout the debate, many MLAs expressed concern that abortion should be provided by private sources, rather than via the NHS. This was particularly stressed by Givan (DUP) in his contributions, who argued that "it is morally abhorrent that vulnerable women and their children, who are in grave physical and mental danger, should pay a private clinic in circumstances in which a life is to be ended." Indeed, a large portion of the debate centred around the issue of how a private healthcare facility might be regulated. MLAs supporting the amendment were concerned that Marie Stopes was outside of their jurisdiction and thus their control. Maginness (SDLP) declared that:

> Accountability is very important. If a private organisation, particularly in a sensitive area such as health, is not publicly accountable, which Marie Stopes is not, how can we trust what they are doing as being right and proper within criminal law?

Some members appeared frustrated at the apparent lack of oversight and expressed a desire for a greater level of insight and knowledge about the workings of the clinic. Jim Wells, future DUP Health Minister, said that "We will now be seeking explanations about why even the small number of abortions is carried out" and that "I want to be very clear in my mind that those figures are absolutely a true reflection of the legal position in Northern Ireland. … that will be good news, when we have that clarity." Then, DUP Health Minister, Edwin Poots, appeared equally distressed about the apparent lack of oversight, acknowledging that DHSSPS "has no jurisdiction whatsoever over Marie Stopes or any other organisation that wishes to establish a clinic to carry out abortions or terminations of pregnancy in the private sector." Later in the debate, Poots said "The problem is that nobody knows whether the law is being breached, because *Marie Stopes is operating under a cloud of darkness*" (emphasis added). The amendment would have passed (by 53 to 40 votes) were it not for the use of the petition of concern.

A second attempt to make Marie Stopes' abortion provision in the province illegal, along essentially identical lines, was amongst a raft of amendments to the Criminal Justice bill debated on the 2 June 2015.[33] Sinn Féin instigated a petition of concern in order to stop the amendment, but still had to emphasise that they are "not in favour of abortion. We opposed and voted against the extension of the 1967 Act to the North when it was proposed in the Assembly" (Ruane, Sinn Féin). Instead, Ruane went on to argue, this amendment discriminates against women's right to healthcare: "it is about limiting a woman's right to have that treatment."

On the whole, the debate is more even handed than most which precede it on abortion—the tone for and against the amendment is fairly evenly split. Many MLAs spoke to point out that if those supporting the amendment want regulation of Marie Stopes, it is very easily within their power:

> Lunn (Alliance): "The fact remains that Marie Stopes is quite prepared to be regulated by whatever means the authorities choose to impose … Whose fault is it that we cannot see what is going on behind those doors? That is the point."
>
> McCrea (NI21): "You want regulation: bring it in. You want some form of guidance: do not take ten years over it."

The debate again took place around the relatively narrow parameters of the Marie Stopes clinic and regulation. Although the petition of concern was used, the amendment also failed, by 41 votes to 39.

The little literature which has been produced on the petition of concern in Northern Ireland tends to approach it as an instrument which is beneficial to the functioning of the Assembly and which has not overly dominated proceedings or been misused by parties (Conley and Dahan 2013; McEvoy 2013). Yet the petition has been used frequently, as illustrated here, on the issue of abortion, an issue which affects women across the communal divide. Furthermore, this is in spite of the way in which, as this chapter and the previous chapter have shown, it has continually been constructed as a *cross*-community issue. A device which was intended to protect communal interests has been used on a non-community-specific issue. As such, elements of a consociational system have been used to hijack discussion on women's rights. As shown previously with regard to the Assembly debates, again the design and ideological underpinnings of the institution restrict the ways in which the discussion of women's rights can be structured.

"Slippery Slope" to Legislative Change? Amendments to the Justice Bill

Although, as outlined above, Marie Stopes' arrival in the province brought a flurry of political, legal and activist activity, it did not, as many pro-life politicians appear to have feared, bring greater calls within the Assembly to reform abortion legislation. Whilst the clinic's opening has helped to keep the issue of abortion in the public eye, it is several women coming forward with very personal stories that have gained the most media attention and encouraged liberalising political movement. In late 2013, two cases of pregnancies with fatal foetal abnormality received much publicity. In October, Sarah Ewart went to the BBC, asking them to highlight her case as she travelled to England for a termination, following a diagnosis of anencephaly. Shortly afterwards, another woman, known only as "Laura," came forward, with a similar situation, only this time pregnant with twins. Although it has long been understood that cases such as these do not fit the legal remit for termination in the province, and key stakeholders have emphasised this, the human face presented by Sarah Ewart's case once again reignited public debate around Northern Ireland's abortion laws.

As a result of these cases, the Justice Minister announced that he would propose legislation on changing the criminal law regarding abortion and fatal foetal abnormality and sexual crime. A document for public consultation was produced in autumn 2014 and a period of public consultation ran until January 2015. The consultation document ("The Criminal Law on Abortion: Lethal Foetal Abnormality and Sexual Crime"[34]) explicitly states at the outset that:

> It is not a debate on the wider issues of abortion law – issues often labelled as pro-choice or pro-life. There is no part of this document which seeks to open up this conversation and no response to this document which addresses these wider issues will be considered relevant to any proposed reform of the criminal law on abortion.

It also stresses that it does not attempt to "open the debate on the regulation of private clinics offering abortion services" as this is an issue for DHSSPS, not for the Department of Justice. Rather, this document is "strictly about the criminal law on abortion in respect of lethal foetal abnormality and sexual crime." The document frames the situation with specific, detailed reference to Sarah Ewart's case and limited reference to the second, anonymous, anencephaly case. It recommends that the decision to allow a termination for fatal foetal abnormality be left to a clinical judgement from a medical professional, as opposed to anything more prescriptive. Adapting the law to cover sexual assault appears more difficult, and the document "does not seek to recommend a clear-cut policy or legislative direction for amending the law to provide for abortion in cases of criminal sexual abuse." Although this area was still included as part of the public consultation, in April 2015 it was announced that the proposed amendments would focus only on fatal foetal abnormality and not sexual assault. Thus, if ever extended to law, these proposals will change provision of abortion services only slightly in the province, as such lethal conditions only affect a very small number of pregnancies.

When officials from the Department of Justice presented the document to the Justice Committee at Stormont[35] the Chair, Paul Givan MLA (DUP) directed the conversation in a very specific fashion. His first question to the two department representatives was "at what point is a foetus not a baby and when does it become a baby?" They stressed that they were following medical guidance on this matter but he continued, asking "How many people does the Department of Justice know who tell someone, 'I am carrying a foetus', right up to the point of birth? Is that language that people use in the public domain?" He then went on to question the officials about when "the baby in the womb [is] regarded as having life," most especially medical professionals' role in this decision: "Why should the medical profession be entrusted with the decision on what a life is and whether a life is worth keeping?" At the close of the hearing, he openly chastised the two officials: "you cannot even say when life exists."

The tone of the rest of the Committee was equally critical. Paul Frew MLA (DUP) asked whether the proposed change opened up the possibility of "a danger that 'incompatible with life' could well become 'incompatible with lifestyle'?" Edwin Poots MLA (DUP) suggested that changing the law in the case of rape was unnecessary due to the availability of the morning after pill: "If you are raped, you can avoid a pregnancy by taking action … I am not being judgemental about it." Committee members also seemed concerned that this might bring about the potential for broader liberalisation:

> Maginness (SDLP): "It does open up the whole conversation in relation to abortion."
>
> Givan (DUP): "When you change the law, the courts will then also exercise their role, and it becomes abortion on demand."

Members thus appeared concerned about not only the nature of what the consultation proposed, but also the potential wider liberalising effects it might have. Again, any liberalising move is constructed by these actors as leading to an "open door" to free, unregulated abortion. Even when the proposed changes are as markedly specific as this (only for women carrying a foetus that is seriously malformed), they are still constructed in political language as inevitably leading to "abortion on demand."

Ford's amendments were brought to the Assembly in February 2016 and failed to pass, by 59 to 40 votes. Sinn Féin and Alliance (with the exception of Kieran McCarthy MLA) voted for the changes; the DUP, SDLP and most of the UUP voted against it. The issue now appears to have moved back to the Health Ministry, with the DUP asking their Health Minister, Simon Hamilton, to set up a working group to discuss abortion. As of spring 2016, it was unclear if such a group had been established.

In a separate movement, the NIHRC announced in December 2014 that they would be seeking a judicial review in a bid to change abortion law to allow for termination in the case of rape, incest or "serious malformation" of the foetus. The case was held at Belfast's High Court in June 2015. The judgement, delivered in November 2015, represented the biggest change to Northern Ireland's jurisprudence on abortion since the 1861 Offences against the Person Act. It ruled that terminations were legal in cases of fatal foetal abnormality, rape and incest, but that it was the responsibility of the Assembly to provide legal change. There has yet to be any political movement on these instructions.

Conclusion

As an institution, the Northern Irish Assembly has been hostile to any liberalising movement on abortion and political debates have spoken little to the lived reality of abortion for women in the province. Furthermore, political discourse around abortion since 2007 in Northern Ireland has increasingly narrowed to focus on issues of regulation and private healthcare, rather than a discussion of the real experiences of women facing unwanted pregnancies. The "problem" (Bacchi 1999) of abortion has been constructed in such a way that any movement for change is implicitly linked to the 1967 Act. Yet it is important to remember that the main issues that have been debated within the Assembly (the guidelines, the Marie Stopes clinic, the proposed changes from the Justice Department) would do little to change the legal situations of abortion in the province. Regardless, political debate always returns to the notion of a "slippery slope" and an understanding that, even in the cases of the smallest legal movements, any change will still bring about an unregulated situation of "abortion on demand." As a result of this construction, even those proposing minor liberalisation, or opposing conservative movements, feel the need to stress that they do not want to see freely available abortion, nor the 1967 Act in Northern Ireland—most especially Sinn Féin in their opposition to the 2013 and 2015 amendments to outlaw private abortion provision.

MLAs have been keen to use these debates as a way to signal to Westminster that it should not interfere on this issue. The successive debates of this period allowed Stormont to illustrate the depth of anti-abortion sentiment and to dissuade any potential external political actions. This chapter thus argues, as did Chapter 4, that the inter-institutional relationships within a multi-level governance structure are important, in that they are part of a gendered power structure. The exact boundaries of where this issue can be addressed can fluctuate (Bache and Flinders 2005), and these debates are a way in which Stormont can signal to Westminster that it does not want it to become involved. As such, women's rights come second place to regional rights.

This is also reinforced in the ways in which the cross-community nature of abortion sentiment is continually evoked in political debate. This is again, as Chapter 6 showed, due to the anchoring that post-Good Friday Agreement politics have in ethno-nationally based politics. Many feminist discourse analysis scholars emphasise that the nature of an institution frames what type of discourse is possible in that institution (Schmidt 2008, 314; Kulawik 2009, 270). By constantly referencing the bi-communal nature of the region in this way, this aspect of Northern Irish society and politics is reinforced through this cross-community construction of the abortion issue and a discussion of abortion as a specifically women's issue gets lost. Furthermore, the petition of concern, an institutional feature designed to protect community-specific interests, was used around both attempts to close Marie Stopes, and DUP MLAs indicated that they would try to use the petition of concern again if Minister Ford's amendments on fatal foetal abnormality are brought to the Assembly.[36] As Chapter 6 argued, the ethno-national basis of the institution, including both the language that this particular type of politics encourage and the formal procedures the power-sharing body contains, can be readily used to stymie movement on women's rights. Indeed, it is notable that the key events that have pushed forward public and political debate on abortion in the post-2007 Assembly have not been initiated within the Assembly or within political parties. Instead, they have come from outside the political institutions in Northern Ireland: most notably, the opening of the Marie Stopes clinic, the Sarah Ewart case and the 2015 High Court ruling. Political debate on this issue appears stuck in a rut, with developments within the political institutions nearly impossible, only achievable instead via exogenous shocks.

This chapter has also illustrated the importance of "critical actors" (Childs and Krook 2009) rather than any concerted political movement from parties or key departments (the Justice Department's movements excepted). Key figures have again been influential on any movement around abortion—Iris Robinson's role as Chairperson of the Health, Social Services and Public Safety Committee allowed her to be of central importance to the issue of the guidelines in the mid-2000s. Jim Wells was able to initiate a debate in 2000, at a period when there was no real attempt to extend the Act from Westminster. The Northern Irish Attorney General from 2010, John Larkin, was widely cited in interviews as having heavily influenced the conservative language of the guidelines and for encouraging Assembly attempts to close Marie Stopes. Conservative movements within the Assembly have been proposed by a handful of key figures (Paul Givan—largely in his role as Chairman on the Committee for Justice, Alban Maginness, Jim Wells—including during his brief period as Minister for Health) and opposed by a similar small number (Caitríona Ruane, Anna Lo, Stephen Agnew, Basil McCrea). With liberalising voices so few in formal politics, and the pro-choice movement so distanced from the Assembly (as shown in Chapter 6), conservative actors exercise a large degree of autonomy and can strike the dominant note in the conversation around abortion. It is therefore not only, as Chapter 6 argued, the institutional design which influences the nature of the debate, but also key individuals. An interplay of structure and agency is important to fully understand this issue: conservative "critical actors" (Childs and Krook 2009) have been important to constructing this issue in the way it has come to be understood.

Finally, this chapter has shown that traditional ethno-national political boundaries have not disappeared from contemporary Northern Irish politics. They have, however, changed, becoming increasingly infected by the "culture wars" debates (Hunter 1992; Mycock and McDaid 2014). Although not entirely a clear-cut issue of DUP–Sinn Féin disagreement, due to the dominance of these two parties in the Assembly, abortion has "permeated" (Horowitz 1985, 7) ethno-national politics in the region. Previous discussion of Northern Ireland's "culture wars" has emphasised that political division is taking on an increasingly gendered dimension. Abortion and same-sex marriage have become key flashpoints in Northern Irish politics (Thomson 2015): issues which are not immediately sectarian are adopting these dimensions in political discussion and party policy. Although this is more pointed in discussions around same-sex marriage (and LGBT rights more broadly) than abortion (ibid.), abortion remains central to the province's formal politics, with both the DUP and Sinn Féin eager to use this as a topic which distinguishes each from the other.

Notes

1. Abortion, Assembly debate, 20 June 2000, http://archive.niassembly.gov.uk/record/reports/000620.htm. Accessed 1 February 2018. Online versions of the Northern Irish Assembly debates do not cite volume or page numbers, so all future references are to this source.
2. Wells resigned from his Ministerial position following comments he made regarding same-sex couples and child abuse at a public hustings prior to the 2015 UK General Election. "Health Minister Jim Wells: Police Investigate Gay Abuse Remarks," BBC News, http://www.bbc.co.uk/news/uk-northern-ireland-32443730. Accessed 1 February 2018.
3. "No Change to Abortion Law," BBC, http://news.bbc.co.uk/1/hi/northern_ireland/799135.stm. Accessed 1 February 2018.
4. Unionist MLA. Personal interview with the author, Belfast. March 2014.
5. Former NIWC activist. Private interview with the author, London (via Skype), May 2014.
6. Director, RCM Northern Ireland. Private interview with the author, Belfast. February 2014.
7. The FPA acted entirely on its own in bringing about the first legal challenge. Director of the FPA interview with the author, March 2014.

8. "Abortion Fact Sheet," FPA, http://www.fpa.org.uk/sites/default/files/northern-ireland-abortion.pdf. Accessed 1 February 2018.
9. Director of the FPA. Private interview with the author, Belfast, March 2014.
10. "Abortion Fact Sheet," FPA, http://www.fpa.org.uk/sites/default/files/northern-ireland-abortion.pdf. Accessed 1 February 2018.
11. "Abortion Fact Sheet," FPA, http://www.fpa.org.uk/sites/default/files/northern-ireland-abortion.pdf. Accessed 1 February 2018.
12. Abortion, Northern Irish Assembly debate, 22 October 2007, http://archive.niassembly.gov.uk/record/reports2007/071022.htm. Accessed 1 February 2018. All future references are to this source.
13. http://news.bbc.co.uk/1/shared/bsp/hi/pdfs/20_03_09_ninursing.pdf. Accessed 1 February 2018. All future references are to this source.
14. Private interview with the author, Belfast, March 2014.
15. http://www.biodiritto.org/index.php/item/download/315_0e416b-233ffa4c88c1317e2195f2b1f5. Accessed 1 February 2018. All further references are to this source.
16. RCN response to guidelines, July 2013, on file with author.
17. RCM response to guidelines, July 2013, https://www.rcm.org.uk/sites/.../TOP%20Response%20July%202013.doc. Accessed 1 February 2018.
18. "Department of Health, Social Services and Public Safety, Draft Termination of Pregnancy Guidance, Summary of Consultation Responses Received," p. 5, https://www.dhsspsni.gov.uk/sites/default/files/consultations/dhssps/termination-pregnancy-responses-2013.pdf. Accessed 1 February 2018.
19. "Draft Abortion Guidelines 'Causing Fear Among Northern Irish Staff,'" BBC, http://www.bbc.co.uk/news/uk-northern-ireland-24550586. Accessed 1 February 2018.
20. "Northern Ireland: Barriers to Accessing Abortion Services," Amnesty International, p. 20, http://www.amnesty.org.uk/sites/default/files/eur_45_0157_2015_northern_ireland_-_barriers_to_accessing_abortion_services_pdf.pdf. Accessed 1 February 2018.
21. Medical professional. Private interview with the author, Belfast. July 2014.
22. Medical professional. Private interview with the author, Belfast. July 2014.
23. In May 2015, whilst standing as a DUP Westminster candidate in South Down, Wells told a public hustings event, "You don't bring a child up in a homosexual relationship. That a child is far more likely to be abused and neglected…." "Health Minister Jim Wells: Police Investigate Gay Abuse Remarks," BBC News, 25 April 2015, http://www.bbc.co.uk/news/uk-northern-ireland-32443730. Accessed 1 February 2018.

24. “Guidance for Health and Social Care Professionals on Termination of Pregnancy in Northern Ireland, Department of Health, Social Services and Public Safety, Northern Ireland.” All references to this document are from https://www.dhsspsni.gov.uk/sites/default/files/publications/dhssps/guidance-termination-pregnancy.pdf. Accessed 1 February 2018.
25. As seen in debate around the 2007 guidelines also—see below.
26. Director, FPA Northern Ireland. Private interview with the author, Belfast. February 2014.
27. Private interview with the author, Belfast. March 2014.
28. “Anti-abortion Activists Protest at Opening of Marie Stopes Clinic,” *The Guardian*, 18 October 2012, http://www.theguardian.com/uk/2012/oct/18/anti-abortion-protest-belfast-clinic. Accessed 1 February 2018.
29. Although paid for via public funds, provision for termination of pregnancy in private facilities (mostly run by the British Pregnancy Advisory Service and Marie Stopes) is the norm in England and Wales. In Scotland, all terminations are provided solely on NHS facilities.
30. The petition is a particular feature of the devolved institution, designed to allow for minority dissent (O’Leary 2004, 290), but which can be employed on any topic as long as there is sufficient support within the Assembly. A petition requires the signature of 30 of the 108 MLAs, and any vote on which the petition of concern is expressing disquiet cannot be held until a day after it is registered. The ensuing vote then needs 60% of the legislature to approve it, including 40% from both the Nationalist and Unionist sides.
31. Criminal Justice Bill: Further Consideration Stage, Northern Irish Assembly debate, 12 March 2013, http://www.niassembly.gov.uk/assembly-business/official-report/reports-12-13/12-march-2013. Accessed 1 February 2018. All further references are to this source.
32. The notion of a “shared future” is a recurring motif in Northern Irish political discourse, across party lines.
33. Amendment 34—Consideration Stage: Justice Bill (Northern Irish Assembly Bill 37/11-15), Assembly debate, 2 June 2015, http://aims.niassembly.gov.uk/officialreport/report.aspx?&eveDate=2015/06/02&docID=236057. Accessed 1 February 2018. All further references are to this source.
34. Available at https://www.dojni.gov.uk/sites/default/files/consultations/doj/the-criminal-law-on-abortion-lethal-foetal-abnormality-and-sexual-crime.pdf. Accessed 1 February 2018. All further references are to this source.

35. Consultation on the Criminal Law on Abortion in Cases of Lethal Foetal Abnormality and Sexual Crime: Department of Justice Officials, Committee for Justice, Stormont, 8 October 2014, http://data.niassembly.gov.uk/HansardXml/committee-10152.pdf. Accessed 1 February 2018. All further references are to this source.
36. Unionist MLA. Private interview with the author, Belfast, 11 March 2014 and 24 March 2014.

Bibliography

Amery, Fran. 2014. Social Questions, Medical Answers: Contesting British Abortion Law. *Social Politics* 21 (1): 26–49.

Bacchi, Carol Lee. 1999. *Women, Policy, and Politics: The Construction of Policy Problems.* New York: Sage.

Bache, Ian, and Matthew Flinders. 2005. Multi-level Governance and British Politics. In *Multi-level Governance*, ed. Ian Bache and Matthew Flinders. Oxford: Oxford University Press.

Chappell, Louise. 2002. *Gendering Government: Feminist Engagement with the State in Australia and Canada.* Vancouver: University of British Columbia Press.

Childs, Sarah, and Mona Lena Krook. 2009. Analysing Women's Substantive Representation: From Critical Mass to Critical Actors. *Government and Opposition* 44 (2) (April): 125–145.

Conley, Richard S., and Charles Dahan. 2013. Legislative Behaviour in the Northern Irish Assembly 2007–2011: Conflict and Consensus in a Developing Consociational Democracy. *Political Studies* 61 (S1): 179–197.

FPA. 2014. Abortion Practice and Provision in Northern Ireland—Factsheet. Available at http://www.fpa.org.uk/sites/default/files/northern-ireland-abortion.pdf. Accessed 31 January 2018.

Horowitz, Donald L. 1985. *Ethnic Groups in Conflict: Theories, Patterns, and Policies.* Berkeley: University of California Press.

Hunter, James Davison. 1992. *The Culture Wars: The Struggle to Define America.* New York: Basic Books.

Kulawik, Teresa. 2009. Staking the Frame of a Feminist Discursive Institutionalism. *Politics and Gender* 5 (2): 262–271.

Mackay, Fiona. 2014. Nested Newness, Institutional Innovation, and the Gendered Limits of Change. *Politics and Gender* 10: 549–571.

Mackay, Fiona, and Mona Lena Krook. 2011. Introduction: Gender, Politics and Institutions. In *Gender, Politics and Insitutions: Towards a Feminist Institutionalism.* Basingstoke: Palgrave Macmillan.

McEvoy, Joanne. 2013. We Forbid! The Mutual Veto and Power-Sharing Democracy. In *Power Sharing in Deeply Divided Places*, ed. Joanne McEvoy and Brendan O'Leary. Philadelphia: University of Pennsylvania Press.

Mycock, Andrew, and Shaun McDaid. 2014. Stem the Tide of Northern Ireland's 'Culture Wars'. https://www.opendemocracy.net/andrew-mycock-shaun-mcdaid/stem-tide-of-northern-ireland%E2%80%99s-%E2%80%98culture-wars%E2%80%99. Accessed 31 January 2018.

O'Leary, Brendan. 2004. The Nature of the Agreement. In *The Northern Ireland Conflict: Consociational Engagements*. Oxford: Oxford University Press.

Schmidt, Vivien. 2008. Discursive Institutionalism: The Explanatory Power of Ideas and Discourse. *Annual Review of Political Science* 11: 303–326.

———. 2010. Taking Ideas and Discourse Seriously: Explaining Change Through Discursive Institutionalism as the Fourth New Institutionalism. *European Political Science Review* 2 (1): 1–25.

Thomson, Jennifer. 2015. Abortion and Same-Sex Marriage: How Are Non-sectarian Controversial Issues Discussed in Northern Irish Politics? *Irish Political Studies* 31 (4): 483–501.

Tonge, Jonathon. 2005. *The New Northern Irish Politics?* London: Palgrave.

CHAPTER 8

Conclusion

The 1967 Abortion Act has never applied in Northern Ireland. With movements for change blocked at the regional level, and national parliament at Westminster showing little interest in forcing legal change, there are few signs that the Act will ever be extended. Although Northern Irish women can now access free terminations in England, Scotland and Wales, the strict legal situation in the region itself looks set to continue. This book has asked why this is the case: Why has the 1967 Act never been extended to Northern Ireland?

Within academic work in the social sciences, Northern Ireland and its politics have only been considered sporadically from a gendered perspective. The majority of politics scholarship on the region has looked at the conflict and its aftermath from the level of elite negotiations. Women have rarely figured in these narratives; neither has a sustained consideration of gender, within both the conflict, and Northern Irish society and politics. Although there is a growing body of work on women's descriptive representation in the Northern Irish Assembly (Braniff and Whiting 2015; Cowell-Meyers 2003, 2011; Galligan 2006, 2013; Matthews 2014), there has been less consideration of gender as a structural force in Northern Irish politics and its institutions.

Furthermore, academic work has shown little interest in women's substantive interests in the region. Within this, abortion has been especially neglected. Abortion has been legal for almost 50 years under the 1967 Act in England, Scotland and Wales. Northern Ireland was exempt from this original legislation and continues to be so. Whilst Northern Ireland

J. Thomson, *Abortion Law and Political Institutions*, Gender and Politics, https://doi.org/10.1007/978-3-319-96169-9_8

also differs from the rest of the UK on a range of social policy issues, abortion has proven especially resilient to change. Furthermore, abortion has rarely been studied from an institutional perspective; in fact, much work on the politics of abortion tends to treat institutions as "natural occurrences" (Halfmann 2011, 5). This book has addressed the issue from an institutional perspective, asking how the particular institutional make-up of Northern Ireland, with its unique multi-level governance set-up, has influenced political debate and the ultimate lack of action around this issue.

This book has also considered a devolved institution and regional politics which have rarely been addressed from a gendered perspective. Feminist institutionalism has had much interest in political institutions in the UK (Kenny 2013; Mackay 2010, 2014) but less so Northern Ireland. The gendered implications of multi-level governance have been explored in this book, particularly in the relationships between central government and the devolved Northern Irish institutions.

This book considered the issue of abortion at two different levels of multi-level governance—the national institution at Westminster and the regional institution at Stormont. Following the introductory chapters, Chapter 4 turned to national government at Westminster. Through a long-term historical narrative, this chapter illustrated how central government has largely ignored, avoided and overlooked the issue of abortion and Northern Ireland since the initial passing of legislation via the 1967 Act. The book then turned to consider regional government in Stormont. Chapter 5 charted the peace process in Northern Ireland from the early 1980s to the Good Friday Agreement. It showed that women, both descriptively and substantively, played little role in the movement towards peace. As such, there was minimal space for a discussion of abortion rights. Chapter 6 then looked at the type of political institution that was created through the peace agreement and devolution in the region. It argued that because the consociational power-sharing basis of Northern Ireland's political institutions privileges ethno-national identity and politics, it becomes difficult to mobilise formal politics around non-ethno-national issues. It further explored the difficulties that pro-choice campaigners have had in trying to encourage movement around the issue at Stormont. Chapter 7 turned to consider the ways in which abortion has been discussed in political debate in the new Northern Irish Assembly. It illustrated how abortion, and especially the 1967 Abortion Act, has always been discussed with mistrust in Northern Irish politics and has continually been presented as a law which allows for "abortion on demand." A key group of individuals have been especially important in ensuring that anti-abortion movements and discussion remain on the political agenda. As a result, this has focused debate in a narrow fashion, centred around the regulation of Marie Stopes and minor policy changes (the guidelines for medical professionals), rather than the broader issue of women's rights and health. The chapter further argues that traditional "green-orange" politics in Northern Ireland are changing, with gendered issues such as abortion taking greater prominence in highlighting the difference between the two dominant political parties, the DUP and Sinn Féin.

Feminist Institutionalism and Abortion

This book is a case study of what feminist institutional theory can learn from an instance when positive gendered change has not happened. Why *hasn't* the Abortion Act been extended? The book has explored the issue of abortion legislation in Northern Ireland from the perspective of political institutions. In its discursive underpinnings, this book made extensive use of Carol Lee Bacchi's "What's the problem?" (1999) methodological framework. Table 8.1 shows how the construction of abortion has been presented in political discourse across the main institutions and debates which have been addressed in this book. The table illustrates the varying ways that the issue has been presented in political discussion, from the minimal reference made to abortion in the period during which Northern Ireland was moving towards the Good Friday Agreement to the devolved Assembly of the present day, where the discussion has focused on specific elements of abortion provision. The table shows how the frameworks used to discuss abortion in Northern Ireland have increasingly narrowed throughout two decades of debate on the issue. The case for Northern Ireland alone, without Westminster's involvement, to make a decision on this issue has grown since devolution. At the same time, debate on the topic has become more constricted, so that discussion is focused around the issue of termination for precise reasons (largely fatal foetal abnormalities) rather than the broader issue of the status of access to terminations in the province at large. The table also shows that, at what was arguably the most important moment in Northern Ireland's political history in the last thirty years—the Good Friday peace negotiations—abortion was entirely absent from discussion.

Table 8.1 Discursive representations of abortion in Northern Ireland from early 1980s to present day

	Peace talks leading up to GFA	*2000 debate*	*2007 Westminster debate*	*2007 to present day*
Representation of abortion	Absent from discussion	Regional issue for Northern Irish concern—change should be left to Stormont; slight discussion of women having to travel for treatment	Regional issue for Northern Irish concern, not a national/women's issue; should not be discussed at Westminster, but rather left to Stormont	Increasing focus on specific parts of the issue (private provision; fatal foetal abnormality); absent from national (Westminster) debate
Consequences for political debate	Not present for discussion so no means for action to be taken	Westminster discouraged from involvement	Westminster discouraged from involvement	Broader issues of access and place of termination in Northern Irish women's healthcare cannot be discussed; Westminster's silence suggests unlikely to act/encourage legal change

As is discussed in greater depth below, this reflects the book's contribution to an understanding of the gendered nature of political structures and decision-making—at the most important political point, this issue was organised out of political debate and was not considered to be an important topic for discussion.

This book has illustrated that multi-level governance in the contemporary UK has gendered implications, in that "blurred boundaries" (Celis *et al.* 2012, 46) are created between the various levels of government. As a result, gender issues such as abortion slip between the gaps of the levels of the complicated governance structures in the UK. In Chapter 4, the book illustrated how central government at Westminster has, since the 1960s, been happy to secede responsibility for this issue to the regional level. Table 8.1 reiterates this understanding, which is seen in both regional- and national-level debates—abortion is a regional issue for Northern Ireland and a topic for discussion that can be addressed at the national level only in the very specific circumstances of a weak government and renewed Westminster interest in Northern Ireland, in 2017. As a result, attempts at real, legal change from London have continually failed. Both Westminster's unwillingness to act and uncertainty over which level of governance in the contemporary UK retains responsibility for the issue mean that, again, the issue falls between the gaps of subnational and national governance. Without one distinct institution "owning" this issue or a fundamental underpinning for abortion provision in national law beyond the 1967 Act (in, for example, a national human rights bill or constitution), there is a lack of possibility for decisive action to be taken on it.

This book has reinforced and expanded the concept of "nested newness" which exists in feminist institutionalist theory. It has shown that the critical juncture presented in the founding of the new Assembly in 1998 did not provide a moment for the creation of a completely "new" body. Instead, the devolved institution remains underpinned by older understandings of politics in Northern Ireland. Chapter 5 explained how the ethno-national underpinnings of the peace negotiations result in a political institutional set-up in the province which privileges ethno-national identity as the dominant political fault line in Northern Irish politics. Chapter 4 illustrated how this was also present in national government's understanding of the region, to the extent that intervention from that level of government on the issue was perceived to be potentially disruptive to the ongoing peace process (see Table 8.1). As such, the new institution is "nested" in an already existing understanding of Northern Irish politics as centred around two ethno-national communities—the space for women to emerge as a cross-cutting political category is weak.

These understandings underpinning the institutional basis of Northern Irish politics rely on a certain "gender regime" (Connell 1987) which sees women's and gendered issues as extraneous to "real" political issues. In Andrew Finlay's words, the consociational set-up creates a political system where "all difference is welcome so long as it's ethnic" (2011, 9). As a result, mobilising women's or gendered identities in the political realm remains difficult, as they do not speak in the customary frame of reference. Chappell's conception of a "gendered logic of appropriateness" (Chappell 2006) thus underlies Northern Irish politics, where issues which fall outside of the main ethno-national division are deemed less important and not of central political concern. Again, this finding maps onto a gendered conception of power and decision-making in the province—what is important (ethno-national) is organised in, what is unimportant (and non-ethno-national, such as gendered or women's issues) is organised out. In this sense, the prolonged non-decision-making and silence around abortion and Northern Ireland are distinctly gendered.

Following on from this argument, this book has explicitly added to the focus that feminist institutionalist theory has on power within political structures. This book has shown that non-decision-making is an important site of gendered power. Although, as shown in Table 8.1, abortion has been discussed as a political issue, especially in the most recent iteration of the Assembly, no liberalising action has actually been taken. Neither national government nor supranational or international bodies have helped to make any progress on expanding abortion provision since the early 1980s. In this sense, this research reiterates the importance of inaction (Chappell 2015) for feminist institutionalist research. This case study illustrates that actions not taken are as important as those that are (Waylen 2014).

It has also added to this discussion of power and decision-making through an engagement with the issue of gendered structure and agency. Through a novel employment of the concept of "critical actors" (Childs and Krook 2006), this book has shown that conservative actors have been responsible for mobilising around this issue in the new institution to keep abortion liberalisation at bay. Whilst often used to refer to small groups of individuals who are responsible for positive change within institutions, this book has used the term "critical actors" to show how a small group of individuals from within the Northern Irish Assembly have managed, with the latent support of the majority of MLAs, to derail any attempts at liberalisation and to encourage movement around more conservative abortion practice in the province. This book has shown how a well-developed concept within the gender and politics literature can be inverted to explain the absence of movement. In this sense, this use of "critical actors" ties in with the previous arguments outlined above that the book also makes, and the role that they have played in supporting an absence of political movement and continued silence around the issue (Chappell 2015; Waylen 2014).

Key Contributions and Future Areas for Research

From this book, the following key conclusions can be drawn:

- *The type of political institution influences the way women's rights are addressed (Chapter 6).* Northern Ireland has been highlighted as a success story of power-sharing government and an exemplar of post-conflict stability: in the words of Rupert Taylor, it "shines as the brightest star in the consociationalist universe" (Taylor 2009, 7). Consociational theory played a key role in conceiving the Northern Irish post-conflict institutions and underpins their framework. Yet, in spite of the wide range of academic work on consociationalism, and a lengthy debate between pro- and anti-consociationalists (Taylor 2006), its effects on "other" political identities have been under-considered. The gendered effects of consociational power-sharing (with a few exceptions: Byrne and McCulloch 2012; Kennedy *et al.* 2016) have been largely ignored. Chapter 5 illustrates how an understanding of ethno-nationalism dominated the movement towards peace in the 1980s and 1990s, with women's groups and gendered issues having trouble making it onto the agenda. As a result, as Chapter 6 shows, consociational governance based around ethno-nationalism as the central political identity makes it difficult for "other" political issues to gain traction. Women's and gendered issues, such as abortion, have thus struggled to create any political momentum.

- This finding points to an exciting new direction for both feminist institutionalism and the literature on power-sharing as a means for post-conflict governance. Feminist institutionalism provides the tools to make key contributions to a gendered critique of consociational governance, by looking at how the institutional make-up of power-sharing bodies impacts descriptive and substantive gendered representation. And whilst the Women, Peace and Security literature is extraordinarily well developed (most especially around the issue of UNSCR 1325: McLeod 2011, 2015; Shepherd 2008a, b, 2011), it has given little consideration to governance structures and political institutions (again, with the exceptions of Byrne and McCulloch 2012; Kennedy *et al.* 2016). This book thus posits that there is the potential for fruitful dialogue between these two bodies of work. There are multiple other case studies through which the gendered impact of consociational governance might be explored. Although there has been much feminist and gender research into post-conflict Bosnia–Herzegovina, there has been little which has looked at the institutional level. Similarly, post-conflict examples of consociationalism, from Lebanon to Iraq and Macedonia, have had little sustained interest from a gendered perspective. Comparative work might be undertaken between these various sites of consociationalism. All are largely conservative with regard to gendered politics: Can this be explained in any way through their institutional design? Is consociationalism impeding female representation and political voice? Furthermore, consociationalism forwards an understanding of post-conflict governance as based around ethnic identity; UNSCR 1325 argues for women's inclusion as women. How do these competing arguments play out in practice? How has consociational design and its implementation in these various contemporary contexts been squared against the developing Women, Peace and Security agenda?
- *Inter-institutional relationships are key to understanding gender and multi-level governance (Chapters 4 and 7).* As outlined in Chapter 2, the majority of work on gender and devolution in the UK is positive in the picture it portrays of women's descriptive and substantive representation. The new institutions in Cardiff and Edinburgh have seen some of the highest levels of women's elected representation in the UK, which, following the advent of Nicola Sturgeon as Scottish First Minister, has grown in prominence and media coverage. Studies report

MSPs and AMs showing a high level of gender awareness in policymaking (Mackay and Charles 2013). The literature considering the gendered effects of devolution in Northern Ireland is far less developed. This case study adds Northern Ireland to the mix and illustrates that the positive effects happening elsewhere have not been echoed in the province. The new iteration of devolved governance at Stormont since 1998 has not seen a greater level of women's elected representation, nor an awareness that this might be a problem. Furthermore, on a range of gendered issues (abortion, same-sex marriage, blood donation by gay men and LGBT rights more generally) Northern Ireland has not enacted changes seen in the rest of the UK. On all of these issues, Westminster has remained quiet (or, in the case of blood donation by gay men, actively pursued the line that this is for Stormont to decide upon, even if it chooses a different policy direction from Westminster[1]). The complex multi-level set-up created by devolution has provided a way by which central government can sidestep controversial issues, many of which have very gendered implications. The relationship between Westminster and Stormont is shown to suffer from a "nested newness" (Mackay 2014), where emphasis from central government is on peace and stability to the detriment of women's rights.

- Indeed, as the debates at Stormont discussed in Chapter 7 showed, the Northern Irish Assembly used these as an opportunity to signal to Westminster that it did not want national government's involvement. Devolution has thus created "blurred boundaries" (Celis *et al.* 2012, 46) for where responsibility for certain policy issues lies. Whilst national government might technically be able to enforce or encourage policy change, it has chosen not to. "Multi-level games" (ibid., 51) and a sidestepping of responsibility around gendered issues have become a part of the relationships between the various levels of British governance. This case study illustrates that it is important for the literature on gender and devolution/multi-level governance to look at the relationships between the various bodies, not just individual bodies on their own which has until now been the tendency (e.g. Chaney 2006; Kenny 2013; Mackay 2010). The relationship between the levels of multi-level governance is gendered, in that differences between national and devolved attitudes to controversial gender issues are far more likely to be ignored, sidelined or brushed under the carpet than other economic or social issues.

- This finding opens up several interesting areas for future research. With devolution now proposed on a much wider scale across the UK, particularly in various city-regions in England, how will gendered issues be incorporated into the newly devolved structures? With abortion now also devolved to Scotland, does this signal a broader move towards the decentralisation of reproductive rights in the UK?
- *"Venue-shopping" (Vickers et al.* 2010, *237) is not always necessarily a useful tool for women's rights campaigns.* Gender scholars (Bashevkin 1998) have largely viewed the ability to move between different political spaces as a positive feature of multilayered democracies. Bashevkin argues that, under the Conservative governance of the 1980s, women's activists in the UK were able to resort to lobbying at the European Union level in order to achieve their goals. Likewise, Chappell (2002) argues that the federal structures of Australia and Canada have aided feminist activism. Vickers *et al.* (2010, 237) argue that "venue-shopping" can mean that a "blockage" at one level means there is opportunity for action elsewhere. Multiple political arenas (Westminster, Stormont, recourse to international bodies and treaties) via which liberalising measures might be encouraged or enacted are not shown to be helpful in this case study. As Chapter 4 illustrated, since the advent of the 1967 Act, Westminster has routinely avoided intervening in this issue. An understanding of Northern Ireland as "different" and a "special case" has dominated Westminster's view of the province, such that action around abortion is deemed unnecessary, with national figures wary that potential movements might somehow destabilise the peace process. As seen most especially in Chapter 7, Stormont has avoided, disincentivised and obstructed any attempts at liberalisation of abortion since devolution. Similarly, and reflecting broader literature on abortion and human rights, international institutions and human rights mechanisms have had a very limited impact on the political discussion around abortion and have not provided key spaces whereby greater liberalisation can be encouraged (Thomson 2017). For abortion in Northern Ireland, more spaces in which political change *might* occur have not resulted in change actually happening. "Blockage at one level of government" (Sawer and Vickers 2010, 11) and a move to lobbying in another locale has only met

with further blockages, including an oversimplification of Northern Irish politics which disadvantages women and a lack of interest from national parliament, and the inability of international mechanisms to have any influence on regional politics (Thomson 2017).

- Furthermore, this inability to move effectively between venues also occurs given the "blurred boundaries" (Celis *et al.* 2012, 46) that the complex multi-level governance set-up in Northern Ireland creates. Gender scholars have argued that, in complex governance situations such as the contemporary UK, the onus for institutions to act on gender issues can get lost. Such is the case with regards to abortion and Northern Ireland. Which institution carries responsibility has become muddled. As Chapters 4 and 7 showed, there is still confusion over where responsibility truly lies. Chapter 4 illustrated that many Northern Irish MPs believed that there were still tensions between national and devolved government around who should address abortion and Northern Ireland, a fact exemplified in the 2017 Westminster decision to provide abortions for Northern Irish women on NHS England. The continually evolving political structure in the contemporary UK—rather than a strictly legally defined division of powers between institutions—is to the detriment of women's rights in this case study.
- Future research might look at other examples of multi-level governance: it might consider how other European Union jurisdictions, such as Poland, have attempted to use the European level to encourage domestic reform of abortion legislation. Similarly, a feminist institutionalist framework might usefully be extended to a study of the USA and abortion legislation: How have pro-life forces used the federal legal and political system to encourage more restrictive legal frameworks?
- *The continuing division in Northern Irish politics between Sinn Féin and the DUP is gendered.* The "culture wars" (Hunter 1992; Mycock and McDaid 2014; Wuthnow 1990) in contemporary Northern Irish politics have, to date, been given little academic consideration. Yet they have much to tell us about the ways that post-conflict formal politics is developing in Northern Ireland. Gendered policy issues, including abortion, have become a new point of friction through which the main strands of formal politics can assert their difference

from one another. Whilst this is seen most pointedly in the case of same-sex marriage, which has largely mapped onto the traditional green-orange political party division (Thomson 2015), abortion is less clearly divided. Sinn Féin, whilst strongly supportive of same-sex marriage and LGBT rights more broadly, can only act defensively in response to conservative attempts to greater restrict abortion. They have provided little in terms of proactive policies that might liberalise legislation in this area. The contemporary dominance of Sinn Féin and the DUP does not appear likely to change in the immediate future. Both parties are keen to highlight differences between them, as DUP members' repeated assertion during the abortion debate that Sinn Féin was an immoral, pro-choice party shows.

- This research thus suggests, not that green and orange politics have gone away, but that they are changing. Rather than positing that Northern Irish politics are entering a post-ethno-national framework, it argues that the framework is increasingly gendered in ways that it was not previously. As Horowitz writes, there is a "salience" to ethnicity, such that "in divided societies … almost any issue, any phenomenon, can suddenly 'turn ethnic'" (1985, 8). Abortion is "politically consequential" (Htun 2003, 2) in contemporary Northern Irish politics, in that it is both encouraging new political relationships that cross the ethno-national divide (Lutz and Farrington 2006) but also acting as a marker between the political sides. This book thus argues that gender is not an "add on" (Ashe *et al.* 2016), but rather more fundamental to our understanding of contemporary politics in Northern Ireland.
- In this finding, it also argues that there is no inevitable link between greater democracy and stability and women's rights. Abortion has become enmeshed in Northern Ireland's ethno-national politics to the detriment of women's rights. As political discussion of the issue has grown, policy inertia has occurred. In this sense, this book also reiterates previous findings that transitions to democracy and stability from conflict or authoritarian rule are not necessarily all that is required for support for women's rights (Anderson 2016; Htun 2003). This finding (that the post-'post-conflict' era is an increasingly gendered political terrain) might be extended to compare other locales with which Northern Ireland has similarity, such as Bosnia–Herzegovina—are gendered issues becoming equally

politicised? Is this unique to Northern Ireland, with its particular brand of Christian-inflected politics, or is an equally conservative attitude to social issues seen more generally in post-conflict societies?

- *For feminist political science, considering instances of a lack of movement around policy issues can be as important as addressing substantial (whether positive or negative) change.* As Chapters 6 and 7 illustrated, the governmental structure of Northern Irish politics and its focus on ethno-nationalism as the dominant political identity renders gendered issues difficult to mobilise around politically. The lack of change on abortion can thus largely be explained through a macro-level, institutional lens. Chapter 7 turned to consider the micro-level of political debate within the devolved institutions. Focusing on the specific actions (and non-actions) of the Assembly since devolution adds greater depth by highlighting the importance of key individuals to the political understanding of abortion. Certain "critical actors" (Childs and Krook 2006) have worked to ensure conservative movement on the issue of abortion. Assembly debates have been instigated by a key group of figures. Jim Wells, whose personal beliefs around abortion are well documented, had the ability to initiate a debate in 2000, at a period when there was no political movement around abortion and was then behind the second attempt to close Marie Stopes via the Assembly in 2015. Key voices in these debates are ones that are heard again and again in political discussion around this issue. The long-drawn-out story of the guidance illustrated across Chapter 7 also illustrates the power that individual politicians and public figures have had. The Health Minister has had clear power and influence over the shape of the guidance. Iris Robinson's role as Chairperson of the Health, Social Services and Public Safety Committee allowed her to be of central importance to the issue of the guidelines, instigating the 2007 Assembly debate. Under Edwin Poots, the guidance was rewritten entirely from the version overseen by the former Health Minister, Michael McGimpsey, in the late 2000s. John Larkin, the Attorney General, is widely perceived as having a key influence on the tone of the 2013 version of the guidance. Similarly, medical professionals stressed the impact they felt that the Attorney General, and not the Chief Medical Officer, had on the 2013 version of the guidelines. Individual "critical actors" (Childs and Krook 2006) have had a huge impact on the shape of the guidance.

- It is thus not only the institutional design which influences the nature of this debate, but also key individuals. Since the birth of the new Assembly, a group of critical actors have worked to impede any liberalisation. Whilst the specific design and nature of the institution are important in explaining why gendered politics struggle to be heard, a micro-level consideration of individual politicians who have acted around abortion provides greater depth to an understanding of why there has been so little change. An interplay of structure and agency is important to fully understand the inaction around this issue. This argument echoes other contemporary feminist institutionalist work which has emphasised the ways in which institutions can be sites of resistance and obstruction to positive gendered change (Chappell 2014a, b, 2015; Kenny 2013; Mackay 2014; Waylen 2014). This book builds upon these works to argue that an understanding of critical actor theory can broaden feminist institutionalist frameworks to help understand why positive change does not occur.
- Indeed, feminist political science has largely been concerned with positive, substantial change. Reflecting the normative underpinnings of feminist politics, feminist political scientists have largely turned their attention to discernible change (such as the prolific literature on quotas for women in formal political institutions: Murray 2010; or the large body of work on domestic violence legislation; Weldon 2002). Feminist social science is often also very rooted in activism and civil society organising: as Campbell and Childs note, "the 'ivory tower' never accurately captured what many feminist scholars including feminist political scientists were, and are, doing" (2013, 185). Work on feminist peace activism is a key example of scholarship which is very pointedly situated within anti-war efforts and organising (Confortini 2012). Feminist political scholarship often carries strong normative underpinnings and is largely concerned with the visible and achievable.
- Yet as much can be learned from things that have not happened—treaties that have not been ratified (Baldez 2014), issues that go ignored (Crenson 1971) and topics that are "organised out" of political conversation (Bachrach and Baratz 1962). This book has implicitly forwarded a case for the contribution that a consideration of a lack of action might have for feminist political science. Indeed, the case of abortion in Northern Ireland largely provides feminist

political science with a negative case study in which very little concrete change has occurred. Yet, as Chappell reminds us, "it is as important to account for ***actions not undertaken*** as it is to analyse those that have" (2014b, 193, emphasis in original). Westminster has dragged its heels on this issue since 1967. Stormont has seen a series of events designed to stop, stall, delay or further inhibit abortion in the province. Looking at why this has been the case has led to further insights about the gendered nature of governance in Northern Ireland, the influence of post-conflict institutional design on gender politics and the key role that individual critical actors have played in this debate. We can learn as much from what institutions have "*failed to do*" (ibid., emphasis in original) as from what they have actually achieved.

Plus ça Change?...

In May 2018, the Republic of Ireland voted overwhelmingly to repeal the 8th amendment to the country's Constitution. This will allow for change to permit legal abortion in Ireland for the first time. Following the referendum in the Republic, Northern Ireland's status as an outlier vis-à-vis its abortion laws was quickly pointed out by the media and politicians, both Irish and British alike. Around 160 Westminster MPs backed a letter calling for Northern Ireland's abortion laws to be liberalised.[2] Yet the government appeared unlikely to intervene, with a spokesperson for Theresa May saying that:

> … it's important to recognise that the people of Northern Ireland are entitled to their own process, which is run by locally elected politicians. Our focus is restoring a democratically accountable devolved government in Northern Ireland so that locally accountable politicians can make decisions on behalf of the public they represent.[3]

The definition of abortion as a devolved issue, and not a women's issue, continues.

To return to the two cases which opened this book provides some optimism. Whilst there has been little discernible legal or political change in the interim, there is clearly a greater openness and discussion around abortion in a contemporary setting. The case of Sarah Ewart saw an outpouring of public soul-searching in the Northern Irish media and public sphere. In the words of Dawn Purvis, former Director of the Belfast Marie Stopes clinic, this represents that "the population are way ahead of their politicians when it comes to this issue."[4] Beyond politics, public sentiment, coupled with the knowledge that Northern Ireland is now unique in Western Europe in its strict legislation, may yet force legal change.

Notes

1. "Stormont to Decide on Whether Gay Men Can Give Blood in Northern Ireland", BBC, 16 March 2016, http://www.bbc.co.uk/news/uk-northern-ireland-35822913. Accessed 12 February 2018.
2. "MPS Call for Theresa May to Permit Poll on Abortion in Northern Ireland", *The Guardian*, 29 May 2018, https://www.theguardian.com/world/2018/may/27/theresa-may-oppose-vote-northern-ireland-abortion-law. Accessed 31 May 2018.
3. "No Plans to Intervene on Northern Ireland Abortion Law, Says No. 10", *The Guardian*, 29 May 2018, https://www.theguardian.com/politics/2018/may/29/no-plans-to-intervene-on-northern-ireland-abortion-law-says-no-10. Accessed 31 May 2018.
4. Dawn Purvis. Private interview with the author, Belfast. March 2014.

Bibliography

Anderson, Miriam J. 2016. *Windows of Opportunity: How Women Seize Peace Negotiations for Political Change*. Oxford: Oxford University Press.

Ashe, Fidelma, Gorana Mlinarevic, Claire Pierson, and Jennifer Thomson. 2016. Gendering Research in Divided Societies: A Conversation. *International Feminist Journal of Politics* 18 (4): 606–613.

Bacchi, Carol Lee. 1999. *Women, Policy, and Politics: The Construction of Policy Problems*. New York: Sage.

Bachrach, Peter, and Morton S. Baratz. 1962. Two Faces of Power. *The American Political Science Review* 56 (4): 947–952.

Baldez, Lisa. 2014. *Defying Convention: US Resistance to the UN Treaty on Women's Rights*. Cambridge: Cambridge University Press.

Bashevkin, Sylvia. 1998. *Women on the Defensive: Living Through Conservative Times*. Chicago: University of Chicago Press.

Braniff, Maire, and Sophie Whiting. 2015. 'There's Just No Point Having a Token Woman': Gender and Representation in the Democratic Unionist Party in Post-agreement Northern Ireland. *Parliamentary Affairs* 69 (1): 93–114.

Byrne, Siobhan, and Allison McCulloch. 2012. Gender, Representation and Power-Sharing in Post Conflict Institutions. *International Peacekeeping* 19 (5): 565–580.

Campbell, Rosie, and Sarah Childs. 2013. The Impact Imperative: Here Come the Women. *Political Studies* 11 (2): 182–189.

Celis, K., Fiona Mackay, and Petra Meier. 2012. Social Movement Organizations and Changing State Architectures: Comparing Women's Movement Organizing in Flanders and Scotland. *Publius: The Journal of Federalism* 43 (1): 44–67.

Chaney, Paul. 2006. Women and Constitutional Reform: Gender Parity in the National Assembly for Wales. In *Representing Women in Parliament: A Comparative Study*, ed. Marian Sawer, Manon Tremblay, and Linda Trimble. Abingdom: Routledge.

Chappell, Louise. 2002. *Gendering Government: Feminist Engagement with the State in Australia and Canada*. Vancouver: University of British Columbia Press.

———. 2006. Comparing Political Institutions: Revealing the Gendered 'Logic of Appropriateness'. *Politics and Gender* 2 (2): 232–235.

———. 2014a. 'New', 'Old', and 'Nested' Institutions and Gender Justice Outcomes: A View from the International Criminal Court. *Politics and Gender* 10 (4): 572–594.

———. 2014b. Conflicting Institutions and the Search for Gender Justice at the International Criminal Court. *Political Research Quarterly* 67 (1): 183–196.

———. 2015. *The Politics of Gender Justice at the International Criminal Court: Legacies and Legitimacy*. Oxford: Oxford University Press.

Childs, Sarah, and Mona Lena Krook. 2006. Should Feminists Give Up on Critical Mass? A Contingent Yes. *Politics and Gender* 2 (4): 522–530.

Confortini, Catia Cecilia. 2012. *Intelligent Compassion: Feminist Critical Methodology in the Women's International League for Peace and Freedom*. Oxford: Oxford University Press.

Connell, R.W. 1987. *Gender and Power*. Cambridge: Polity.

Cowell-Meyers, Kimberley. 2003. Women Legislators in Northern Ireland: Gender and Politics in the New Legislative Assembly. http://www.qub.ac.uk/cawp/research/assembly.PDF. Accessed 21 April 2015.

———. 2011. A Collarette on a Donkey: The Northern Ireland Women's Coalition and the Limitations of Contagion Theory. *Political Studies* 59 (2): 411–431.

Crenson, Matthew A. 1971. *The Un-Politics of Air Pollution: A Study on Non-decision-making in the Cities*. Baltimore: John Hopkins University Press.

Finlay, Andrew. 2011. *Governing Ethnic Conflict: Consociation, Identity and the Price of Peace*. Abingdon: Routledge.

Galligan, Yvonne. 2006. Women in Northern Ireland's Politics: Feminizing an 'Armed Patriarchy'. In *Representing Women in Parliament: A Comparative Study*, ed. Marian Sawer, Manon Tremblay, and Linda Trimble. Abingdon: Routledge.

———. 2013. Gender and Politics in Northern Ireland: The Representation Gap Revisited. *Irish Political Studies* 28 (3): 413–433.

Halfmann, Drew. 2011. *Doctors and Demonstrators: How Political Institutions Shape Abortion Law in the United States*. Chicago: University of Chicago Press.

Horowitz, Donald L. 1985. *Ethnic Groups in Conflict: Theories, Patterns, and Policies*. Berkeley: University of California Press.

Htun, Mala. 2003. *Sex and the State: Abortion, Divorce and the Family Under Latin American Dictatorships and Democracies*. Cambridge: Cambridge University Press.

Hunter, James Davison. 1992. *The Culture Wars: The Struggle to Define America*. New York: Basic Books.

Kennedy, Ronan, Claire Pierson, and Jennifer Thomson. 2016. Challenging Identity Hierarchies: Consociational Power-Sharing and Gendered Political Representation. *British Journal of Politics and International Relations* 18 (3): 618–633.

Kenny, Meryl. 2013. *Gender and Political Recruitment: Theorizing Institutional Change*. London: Palgrave Macmillan.

Lutz, Karin, and Christopher Farrington. 2006. Alternative Ulster? Political Parties and the Non-constitutional Policy Space in Northern Ireland. *Political Studies* 54 (4): 715–742.

Mackay, Fiona. 2010. Devolution and the Multilevel Politics of Gender in the UK: The Case of Scotland. In *Federalism, Feminism and Multilevel Governance*, ed. Melissa Haussman, Marian Sawer, and Jill Vickers. London: Ashgate.

———. 2014. A Feminist Institutionalist Approach. *Politics and Gender* 10 (4): 679–684.

Mackay, Fiona, and Nickie Charles. 2013. Feminist Politics and Framing Contests: Domestic Violence Policy in Scotland and Wales. *Critical Social Policy* 33 (4): 593–615.

Matthews, Neil. 2014. Gendered Candidate Selection and the Representation of Women in Northern Ireland. *Parliamentary Affairs* 67 (3): 617–646.

McLeod, Laura. 2011. Configurations of Post-conflict: Impacts of Representations of Conflict and Post-conflict upon the (Political) Translations of Gender Security Within UNSCR1325. *International Feminist Journal of Politics* 13 (4): 594–611.

———. 2015. *Gender Politics and Security Discourse: Personal-Political Imaginations and Feminism in 'Post-conflict' Serbia*. London: Routledge.

Murray, Rainbow. 2010. *Parties, Gender Quotas and Candidate Selection in France*. Basingstoke: Palgrave.
Mycock, and McDaid. 2014. Stem the Tide of Northern Ireland's 'Culture Wars'. https://www.opendemocracy.net/andrew-mycock-shaun-mcdaid/stem-tide-of-northern-ireland%E2%80%99s-%E2%80%98culture-wars%E2%80%99. Accessed 29 January 2018.
Sawer, Marian, and Jill Vickers. 2010. Introduction: Political Architecture and Its Gender Impact. In *Federalism, Feminism and Multilevel Governance*, ed. Melissa Haussman, Marian Sawer, and Jill Vickers. London: Ashgate.
Shepherd, Laura. 2008a. Power and Authority in the Production of United Nations Security Council Resolution 1325. *International Studies Quarterly* 52 (2): 383–404.
———. 2008b. *Gender, Violence and Security: Discourse as Practice*. London: Zed Books.
———. 2011. Sex, Security and Superhero(in)es: From 1325 to 1820 and Beyond. *International Feminist Journal of Politics* 13 (4): 504–521.
Taylor, Rupert. 2006. The Belfast Agreement and the Politics of Consociationalism: A Critique. *The Political Quarterly* 77 (2): 217–226.
——— (ed.). 2009. *Consociational Theory: McGarry and O'Leary and the Northern Ireland Conflict*. Abingdon: Routledge.
Thomson, Jennifer. 2015. Abortion and Same-Sex Marriage: How Are Non-sectarian Controversial Issues Discussed in Northern Irish Politics? *Irish Political Studies* 31 (4): 483–501.
———. 2017. Thinking Globally, Acting Locally?: The Women's Sector, International Human Rights Mechanisms and Politics in Northern Ireland. *Politics* 37 (1): 82–96.
Vickers, Jill, Melissan Haussman, and Marian Sawer. 2010. Conclusion. In *Federalism, Feminism and Multilevel Governance*, ed. Melissa Haussman, Marian Sawer, and Jill Vickers. London: Ashgate.
Waylen, Georgina. 2014. Informal Institutions, Institutional Change and Gender Equality. *Political Research Quarterly* 67 (1): 212–223.
Weldon, Laurel. 2002. *Protest, Policy and the Problem of Violence Against Women: A Cross-National Comparison*. Pittsburgh: University of Pittsburgh Press.
Wuthnow, Robert. 1990. *The Restructuring of American Religion: Society and Faith Since World War II*. Princeton: Princeton University Press.

Appendix A—The 1967 Abortion Act

The 1967 Abortion Act as Amended by the 1990 Human Fertilisation and Embryology Act Medical Termination of Pregnancy

1. (1) Subject to the provisions of this section, a person shall not be guilty of an offence under the law relating to abortion when a pregnancy is terminated by a registered medical practitioner if two registered medical practitioners are of the opinion, formed in good faith: (a) that the pregnancy has not exceeded its twenty-fourth week and that the continuance of the pregnancy would involve risk, greater than if the pregnancy were terminated, of injury to the physical or mental health of the pregnant woman or any existing children of her family; or (b) that the termination is necessary to prevent grave permanent injury to the physical or mental health of the pregnant woman; or (c) that the continuance of the pregnancy would involve risk to the life of the pregnant woman, greater than if the pregnancy were terminated; or (d) that there is a substantial risk that if the child were born, it would suffer from such physical or mental abnormalities as to be seriously handicapped.

1. (2) In determining whether the continuance of a pregnancy would involve such risk of injury to health as is mentioned in paragraph (a) or (b) of subsection (1) of this section, account may be taken of the pregnant woman's actual or reasonably foreseeable environment.

J. Thomson, *Abortion Law and Political Institutions*, Gender and Politics, https://doi.org/10.1007/978-3-319-96169-9

1. (3) Except as provided by subsection (4) of this section, any treatment for the termination of pregnancy must be carried out in a hospital vested in the Minister of Health or the Secretary of State under the National Health Service Acts, or in a place for the time being approved for the purposes of this section by the said Minister or the Secretary of State.

1. (3A) The power under subsection (3) of this section to approve a place includes power, in relation to the treatment consisting primarily in the use of such medicines as may be specified in the approval and carried out in such manner as may be so specified, to approve a class of places.

1. (4) Subsection (3) of this section, and so much of subsection (1) as relates to the opinion of two registered medical practitioners, shall not apply to the termination of a pregnancy by a registered medical practitioner in a case where he is of the opinion, formed in good faith, that the termination is immediately necessary to save the life or to prevent grave permanent injury to the physical or mental health of the pregnant woman.

Notification

2. (1) The Minister of Health in respect of England and Wales, and the Secretary of State in respect of Scotland, shall by statutory instrument make regulations to provide—(a) for requiring any such opinion as is referred to in section 1 of this Act to be certified by the practitioners or practitioner concerned in such form and at such time as may be prescribed by the regulations, and for requiring the preservation and disposal of certificates made for the purposes of the regulations; (b) for requiring any registered medical practitioner who terminates a pregnancy to give notice of the termination and such other information relating to the termination as may be so prescribed; and (c) for prohibiting the disclosure, except to such persons or for such purposes as may be so prescribed, of notices given or information furnished pursuant to the regulations.

2. (2) The information furnished in pursuance of regulations made by virtue of paragraph (b) of subsection (1) of this section shall be notified solely to the Chief Medical Officers of the Ministry of Health and the Scottish Home and Health Department, respectively.

2. (3) Any person who wilfully contravenes or wilfully fails to comply with the requirements of regulations under subsection (1) of this section shall be liable on summary conviction to a fine not exceeding one hundred pounds.

2. (4) Any statutory instrument made by virtue of this section shall be subject to annulment in pursuance of a resolution of either House of Parliament.

Application of Act to Visiting Forces, Etc

3. (1) In relation to the termination of a pregnancy in a case where the following conditions are satisfied, that is to say: (a) the treatment for termination of the pregnancy was carried out in a hospital controlled by the proper authorities of a body to which this section applies; (b) the pregnant woman had at the time of the treatment a relevant association with that body; and (c) the treatment was carried out by a registered medical practitioner or a person who at the time of the treatment was a member of that body appointed as a medical practitioner for that body by the proper authorities of that body, this Act shall have effect as if any reference in section 1 to a registered medical practitioner and to a hospital vested in a Minister under the National Health Service Acts included, respectively, a reference to such a person as is mentioned in paragraph (c) of this subsection and to a hospital controlled as aforesaid, and as if section 2 were omitted.

3. (2) The bodies to which this section applies are any force which is a visiting force within the meaning of any of the provisions of Part I of the Visiting Forces Act 1952 and any headquarters within the meaning of the Schedule to the International Headquarters and Defence Organisations Act 1964; and for the purposes of this section—(a) a woman shall be treated as having a relevant association at any time with a body to which this section applies if at that time—(i) in the case of such a force as aforesaid, she had a relevant association within the meaning of the said Part I with the force and (ii) in the case of such a headquarters as aforesaid, she was a member of the headquarters or a dependant within the meaning of the Schedule aforesaid of such a member; and (b) any reference to a member of a body to which this section applies shall be construed—(i) in the case of such a force as aforesaid, as a reference to a member of or of a civilian component of that force within the meaning of the said Part I and (ii) in the case of such a headquarters as aforesaid, as a reference to a member of that headquarters within the meaning of the Schedule aforesaid.

Conscientious Objection to Participation in Treatment

4. (1) Subject to subsection (2) of this section, no person shall be under any duty, whether by contract or by any statutory or other legal requirement, to participate in any treatment authorised by this Act to which he has a conscientious objection: provided that in any legal proceedings, the burden of proof of conscientious objection shall rest on the person claiming to rely on it.

4. (2) Nothing in subsection (1) of this section shall affect any duty to participate in treatment which is necessary to save the life or to prevent grave permanent injury to the physical or mental health of a pregnant woman.

4. (3) In any proceedings before a court in Scotland, a statement on oath by any person to the effect that he has a conscientious objection to participating in any treatment authorised by this Act shall be sufficient evidence for the purpose of discharging the burden of proof imposed upon him by subsection (1) of this section.

5. (1) No offence under the Infant Life (Preservation) Act 1929 shall be committed by a registered medical practitioner who terminates a pregnancy in accordance with the provisions of this Act.

5. (2) For the purposes of the law relating to abortion, anything done with intent to procure a woman's miscarriage (or, in the case of a woman carrying more than one foetus, her miscarriage of any foetus) is unlawfully done unless authorised by section 1 of this Act, and in the case of a woman carrying more than one foetus, anything done with intent to procure her miscarriage of any foetus is authorised by that section if: (a) the ground for termination of the pregnancy specified in subsection (1) (d) of that section applies in relation to any foetus and the thing is done for the purpose of procuring the miscarriage of the foetus, or (b) any of the other grounds for termination of the pregnancy specified in that section applies. Interpretation.

6. In this Act, the following expressions have meanings hereby assigned to them: "the law relating to abortion" means sections 58 and 59 of the Offences against the Person Act 1861, and any rule of law relating to the procurement of abortion; "the National Health Service Acts" means the National Health Service Act 1946 to 1966 or the National Health Service (Scotland) Acts 1947 to 1966.

Short Title, Commencement and Extent

7. (1) This Act may be cited as the Abortion Act 1967.

(2) This Act shall come into force on the expiration of the period of six months beginning with the date on which it is passed.

(3) This Act does not extend to Northern Ireland.

Appendix B—List of Westminster/Northern Irish Assembly Debates and Proceedings Referred to in the Text

Westminster

Medical Termination of Pregnancy Bill, House of Commons, 22 July 1966, vol. 732
Abortion, House of Commons, 8 June 1972, vol. 838
Abortion, House of Commons, 25 November 1972, vol. 882
Abortion Law, House of Commons, 9 May 1980, vol. 984
Northern Ireland: Abortion Law, House of Lords, 19 July 1982, vol. 433
Abortion Act 1967, House of Commons, 10 November 1982, vol. 31
Abortions, House of Commons, 5 March 1984, vol. 55
Abortion Act 1967, House of Commons, 18 June 1984, vol. 62
Abortion, House of Commons, 5 July 1984, vol. 63
Abortion, House of Commons, 22 October 1984, vol. 65
Abortion, House of Commons, 7 March 1985, vol. 74
Births and Abortions, House of Commons, 12 June 1986, vol. 99
Abortions, House of Commons, 26 November 1986, vol. 106
Abortions, House of Commons, 13 July 1987, vol. 119

J. Thomson, *Abortion Law and Political Institutions*, Gender and Politics, https://doi.org/10.1007/978-3-319-96169-9

Abortion, House of Commons, 12 November 1987, vol. 119

Abortion, House of Commons, 12 November 1987, vol. 122

Abortion, House of Commons, 19 July 1988, vol. 137

Abortion (amendment) Bill, House of Commons, 22 January 1988, vol. 125

Human Fertilisation and Embryology Bill (Lords), House of Commons, 2 April 1990, vol. 170

Abortion, House of Commons, 29 October 1992, vol. 212

Brook Advisory Centres, House of Commons, 20 May 1993, vol. 225

Abortion, House of Commons, 5 July 1993, vol. 228

Abortion, House of Commons, 24 January 1994, vol. 236

Birth Control and Abortion, House of Commons, 25 May 1994, vol. 244

Abortion, House of Commons, 18 July 1994, vol. 247

Abortions, House of Commons, 30 January 1995, vol. 253

Abortion, House of Commons, 25 May 1995, vol. 260

Abortions, House of Commons, 7 November 1995, vol. 265

Abortion, House of Commons, 2 May 1996, vol. 276

Abortion Legislation, House of Commons, 14 November 1996, vol. 285

Northern Ireland: Abortion Law, House of Commons, 23 February 1998, vol. 586

Abortions, House of Commons, 2 March 1998, vol. 307

Reserved Matters, House of Commons, 31 March 1998, vol. 309

Reproductive Health Care, House of Commons, 1 June 1998, vol. 313

Abortion, House of Commons, 21 July 1998, vol. 316

Northern Ireland: Abortion Laws, House of Lords, 19 October 1998, vol. 593

Abortion, House of Commons, 18 January 1999, vol. 323

Abortion and Contraceptive Services, House of Commons, 19 July 2000, vol. 354

Abortion, House of Commons, 9 November 2001, vol. 374

Abortions, House of Commons, 15 September 2004, vol. 424

Human Fertilisation and Embryology Bill, House of Commons, 22 October 2008, vol. 481

Abortion Law (Northern Ireland), Westminster Hall Debate, 15 July 2009

Northern Irish Assembly

Abortion Legislation, Assembly, Stormont, 29 February 1984

Abortion, Assembly, Stormont, 20 June 2000

Abortion, Assembly, Stormont, 22 October 2007

Abortion Statistics in Northern Ireland: Results of Audit on 2008/09, 2009/10 and 2010/11 Data, Health Social Services and Public Safety, Written Ministerial Statement, Minister of Health, Social Services and Public Safety, 22 August 2012

Criminal Justice Bill: Further Consideration Stage, Assembly, Stormont, 12 March 2013

Amendment 34—Consideration Stage: Justice Bill (NIA Bill 37/11-15), Assembly, Stormont, 2 June 2015

Marie Stopes International: Compliance with Criminal Law on Abortion in Northern Ireland, Committee for Justice, Stormont, 10 January 2013

Consultation on the Criminal Law on Abortion in Cases of Lethal Foetal Abnormality and Sexual Crime: Department of Justice officials, Committee for Justice, Stormont, 8 October 2014

Justice Bill: CARE NI, Evangelical Alliance Northern Ireland and Christian Medical Fellowship, Committee for Justice, Stormont, 26 November 2014

Justice Bill: Amnesty International UK, Committee for Justice, Stormont, 26 November 2014

Justice Bill: Regulation and Quality Improvement Authority, Committee for Justice, Stormont, 14 January 2015

Index

J. Thomson, *Abortion Law and Political Institutions*, Gender and Politics, https://doi.org/10.1007/978-3-319-96169-9

FSC
www.fsc.org
MIX
Papier | Fördert gute Waldnutzung
FSC® C083411

Kolibri 360 GmbH
Ferdinand-Jühlke-Straße 7
99095 Erfurt, Deutschland
produktsicherheit@kolibri360.de